Reconciliation
Restoring Justice

Reconciliation
Restoring Justice

John W. de Gruchy

Fortress Press
Minneapolis

RECONCILIATION
Restoring Justice

ISBN 0-8006-3600-7

Cover design: Andrea Purdie
Cover photo: Harald Sund, courtesy of Getty Images

The paper used in this publication meets the minimum requirements of American National Standard for Information Sciences—Permanence of Paper for Printed Library Materials, ANSI Z329.48-1984.

Manufactured in the U.S.A.

06   2   3   4   5   6   7   8   9   10

To
Lynn Holness
in appreciation

Contents

Part Three: Process and Goal

Introduction

If there is any need to justify another book on reconciliation, or on the use of the Truth and Reconciliation Commission (TRC) in South Africa as a case study, this is given in the first chapter. In a world torn apart by conflict in so many places, reconciliation is a theme that demands constant consideration in ways that relate to the context in which we live. For Christians it is a subject at the centre of our faith. The reason is not difficult to discern, for the gospel is about overcoming alienation and estrangement between God and ourselves, between us and others, and between all of us and creation. Immediately we put it in this way we recognize that this is a claim that has social and political consequences, as well as some more obvious interpersonal ones. So it would be a theological travesty if we tried to give an account of the Christian doctrine of reconciliation in a way that confined it to the realm of personal piety and relations, or to the sphere of the Church. If there was ever a theological theme that had to be developed in relation to the world in all its agony and hope, this is that theme.

Yet reconciliation remains a much misunderstood and elusive notion, one that is abused in rhetoric and difficult to achieve in reality. Part of the reason for this is that we too often read into the notion what we want to find there thus ending up with the confirmation of our own position. The meaning of reconciliation seems so obvious to us until we really get into serious discussion with those alienated from us, and begin to explore the issues in more depth.

At the heart of my argument is the conviction that reconciliation is about the restoration of justice, whether that has to do with our justification by God, the renewal of interpersonal relations, or the transformation of society. At first sight this might seem a very cold way of understanding reconciliation. But that has much to do with our reduction of justice to forensic and legal ideas and processes. The justice meted out by courts of law is necessary for the sake of order in society. How that is to be done is a matter of serious concern. But that there should be such justice is not a matter of debate. What is a matter of considerable debate, however, is the nature of justice and its application when reconciliation becomes part of the equation. This introduces the concept of restorative justice, a form of justice that has to do with healing relationships, whether they be personal or political. Yet the phrase 'restorative justice' does not carry the wealth or the warmth of meaning embedded in the word 'reconciliation'. What needs to be done, then, is to recover the full meaning and rich texture of reconciliation, and to demonstrate its inseparable connection with the restoration of justice.

The issues discussed in the book are not purely theological nor of sole interest to people of religious faith or Christian conviction. But they are explored from a specifically Christian perspective. If there were a subtitle to the volume it would probably refer in some way to 'the Christian tradition'. Of course, the Christian tradition is not monolithic, comprised as it is of many different Christianities. This is comparable to the many differences within most other major religious traditions, and the diversity in secular ideologies and world-views. Some of the diverse strands in Christianity are in tension with others, and they often break apart as the multiplicity of denominations and confessions indicate. Thus when I speak of *the* Christian tradition, it is always with an awareness it is made up of many strands. Nonetheless, I have endeavoured to represent a perspective in 'Christian tradition' that I believe does have ecumenical support.

Christianity is only one of several world religions, so although my focus is on Christian tradition I am fully aware that the issues need to be explored aware of the multicultural character of virtually all societies today, and the dynamics of multi-faith relationships. I have endeavoured to contribute in some way to this discussion by including a chapter on reconciliation in relation to the family of Abrahamic religions, Judaism, Christianity and Islam. This selection is not meant to imply that other religious traditions outside of the Abrahamic household are not significant or have little to contribute to the issues at hand. The contrary is true, but to do justice to this wider dimension of the subject would have required a much larger volume or, at least, a quite different format.

In approaching my task I have benefited immensely from the labours and insights of others. There is an already extensive and continually expanding literature on the issues that I have explored. My use of some key essays and books will be evident to the reader, and I have sought to acknowledge my indebtedness wherever appropriate in the text, endnotes and select bibliography. I am aware that there is much more that could have been consulted, not least the literature in languages other than English.

Before embarking on the journey ahead, I would like to invite the reader to consider the structure of the book and the way in which the chapters relate to each other. In doing so I will also introduce the main themes that will be addressed.

The structure of the book

The book is divided into three parts, each of which has two chapters. Part 1, entitled 'Discourse', is about the language we use in speaking about reconciliation, and especially about the relationship between theological and political speech. Part 2, entitled 'Agency', deals with the Christian Church as an instrument in enabling and embodying reconciliation in the world, and then with the relationship between Christianity, Judaism and Islam in promoting reconciliation and social justice. Part 3, entitled 'Process and Goal', is about the reconciliation process and the goal of restoring justice within a new covenantal relationship. With this structure in mind, let us consider an outline of the chapters themselves.

In Chapter 1, 'How Dare We Speak of Reconciliation?' I introduce the problem of speaking about reconciliation and seek to clarify the various ways in which we do so at the different levels of personal and social life. I also stress the need to distinguish between reconciliation understood theologically and politically while acknowledging the important and necessary connections between these two genres. This relationship is then illustrated with respect to the way in which understandings of reconciliation have been constructed in South Africa both during the struggle against apartheid and in more recent times in relation to democratic transition and national reconstruction. In doing so I pay special attention to the work of the TRC. The importance of the TRC as a case study for reconciliation is widely accepted around the world and thus has wider than South African significance. This is important to note, for what I have attempted to do is something much broader than both the TRC and South Africa. Nonetheless, reference to the TRC gives contextual continuity and concreteness to the discussion throughout the book.

In Chapter 2, 'Reconciliation in Christian Tradition', I interpret the Christian doctrine of reconciliation in a way that relates to the broader social and political discussion. In order to do this I highlight the importance as well as the substance of St Paul's teaching on reconciliation and its connection with restorative justice. I then proceed to examine the various ways in which the doctrine of reconciliation has developed in the course of the history of Christian doctrine. The Christian tradition has developed some very specific ways of understanding reconciliation that need to be taken into account if we are to make the connection between theology and politics around this theme. Notions such as covenant and creation, sin, guilt and forgiveness, vicarious suffering, grace and redemption, love, power, justice and hope are fundamental to Christianity, but also have important political significance when it comes to speaking about national or social forms of reconciliation. The chapter ends with a discussion on how the theology and politics of reconciliation should be related to each other.

In Chapter 3, 'Reconciliation Embodied', I take the discussion of Chapter 2 a step further by considering how, from a Christian perspective, the Church is fundamental to the doctrine of reconciliation. Reconciliation is not an ahistorical idea or an academic theory but a tangible experience of living together in community. Theologically speaking, this refers to the sacramental embodiment of the new humanity. Understood in this way, the Church is an agent of reconciliation, representing its embodiment in history. But the Church is by no means a paragon of reconciliation, quite the contrary is too often true. So the relationship between the Church as empirical reality and its struggle to be true to its sacramental nature is of critical importance. This leads us to a consideration of the place of the sacraments of reconciliation in the life of the Church: baptism, Eucharist and confession or penance. The latter is specifically included both because of its analogical significance for understanding the TRC and the broader processes of reconciliation, and because its absence, or the absence of any meaningful alternative, from the life of many Churches has had serious consequences. Following on from this, the chapter ends with a discussion of the Church's role in acknowledging and confessing both its own guilt and, vicariously, that of the nation, as an important step towards political reconciliation.

In Chapter 4, 'Reconciliation and the Household of Abraham', I briefly explore the historical relationship between Christianity, Islam and Judaism, their relationship in South Africa and their response to the TRC. I then examine some attempts to engage in dialogue, compare the way in which each faith understands reconciliation, and conclude with comment on their mutual responsibility as 'children of Abraham' to work for social justice. The importance of this discussion needs no apology given the current global situation, of which the conflict in the Middle East is the epicentre. Judaism, Islam and Christianity have a special relationship to each other, and share a common prophetic responsibility as agents of justice and reconciliation in the world. They all derive from the same covenantal stem, represented by Abraham, and as such they should be a force for international healing rather than a source of continuing violent conflict. In view of these relationships, my treatment of Judaism as such, as well as its relationship to Christianity, receives far less attention than it deserves. Christianity, I would assert, can only be truly understood in terms of its Jewish origins.

In Chapter 5, 'The Art of Reconciliation', I begin by referring to the role of artists in the process of reconciliation as creating space within which the process of reconciliation can take place. This was part of the value of the TRC as a place in which victim and perpetrator could speak face-to-face, telling the truth about the past and offering or withholding the word of forgiveness and absolution. Listening to the 'other' also means seeking to understand the 'sound of fury', those actions of vengeance that express legitimate rage rather than pardon. But above all, it points to the need for perpetrators and beneficiaries to recognize that victims have the right to know the truth as well as the right to decide about and pronounce forgiveness. Within that framework we can begin to see the spiritual and political wisdom and power of forgiveness as essential to the process of reconciliation. In examining this process, I will show how the relationship between the various parties, often described though inadequately and problematically, as victims, perpetrators and beneficiaries, is a dialectical one.

In Chapter 6, 'Covenanting together to Restore Justice', I propose that the notion of covenant, which is fundamental to the Christian doctrine of reconciliation and which also relates the Abrahamic family of religions to each other, has considerable significance in developing notions of political reconciliation. In South Africa, covenant has been a problematic idea because of its association with the ideology of apartheid, but its potential as a framework within which national reconciliation can be pursued is something that needs to be seriously explored. Covenanting implies accepting responsibility for the past and committed participation in its healing, sharing together in the task of restoring justice in the present, and keeping hope alive for greater reconciliation in the future. This is a task which demands the participation of all citizens, irrespective of whether they are people of faith or not, but it certainly is a special responsibility for those who believe they are called to be God's agents of reconciliation and justice in the world.

During 2001 I was privileged to give a public lecture at the University of Cambridge on 'The Rhetoric and Reality of Reconciliation.' The then editor of SCM Press, Alex Wright, was present and, at the conclusion of the lecture, asked if I would turn my paper into a book. I was delighted to agree, and am grateful to him and to all at SCM Press who have made this book a reality.

Shortly after the contract with SCM was concluded, friends at Cambridge encouraged me to apply for the Hulsean Lectureship. My application was successful and I was honoured to present the Hulsean Lectures in May 2002 on the theme of Reconciliation and the Christian Tradition. This provided an ideal opportunity to develop and test my ideas and prepare the manuscript for this volume. I am grateful to the Electors of the Hulsean Lectureship for electing me to this position, and to Dr. Peter Harland, Secretary to the Electors, for his help with the arrangements. My thanks are also due to Wolfson College for providing accommodation for my wife and I, and inviting me to be a Senior Visiting Scholar, during the period of the Lectureship.

The lectures were hosted by the Faculty of Divinity at Cambridge and took place in the splendid new Faculty buildings. My thanks are due to all those in the Faculty, especially the current Dean, Professor Graham Stanton, who made us so welcome and who participated in the lectures. In particular I wish to thank Rosalind Paul, Administrative Secretary and Secretary to the Faculty Board, who took care of the many practical details and who was always available with helpful advice.

The book is dedicated to Lyn Holness my personal assistant for the past seven years. During that time her job description seems to have expanded on a daily basis, yet despite the pressures of office, family and her own research, her dedication, enthusiasm and support have enriched and enabled my own work immeasurably.

Part One

Discourse

How Dare We Speak of Reconciliation?

In February 2002 a special group of 22 international students enrolled in the Graduate School in Humanities at the University of Cape Town. They came from Burma, Burundi, the Democratic Republic of the Congo Uganda, East Timor, Sierra Leone, Zimbabwe, Nigeria and Indonesia. Numbered amongst them were lawyers, journalists, television producers, an agronomist, political scientists and teachers. Most were human rights activists and some were leaders within NGOs in their home countries. What brought them to Cape Town was a new initiative for training leaders engaged in democratic transition and transformation in their home countries.[1] Most of their time in Cape Town was spent working with human rights organizations and NGOs engaged in justice and reconciliation issues. But for part of their time they participated in our graduate programme on societies in transition. They were the first cohort of what might well be many others. The reason why they came to South Africa for this purpose will not surprise any aware of the changes that have taken place there during the past decade.

The relatively peaceful ending of apartheid and the transition to democratic rule in South Africa did, however, take the world by surprise. It also set in motion a process that has attracted global attention, namely the Truth and Reconciliation Commission (TRC) established to seek the truth about the past in order to facilitate national reconciliation. This captured the imagination and interest of many observers, especially people engaged in similar struggles for democratic change elsewhere. Indeed, the

TRC has evoked as much if not more interest in other countries than it has in South Africa itself. As a result South Africa has hosted many groups, including some from Northern Ireland, the Democratic Republic of the Congo and the Middle East who, like this group of international students, have come to learn from our experience. Yet we, their hosts, know only too well that we ourselves have a long way to go in achieving our own goal of national reconciliation and democratic transformation. We also know that there is much we can learn from the experience of others. The problems we face are global, and the solutions can only be found as we tackle them together as citizens of a world threatened by alienation, enmity and violence. Whatever the role of nation states today, or the importance of contexts for understanding and dealing with issues, borders and boundaries cannot and should not be allowed to insulate people or universal concerns for justice and peace.

There have been many truth commissions held in different countries during the past few decades. This phenomenon has been documented and discussed by Priscilla Hayner in her comprehensive study entitled *Unspeakable Truths.*[2] Since her work was published several new commissions have been established, and there are now important mechanisms and institutions dedicated to assisting them and training their personnel. In pursuing their task, these commissions have raised questions and issues for which there are few precedents, and some that are specific to particular contexts and circumstances. After all, every conflict situation is different and each requires its own specific ways and means for dealing with it. Yet there are commonalities that are easily recognizable. We in South Africa learnt a great deal from the experience of other countries in the process leading up to the establishment of the TRC,[3] just as others have subsequently studied and learnt much from the TRC. It would be remarkable if this mutuality were not so, given the characteristic traits of human nature and of social forces. Why, then, did the South African TRC attract such attention?

There are several reasons for this, but one is surely its emphasis on reconciliation. Most truth commissions prior to the South

African TRC were precisely that, instruments for getting at the truth about the past and seeking ways to deal with it. But the goal of the TRC was defined in terms of the future, that is as a project to facilitate the process of national reconciliation and, as such, its mandate went beyond investigating past abuses. In doing so it has sparked off much discussion about the meaning and process of reconciliation, a theme that relates to many situations of conflict around the globe, encompasses many dimensions, and affects our lives on many different levels.

Attempts by world leaders to resolve the enduring conflicts in Northern Ireland, Kashmir, the Balkans, the Middle East, Malaysia, the Sudan, Burundi, Columbia, Afghanistan and the Democratic Republic of the Congo and elsewhere, have increasingly topped the agenda of the United Nations and other political forums. But the need for reconciliation between alienated people and communities is much wider than these obvious examples might suggest. There is a temptation to think of the politics of reconciliation as largely confined to countries and contexts where violent conflict seems endemic. When we do so we fail to recognize the extent to which the need for reconciliation is something that is pertinent in every human community where alienated and estranged people cry out for healing and a reason for hope. This is not a new insight for people of faith, but it is one that is being freshly appreciated far beyond the confines of the Christian Church. Indicative of this discussion is a site on the World Wide Web entitled *A Campaign for Forgiveness Research*[4] that supports projects, ranging from interpersonal relations and health to local and international politics, in which the relevance of forgiveness and reconciliation is researched. Also indicative of this growing focus is the constantly expanding literature around these issues.[5]

Although the work of the TRC in South Africa is now complete, the task of national reconciliation and the debate about what it means will continue for a long time yet. After all, how does one evaluate such a project? Only time will tell the extent to which the TRC did in fact get at the truth about apartheid's murky past and promote national reconciliation. There is much debate about its success and achievements. Yet it has been a remarkable catalyst for dealing with the past and seeking a way into the future. In the process it has raised a wide range of issues that need further research, many of them reopening classical moral, philosophical and theological debates.

Perhaps the most difficult of these is that of moral symmetry. Can one equate the violations of human rights by the perpetrators of oppression with those of the oppressed who were engaged in a struggle for liberation? What is the relationship between truth-telling, justice and reconciliation in a world where moral symmetry is seldom the case? What does 'fairness' mean under such circumstances? Can any moral principle be applied without taking context into account? Further, in seeking to adjudicate between moral absolutes and context it became necessary for the TRC to take cognizance of a range of related legal and ethical issues. Was an act legitimately political? What were the consequences of the deed? On what conditions can amnesty be granted for crimes committed against humanity without undermining the rule of law and the establishment of justice? What about the restitution of land and the honouring of property rights in seeking reconciliation? Or gender relations, and the rights of children? There are also questions that have generally been regarded as more strictly theological. Must victims always forgive their oppressors, and what is necessary, if anything, by way of remorse? Can we speak of corporate guilt, or is guilt something confined to individuals? What is the role of religious communities in working for reconciliation. Indeed, is there a connection between what Christians proclaim, and what divided and strife torn societies seek? Which brings me to the major reason for undertaking this project. My concern is to explore the relationship between the politics of reconciliation and the Christian doctrine of reconciliation and, in doing so, to explore issues such as we have just raised.

Holy Grail or secular pact?

Each word in the title of this chapter is significant and calls for comment. *Reconciliation* is our theme, but what does it signify and in what sense or senses will we refer to it? National reconciliation was the stated goal of the TRC, yet the meaning of the phrase was hotly contested in the struggle against apartheid, during the work of the TRC, and it remains controversial. In her account of the TRC entitled *Country of My Skull*, Antjie Krog observed that reconciliation does not seem to be the right word in a country where 'there is nothing to go back to, no previous state or relationship one would wish to restore'.[6] But is that what reconciliation means? Or is it rather, as Krog intimates, the recovery of a lost humanity squandered in the violent pursuit of racial purity and ethnic self-interest? Reconciliation is clearly an ambiguous and contested term, one heavily laden with theological and political meaning and historical legacy.

Reflecting on the TRC and the debate about reconciliation in South Africa, Jakes Gerwel, a senior advisor to former President Mandela, observed that there is a 'seemingly unworried crossing of genre boundaries' in the debate about reconciliation in South Africa.[7] Gerwel's concern about confusing genre led him to question whether the very 'concept of national reconciliation does not in fact contribute to a discourse of division'. The reason being because 'it focuses in a theoretically deficient and empirically unsubstantiated manner on racial groups as the primary subjects of reconciliation and encourages abiding deficiency assumptions in the national self-consciousness'. For this reason Gerwel suggests that a 'critically refined elaboration of the notion of national unity may prove more purposeful in defining and practically advancing the major post-apartheid national project'.[8] Hence his appeal that 'we do not pathologize a nation in relatively good health by demanding a perpetual quest for the Holy Grail of reconciliation'.[9] Implicit in this appeal is Gerwel's concern to avoid confusing politics and theology in defining and determining the contours of national reconciliation. To put it in his own words, is national reconciliation in South Africa a 'Holy Grail or a secular pact'?

The search for the 'Holy Grail' of 'national reconciliation' is always in danger of confusing political realities with Christian eschatological and messianic hope. But does this mean, as Gerwel suggests, that the notion of 'national reconciliation' should be discarded for that of national unity? Are these two notions really that far apart as to provide alternative choices? Is it not more the case that we need to examine more carefully the meaning of reconciliation understood both theologically and politically, and to discern the relationship between the two in the interests of national unity? After all, what we are attempting in South Africa is more than a secular pact or social contract; it is akin to a covenant relationship. We are not speaking about a negotiated compromise, such as was necessary to start the process of transition in South Africa; we are speaking of something that goes well beyond that step. Namely a process in which there is a mutual attempt to heal and overcome enmities, build trust and relationships, and develop a shared commitment to the common good. Otherwise we should avoid the word, and recognize at the same time that national unity will always elude us.

Given the range of secular ideological positions in every modern society, multiple identities, loyalties and affiliations, political discourse is inevitably multilingual in character.[10] Yet, because religion and theology tend to deal with absolutes and ultimates, the crossing of boundaries between religion and politics can lead to conceptual confusion and worse, to undesirable religious and political consequences. So what is required in speaking about reconciliation at the interface between the theology and politics of reconciliation is to find ways that make the connections without confusing the genre and ending up in a futile quest that cannot be fulfilled.

But even so *dare* we Christians speak about reconciliation as though we have a monopoly on the word and its basis, as though we all agree on what it means, and as though the Church has been a shining example of a community of reconciliation? In a world of many Christianities and many faiths, what is it that we have to say that must be said, and which others might find worth hearing?

Many voices speak of reconciliation, but what they say depends on who is speaking, on their experience, their location in society, their perception of the past, the audience they are addressing, and the reason why they are speaking. Whose reconciliation is at stake and for what purpose? On whose terms are we seeking to achieve it? Do we speak from a position of power or out of weakness? Who, then, are *we* who dare to speak about reconciliation? Are we speaking for ourselves, on behalf of others, or with others? Who are we listening to before we speak, or are we not listening at all? Hearing the truth from the alienated 'other' is a prerequisite for daring to speak about reconciliation. But is our speech about reconciliation forcing some to remain silent, perhaps nursing grievances or even plotting revenge? The absence of speech is often more significant than its presence. The absence of speech about reconciliation forces us to consider the silence of those who refuse to participate in the discussion and their reasons for doing so. Could it be that the good news of reconciliation is simply wishful thinking, a way of escape from the harsh realities of conflict confronting us? Are we speaking about reconciliation in order to forget the past, or in order to deal justly with its legacy? Dare we proclaim such a message if in doing so we reinforce structures of injustice and undermine the will to resist and transform? Could it be that the message of reconciliation has become a rhetorical tool in the hands of politicians and preachers combining to prevent the birth of a more just world? In what sense, then, can Christians fulfil their mandate to proclaim the gospel of reconciliation?

Daring to speak may suggest foolhardiness, the action of those who speak before thinking, speak before listening and without concern for the consequences of what is said. But it may also reflect a deeper concern that reflects the ambiguity of our task. For how dare we speak of reconciliation in a world in which there is little justice for the victims of oppression, an immodest haste to forget atrocities and forgive perpetrators for their crimes? How dare we speak of reconciliation to a woman who has been raped by someone with HIV/AIDS? How dare we speak of reconciliation in a world where its rhetoric is hijacked by oppressors to prevent their prosecution and punishment? How dare we who are the beneficiaries of centuries of colonial injustice, speak of reconciliation between the races, between North and South? As an Argentinian journalist, reflecting on the attempt in his country to subvert attempts to get at the truth about the disappeared, put it: 'The political discourse of reconciliation is profoundly immoral, because it denies the reality of what people have experienced.'[11]

We must recognize the danger of speaking about reconciliation. There is certainly a time for remaining silent, and sometimes silence can express our concern even better than words. But that is no excuse for not speaking, for not daring to speak when the time demands it. Sensitive to the questions we have raised, we dare to speak of reconciliation because we dare not remain silent in a world torn apart by hatred, alienation and violence. We dare not remain silent whether as citizens or as Christians.

But even if we dare to speak, as we must in a world increasingly torn apart by enmity and violence, *how* should we speak? *Speaking* assumes a particular form of discourse, a language, a style of rhetoric. What language should we employ? What is the appropriate way for those of us who are citizens and Christians, as well as the heirs of colonial privilege, to speak about reconciliation? Should we confine ourselves to the language of tradition or search for new ways of speaking? Or is it possible to critically retrieve the tradition in a way that speaks with new potency for today?

Christians dare to claim with St Paul that 'God was in Christ reconciling the world to himself', and that this is the point of departure for understanding its meaning. As such, reconciliation is a reality we appropriate now by faith, and we do so in anticipation of its eschatological fulfilment. This conviction is at the heart of the Christian tradition. Sceptics are swift to point out, however, that the world is more engulfed by violence today than when the gospel of reconciliation was initially announced, and that the Church as the bearer and embodiment of that gospel is itself hopelessly divided and compromised. Theologians themselves admit that 'appearances and the lessons of world history do not seem to support' the belief that God has reconciled the world.[12]

Theologically it is appropriate to speak about reconciliation as a God-given reality that can be appropriated, and to claim that, in the end, God will reconcile all things to himself. But it can be highly inappropriate and counter-productive when such faith language is uncritically or directly attached to political discourse. Failure to recognize this inevitably leads to misunderstanding, disappointed expectations and criticism, the abuse of power relations, as well as religious dissension. Part of the reason for this is that the Church's witness to reconciliation relates to a promise that has yet to be fulfilled in social and political terms. Hence there is the need to distinguish between what Dietrich Ritschl refers to as the 'levels of primary and secondary statements':

> At a primary level of expression the content of reconciliation is invisible and undemonstrable; but it can also be stated in the linguistic form of the hopes and recollections of Israel and the early church. For anyone to whom this language is alien, the primary talk of reconciliation also remains incomprehensible and uninteresting. On the level of secondary statement we have the signs set up by believers and the words that comment on them. For their part believers arrive at an insight into a reconciled relationship with God through their perception of the statements and signs on the secondary level . . .[13]

Primary expressions about reconciliation in the Christian liturgy and confessions of faith may well become carefully articulated doctrine, but they remain faith convictions and cannot be verified except on the basis of Scripture. As faith convictions they cannot be directly equated with reconciliation as a political policy and objective without creating conceptual confusion. Secondary expressions on the contrary are visible in social and political reality even though, for the Christian they have their basis in that which is beyond empirical verifiability. Ritschl refers to 'acts of love, the pressure to free the oppressed, the healing of the sorrowful and sick, the reconciliation of enemies, support of justice in hope of the kingdom of God'.[14] Such acts contribute to the creation of a new reality. All 'rational and responsible human beings', says Ritschl, have access to these signs of reconciliation even if they cannot accept what Christians claim is their basis.[15] The challenge in speaking about reconciliation from a Christian perspective is not simply that of proclaiming primary expressions of reconciliation, but engaging in public life in ways that make God's gift of reconciliation and Christian hope a reality through secondary expressions.

Much has been written about the Christian doctrine of reconciliation at a primary level, not least by one of the twentieth century's greatest theologians, Karl Barth, who devoted four hefty volumes to the subject. It has also long been a major theme in ecumenical theology and practice, reflecting the war-torn and conflict-ridden historical context in which the ecumenical movement was conceived and developed. Despite this, not all Christians agree on the meaning of reconciliation, and they disagree most when it comes to relating reconciliation to the political arena. All would agree that it has to do with our personal relationship with God and that this is connected to relationships with others. But how these are connected, and what this might mean on the broader canvas of social relations and political realities is a matter of contention. Is reconciliation with God primary, irrespective of reconciliation with the alienated 'other', or is the latter an essential element in being reconciled with God? Does reconciliation with the 'other' extend beyond estranged individuals so that reconciliation with God is intrinsically connected to the overcoming of ethnic, racial and other forms of alienation? How do we relate faith in God's gift of reconciliation to the overcoming of social enmities and conflicts? In other words, how do we make the connection between the primary and secondary expressions of reconciliation in both our theological endeavours and in our practical contribution to public life?

There is a constant need to rethink the Christian understanding or doctrine of reconciliation in the light of both critical theological thinking and the radically changing political scenario of the contemporary world. Just as the TRC raised a series of moral and philosophical issues, so too it raised key theological issues, and did so in a way that must be taken into account in restating the doctrine of reconciliation in our context. These include covenant and creation, sin and guilt, grace and forgiveness, the reign of God's justice and human hope, all of which have political significance. What Christians believe about reconciliation cannot be understood in isolation from these primary themes. Moreover the Christian contribution to the debate about reconciliation would lose its value and relevance if they were not central to the discussion. Religion, as Bhikhu Parekh so rightly points out, 'is best able to contribute its insights and enrich political debate when it is allowed to speak in its authentic idioms'.[16] In other words, even though others may not accept the faith claims on which Christians base their understanding of reconciliation, we cannot avoid using primary expressions of reconciliation in seeking to give an account of its social significance. Joseph Liechty and Cecelia Clegg demonstrate this well in their perceptive study on Northern Ireland entitled *Moving Beyond Sectarianism*. A true understanding of reconciliation, they argue, has to be 'built on the interlocking dynamics of forgiveness, repentance, truth, and justice, understood in part as religiously-rooted virtues, but also as basic dynamics (even when unnamed or unrecognized) of human interaction, including public life and therefore politics'.[17] Put differently, reconciliation is both 'the theological remainder of politics, the leap that comes when realism confronts total conflict . . . and the political remainder of theology, a form of action that endows hope with content'.[18] Reconciliation, in other words, is a human and social process that requires theological explanation, and a theological concept seeking human and social embodiment.

No one understood the problem of proclaiming the gospel of reconciliation in a strife-torn and sceptical world better than the German theologian and martyr of the Third Reich, Dietrich Bonhoeffer. In a sermon prepared in prison for the baptism of his nephew, Bonhoeffer wrote these words:

Reconciliation and redemption, regeneration and the Holy
Spirit, love of our enemies, cross and resurrection, life in
Christ and Christian discipleship – all these things are so difficult and so remote that we hardly venture to speak any more
of them. In the traditional words and acts we suspect that there
may be something quite new and revolutionary, though we
cannot as yet grasp or express it.[19]

The problem, for Bonhoeffer, did not lie with the reality of
reconciliation or the other great themes of the Christian tradition
of which it is an integral part. Bonhoeffer remained convinced
that they stood for something 'new and revolutionary', something as pertinent today as when they were first used to express
the gospel. The problem was that the Church in Germany, and
by inference elsewhere, had become captive to bourgeois culture,
and thus its use of biblical concepts confirmed rather than challenged the status quo. The great doctrines of Christian faith had
been debased and lost their value. Nonetheless, the day would
come, Bonhoeffer predicted, when they would find expression in
a new liberating and redeeming language of 'righteousness and
truth'. Hence his call to the Church to proceed by engaging in
acts of justice and prayer, for out of such action the great words
of Christian faith would be set free, both shocking people and
overcoming them by its power. There is, then, a certain irony in
giving lectures or writing a book on reconciliation. How dare we
speak about reconciliation if the way to give expression to its
transforming power is, as Bonhoeffer suggests, through struggling for justice in a way sustained by a disciplined spirituality?

Reconciliation is, indeed, an action, praxis and movement
before it becomes a theory or dogma, something celebrated
before it is explained. Understood only or primarily as political
theory or theological doctrine reduces it to an ahistorical idea
that can be debated at length and in the abstract. But reconciliation is properly understood as a process in which we become
engaged at the heart of the struggle for justice and peace in the
world. That is why any discussion of reconciliation must be
historically and contextually centred, a reflection on what is

happening on the ground by those engaged in the process. Only then can we critically engage the rhetoric and practice of reconciliation in order to challenge its abuse and to act in ways that contribute to the healing of people and nations.

Fortunately, alongside the rhetorical misuse of reconciliation, there is also a remarkable story to be told of men and women, as well as communities of faith, who have opened up a path to reconciliation and left us a legacy of actions that provide signposts of what reconciliation means. Their actions undoubtedly speak louder than words. But words rightly chosen have their own power. Reconciliation is something that occurs through the interplay of speech, listening and action motivated by hope and love. The *way* in which we speak with and listen to the alienated 'other' is already an action that makes reconciliation a possibility. Both words and deeds are necessary if we are to rescue reconciliation from banality and recover its costly connection with telling the truth and social justice. Desmond Tutu demonstrated this connection vividly, which is why his account of the TRC, of which he was chair, entitled *No Future Without Forgiveness*,[20] carries weight, transforming traditional words into something fresh and revolutionary. Even those who may challenge his interpretation of events, reject his faith claims, and remain sceptical of his optimism, cannot deny the integrity of his witness born out of the struggle for justice sustained by a profound spirituality.

From a Christian perspective the best way to speak about reconciliation is through story-telling rather than through systematic expositions of dogma. Christian tradition is all about the handing on and celebration of a story. For many centuries, long before theologians attempted to construct theories of redemption or atonement, the 'doctrine' of reconciliation was narrated, proclaimed and celebrated as the story of God's salvation. Contemporary Jews recount the story of the Exodus in celebrating Passover as though they themselves are experiencing it here and now. Christians celebrate the Eucharist in actions that recount what happened on the 'night Jesus was arrested'. This does not mean that narrative replaces critical reflection and the need for cogent rational and systematic thought.[21] But neither do we mean to imply that narrative is pre-critical, having no inner coherence and recognizable logic.

Truth in the biblical sense is communicated primarily through remembering and retelling past events in ways that relate to present issues and struggles. Jesus restated received wisdom through parables that breathed new life into the truth about God's reign for his hearers – and for us. Story-telling is, in fact, the most appropriate genre for introducing the Christian understanding of reconciliation; it was also the primary form of discourse at the TRC. This was not an easy exercise, as though people who have experienced great suffering and anguish relish the idea of reliving the past, and doing so in front of the glaring lights of public television. Nevertheless, it was often true that in telling their painful stories victims of oppression were able to enter the process of remembrance and healing, and perpetrators came face to face with their guilt, acknowledged or not, and therefore with an opportunity for change.

For many victims their stories related to the Christian narrative of salvation history. In other words, through story-telling primary and secondary expressions of reconciliation made connection. Their stories were personalized cameos of lives shaped by faith, forgiveness and hope derived from the gospel but lived out amidst the social and political traumas of our time and not exempt from feelings of vengeance. Sometimes they were stories that jolted our understanding of the Christian grand narrative and, like the story of Job, made us recognize that the answers to human pain, anguish and suffering are never facile and seldom straightforward. In the light of their stories we could better understand why some people lost faith in the God of justice even while others were sustained by faith in the God of grace. Moreover, through the telling of these stories the 'master narrative' of colonial and apartheid South Africa was undermined, contradicted, and replaced by the story of struggle, suffering and the 'miracle story' of transition to democracy. There can be no doubt, to quote Jakes Gerwel again, that the TRC redirected the 'public understanding of national reconciliation from the formal statist view, which seemed to dominate during and immediately after the epoch-making negotiation phase, to a more human substantive understanding based on social history and biography'.[22]

This insight, along with others that we have now introduced, suggests that no matter what the problems might be in speaking about reconciliation theologically in conjunction with political discourse about national reconciliation, the two are connected and there is good reason for the project at hand. But we need to explore this interface further to see how we can make necessary connections in our understanding and practice of reconciliation without confusing the genre.

Clarifying the genre

There is more to understanding the meaning of a word than studying its genealogy and etymology. Nonetheless, that is an important place to begin. The word reconciliation entered Christian discourse through the Vulgate's use of the Latin *reconciliatio* to translate Paul's choice of καταλλαγη, a word used to describe God's saving work in Jesus Christ. It then entered Anglo-Saxon through the French and appeared in English print in the late fourteenth century in the writings of Chaucer, who used it in the sense of reconciling estranged persons. About the same time it was used in the Church in the sense of peace with God and one another, hence the choice of the word by the translators of the King James Version of the Bible. Those meanings have remained central in English usage. However, already by the seventeenth century the word was used in a variety of ways. Amongst these was restoring someone to favour, reconciling penitents to the Church, purification of sacred objects such as church buildings after their desecration, overcoming the estrangement of married partners, or simply the act of reaching agreement.

Reflection on its current usage in different contexts helps us recognize that while reconciliation has retained its core religious sense, it has also gathered a layered set of possible meanings reflected in the rhetoric of pulpit, parliament and the press, as well as embodied in literature, art and popular discourse. For many people today reconciliation may only refer to sorting out their banking accounts, a difficult enough task in itself for most of us, but a use of the word that only entered English in the nineteenth century. In places where social order is taken for granted the use of the word is often bland or even banal, having become, as Rowan Williams puts it, 'a seductively comfortable word, fatally close to "consensus"'.[23] As such, reconciliation evokes little thought or comment.

The word is so overloaded with ambiguity in some contexts and so emptied of significant meaning in others, that we may well wonder whether it remains a useful term in universal discourse. On occasion its meaning may even receive a new twist that alters its sense, thereby indicating how difficult it can be to communicate its meaning, let alone achieve reconciliation in reality. But all of this suggests a clue to its possible value and significance. Talk about reconciliation becomes meaningful when the circumstances and context are such that the overcoming of hostility and enmity, often expressed through violence, demand that we find a solution. Such circumstances and contexts force us beyond the facile and banal uses of the word. Alternative possibilities, 'reaching consensus', for example, are then seen to be inadequate to cover the full range of meaning that we are seeking to express.

Consensus building may be an important part of the process of reconciliation, but reconciliation is far more than arriving at such an agreement. Reconciliation implies a fundamental shift in personal and power relations between former enemies. To quote from Nelson Mandela's speech on receiving the TRC Report, reconcili-ation was the 'search for a nation at peace with itself' and the building of a better life for all.[24] Thus, within South Africa, reconciliation is part and parcel of what we refer to as democratic transformation and reconstruction. Reconciliation, as we shall argue, is about restoring justice. But the notion of reconciliation also pushes us to deeper than structural levels, to interpersonal and social healing and the restoration of humanity. And it is precisely there that we begin to see the way in which the different levels of reconciliation connect and inform each other.

There are four interrelated ways in which we will speak about reconciliation, each of which refers to the overcoming of a relationship of enmity and alienation. The first or *theological* refers to reconciliation between God and humanity, and what this means in terms of social relations. For Christians, the theology of reconciliation is 'mediated in the objective form of a shared life and language, a public community of men and women, gathering to read certain texts and perform certain acts'.[25] What this means will be considered more fully in the next two chapters. But we must note here that for many people the theological meaning is irrelevant, and because it can so easily cloud the issues, the religious discourse that embodies it is also regarded as unhelpful. For them, reconciliation refers to the overcoming of enmity between people whether we speak of interpersonal relations, or the broader social and political situation, without reference to God or divine activity. But even then it is difficult to speak about it without recourse to theological and religious terms as we previously noted. Primary and secondary expressions of reconciliation keep on intersecting.

The second or *interpersonal* way of speaking about reconciliation refers to relations between individuals, as, for example, in restoring a marriage relationship, or the relationship between a victim and a perpetrator of crime. The third or *social* refers to reconciliation between alienated communities and groups at a local level, such as the healing of race relations in a housing estate or at a school, especially in the wake of an outbreak of violence. The fourth or *political* refers to projects such as the process of national reconciliation in South Africa, the overcoming of sectarianism in Northern Ireland, or the achievement of sustainable peace in the Middle East. Each of these ways of speaking about reconciliation and the realities to which they refer overlap thus making the process far more complex than would appear to be the case if we thought in separate spheres. Part of the value of the word, despite the danger of confusing the genre and its inevitable ambiguities in usage, is that reconciliation can meaningfully relate to each of these separately or together.

The breakdown of a marriage between people of different religious traditions or ethnic communities in Burundi or Kosovo will inevitably be related to the wider social situation, and the healing of those relationships will be contingent to a large degree on the political climate at any given time. Likewise, the outbreak of racial tension in a high school could well be the result of conflict between two pupils who simply do not like each other, hence interpersonal, but it may well reflect social tensions that require resolving at another level. The task of national reconciliation in South Africa is an ongoing challenge that not only has to deal with the past crimes of apartheid or overcoming continued forms of alienation and discrimination, but also the healing of interpersonal relationships. The healing of such relations is vital for the national project, and the process of national reconciliation undoubtedly facilitates the healing of interpersonal relationships. At the same time the process in each case is somewhat different, requiring different actions. As Hayner has suggested, the dynamics of reconciliation at an interpersonal level may be more complex for the reason that 'forgiveness, healing, and reconciliation are deeply personal processes, and each person's needs and reactions to peacemaking and truth telling may be different'.[26] Yet this is obviously made more difficult when social and political enmity and conflict compound personal experience. Indeed, political reconciliation has its own complexities that need to be taken into account when seeking the reconciliation of people at an interpersonal level within situations of social conflict.

Irrespective of whether we speak about reconciliation theologically, interpersonally, socially or politically, we need to recognize that we are invariably talking about a sequential process. Reconciliation is a way of dealing with and overcoming past alienation, enmity and hurt. But it is also a way of relating to the 'other' in the present, and a goal that is always ahead of us in the future however much we may experience it here and now. Much of the confusion in speaking about reconciliation, not least in discussions about the TRC, derives from a failure to recognize these sequential distinctions. To assume that the TRC could produce reconciliation in South Africa in the sense of a society in which all past alienation was overcome is grossly misleading. But the TRC did contribute to that goal in becoming a catalyst for the healing of the past and enabling at least some people to experience forgiveness and reconciliation in the present.

Reconciliation is, if you like, a journey from the past into the future, a journey from estrangement to communion, or from what was patently unjust in search of a future that is just. Along the path certain events and moments are both intimations of what reconciliation means and catalysts for taking the process further. The release of Nelson Mandela from prison was such an event. His inauguration as the president of South Africa was a remarkable moment of reconciliation as were the days on which South Africa won the World Rugby Cup and later the African Football Cup of Nations. But these events, like a marriage ceremony in which 'two become one' inevitably lead after the honeymoon to the task of learning to live together. Then begins a process in which husband and wife, or groups of people, have to learn how to live at peace with each other, overcoming times of severe disagreement and even thoughts of divorce, the latter always being a possibility. Likewise, national reconciliation is always a goal ahead of us, yet one inseparable from the process of achieving it.

The goal of reconciliation might be achieved at various stages along the way following estrangement and even divorce, when a restoration of relations is reached. But reconciliation as a final achievement is, in a sense, always beyond our grasp. It is, if you like, a gift that we experience and live by even now, but for most of us, nations included, it is always something ahead of us. It is work in progress, a dynamic set of processes into which we are drawn and in which we participate. So it is important to recognize the relationship and distinction between reconciliation as an event, a process and a goal, and not to confuse our ultimate hopes with realistic possibilities even if they are connected. In Christian theology there is always a tension between the 'here and now' and the 'not yet', between the language of the penultimate and that of the ultimate, between the secondary and primary expressions of reconciliation.

Once we recognize such distinctions we can begin to ask questions about what constitutes the process and how do we know when we have achieved a situation when it is appropriate to say we have achieved some degree of reconciliation. These are obviously linked on a continuum. For example, essential to the process is a commitment to bring an end to violence, whether domestic or political. If a situation is reached when sustainable peace is attained, then we may surely speak meaningfully of reconciliation even if only tentatively. Or, to take another example, a willingness to change or repent is part of the process of reconciliation, and it becomes appropriate to speak of reconciliation when that repentance, that turning away from the past, results in acts of restitution and reparation.

In seeking to clarify the genre, there is another matter that needs comment. Part of the difficulty in speaking about reconciliation, especially in multicultural contexts, is that it is an English word with its own cultural history. Its equivalents in other languages do not always convey the same meaning or have the same legacy. This is not a minor problem, for in many contexts where reconciliation is most necessary and yet so elusive, the politics of cultural identity and therefore language play a critical role. Do Protestants and Catholics hear the same thing in Northern Ireland when mediators speak of the need for reconciliation? How much more problematic this is in the Middle East where English is not the language of either Palestinians or Israelis, but is the language of diplomacy. Or consider the fact that there are eleven official languages in South Africa reflecting a variety of cultures and historical experience, some of them profoundly affected by particular religious traditions in which the term 'reconciliation' carries different meaning and weight. Consulting the ancestors about reconciliation is not part of Western secular culture, but for many Africans it is important. Moreover, when the word 'reconciliation' is translated into some African lan-guages there are subtle changes in what is meant.[27]

Some years ago I supervised the Master's dissertation of a Catholic priest.[28] His research focused on how reconciliation was understood amongst the members of his large sprawling parish of six congregations located on the Cape Flats and comprised of so-called 'coloured' people, a community to which he also belonged. The reason behind his research was a desire to know how to speak about reconciliation to his parishioners. So he set out to compare their understanding of reconciliation with that expressed in various documents produced by the Southern African Catholic Bishops' Conference. The way in which the bishops understood reconciliation was in keeping with traditional Christian teaching, though contextually related. But this was not the case amongst the members of the parish. For them reconciliation had to do with recovering their identity as people of colour. Whenever their priest preached on the need for reconciliation in South Africa, exhorting them to become reconciled to other ethnic groups, they heard him say that they should recover their own self-respect.

This understanding of reconciliation has, on reflection, a certain logic, for how can South Africans overcome the legacy of apartheid and create a genuinely just and sustainable society unless those who were previously oppressed and who still suffer from the indignities of the past regain respect for their own identity? By the same token, there can be little chance for reconciliation in South Africa unless those of us who were privileged by apartheid because of our skin colour renounce an immoral past and seek to develop a fresh identity as members of a new country in search of transformation.[29] So the question of identity, whether it prevents us from relating to the 'other', or whether it is transcended through identification with the 'other' in the fashioning of a new identity, is a critical issue in understanding the dynamics of reconciliation. Many of the conflicts around the world have to do with the attempt to defend identity at the expense of the 'other'. Apartheid in South Africa and sectarianism in Northern Ireland are obvious but not the only examples.

Genuine reconciliation does not mean the obliteration of difference and diversity in the cause of national unity or the healing of a marriage. Reconciliation has to do with the recovery, not the loss, of cultural or other identities, and at the same time the encouragement of multiple identities that build bridges rather than reinforce divisions. The struggle over identity, and the attempt to construct a common South African identity within which other identities are recognized and respected, is at the heart of national reconciliation. Indeed, it is often said that *the* 'national question' has to do with 'who is an African' within the South African context, a question that does not have to do so much with ethnicity as it does with commitment and building relationships.

All of this suggests that our understanding of reconciliation requires more than semantic precision. It is not enough to know the genealogy of the word in order to appreciate its meaning; we have to discern how the word has been constructed within various historical contexts. What do people hear us saying when we dare to speak about reconciliation? For this reason it is impossible to appreciate the meaning and significance of reconciliation in South Africa or any other context where it is a contested term without an understanding of its social history. With that in mind, and mindful of our reference to the TRC as a case study for our explorations, we turn now to consider the way in which reconciliation has been contested and constructed in South Africa. As we have previously suggested, in order to discuss reconciliation meaningfully we need to consider it in relation to particular circumstances and contexts.

Reconciliation: constructed and contested

Both British colonial policy and Afrikaner nationalism were premised on the separation of the white settler from the black indigenous communities. Following the Anglo–Boer War, every effort was made by the British colonial authorities to reconcile the two settler communities in a united white nation. Blacks were excluded by the Constitution of the Union of South Africa in 1910, and subsequently systematically deprived of their land and rights. This led, in response, to the formation of the African National Congress (ANC) in 1912, a movement that sought to unite all blacks, irrespective of ethnic background in the struggle against their exclusion and deprivation. After centuries of gestation scarred by violent conflict, 'two nations' were thus born. Ever since then the fundamental 'national question' facing South Africa has been around the relationship between them, with the 'white nation' seeking to be exclusively European, and the 'black nation' seeking to build an inclusive African identity. Apartheid was the logical outcome of the first; the struggle for liberation and a non-racial democracy was the inevitable project of the second.

The rise of Afrikaner Nationalism and its achievement of political power in 1948 did not fundamentally alter the dynamics of what had been achieved in the Union of 1910. But white hegemony was now driven by Afrikaner interests and supported by a more refined ideology of racial superiority, namely apartheid. The future and the security of whites, according to apartheid's ideologists, lay along the path of segregation rather than any eventual reconciliation between the races. That required, in turn, ensuring that whites retained and consolidated the power that they had achieved through colonial conquest. Such power relations became the corner-stone of apartheid policy and practice, an essential element in maintaining separation.

Given the extent to which Afrikaner nationalism was nurtured within the womb of the Dutch Reformed Church, its policies both needed and received its theological sanction. Racial segregation, originally understood as socially permissible, was decreed to be the will of God. By contrast, the English-speaking Churches, products of colonial and missionary enterprise, hesitatingly hovered between endorsing existing patterns of segregation and a paternalistic practice of limited ecclesiastical inclusion and political enfranchisement. But reconciliation between the races, with all that meant in terms of interpersonal relationships or social and political change, as well as the unity of the Church, was not a priority on their agenda. This was so despite prophetic voices repeatedly warning of the dangers to come if whites continued to entrench their power and develop their wealth to the exclusion and impoverishment of blacks.

The first South African Nobel Peace Prize winner, Chief Albert Luthuli who received the award in 1961, wrote these words towards the end of his autobiography, *Let My People Go!*:

From the beginning our history has been one of ascending unities, the breaking of tribal, racial and creedal barriers. The past cannot hope to have a life sustained by itself, wrenched from the whole. There remains before us the building of a new land, a home for men who are black, white, brown, from the ruins of the old narrow groups, a synthesis of the rich cultural strains we have inherited.[30]

Luthuli went on to speak of the way in which Africans had suffered oppression at the hands of European colonialism and yet, despite this, sought peace and concord rather than vengeance. This was a profound statement of what national reconciliation might mean from one who was both a leading politician, as president of the African National Congress, and a devout Christian. But Luthuli expressed the fear that the outstretched hand that he and others offered to the apartheid regime would be rejected and the struggle would have to continue and possibly intensify.

That, indeed, was the case. In the wake of the Sharpeville Massacre and the subsequent banning of the ANC and the Pan Africanist Congress, the armed struggle that Luthuli and others had tried to prevent through non-violent resistance, was launched. The story of the struggle is now widely known.[31] Less widely known but well documented is the response of the South African member Churches of the World Council of Churches to the Sharpeville Massacre, notably at the Cottesloe Consultation.[32] This, together with the formation of the Christian Institute in 1963 under the leadership of Beyers Naudé, signalled the beginning of the church struggle against apartheid.

At the heart of this struggle was a theology of reconciliation that fundamentally challenged both the politics and theology of racial separation. God's will, as expressed in the gospel of Jesus Christ, was not apartheid but the reconciliation of the peoples of South Africa in one nation. This was most clearly and fully expounded in *The Message to the People of South Africa* published by the South African Council of Churches in 1968.[33] *The Message* was not the first church statement critical of apartheid, but it was the most trenchant, unambiguous, and ecumenical to date. 'Separate development', as apartheid was euphemistically called, was categorically rejected as a false gospel. Whereas the gospel of Jesus Christ reconciled people to each other, apartheid drove them apart.

The ensuing debate about the *Message* embroiled not only the Churches but also politicians, reaching into the chambers of parliament. While many understood reconciliation in the traditional English sense as a private affair between God and the individual with, at most, some consequences for interpersonal relations, for others it had far-reaching social and political implications. But the debate was almost entirely one between white Christians, reflecting the theological divide between conservative and liberal. It was only subsequent to the rise of Black Consciousness, the emergence of Black theology, and the Soweto Uprising in 1975, that its parameters radically shifted. From this perspective reconciliation between white and black South Africans was regarded as impossible as long as apartheid existed. This was not denied by the drafters of the *Message*, or by its follow-up in the Study Project on Christianity in Apartheid Society (Spro-cas). But the question of the relationship between reconciliation and liberation was not resolved.

For the proponents of Black Consciousness any talk of reconciliation or social integration prior to achieving liberation was regarded as undermining liberation, hence the rhetoric of reconciliation was suspect. The suspicion deepened when the apartheid regime itself began to speak of reconciliation within the framework of its own 'reformist' policies as pursued by P. W. Botha in the late 1970s and early 1980s. Botha's policies were designed to perpetuate the regime's control and hegemony in a new guise. As such they plunged South Africa into turmoil, leading to a State of Emergency and the intensification of the armed struggle. As international economic and political sanctions tightened and resistance inside the country became increasingly militant, so the government embarked on its strategy of destroying all agents of what it perceived to be the 'total onslaught' of communism. Detention without trial, torture, the murder of political activists, the fomenting of violence in black townships, and much more became the day-to-day business of various state security agencies.

One Christian response to this crisis was the National Initiative of Reconciliation (NIR) launched in September 1985 by African Enterprise, an evangelical para-church organization. The NIR managed to gather together a wide range of Christian leaders, including white Dutch Reformed Church leaders and SACC representatives. Its 'Statement of Affirmation' acknowledged the connection between reconciliation as a theological concept and the struggle for justice. The struggle for justice and the ministry of reconciliation were not equated, but neither were they separated.[34] At the same time, many involved in the NIR regarded reconciliation as a gift that could be appropriated here and now between black and white, especially at the interpersonal level. Reconciled communities following the 'third-way' of the gospel provided the key to overcoming the political crisis.[35]

A more radical response was expressed in the *Kairos Document* published in 1986. For the *Kairos* theologians, reconciliation was not a means to an end, that is, a process, but rather the goal of the liberation struggle. Justice and the ending of apartheid were preconditions for reconciliation. Recognizing that the basic difference between Christians in South Africa was not primarily denominational or confessional, but political and economic, the *Kairos Document* perceived that the Church itself was a site of the struggle. The key word in that struggle was precisely reconciliation. Thus the *Kairos Document* not only attacked the 'state theology' of those who gave their support to apartheid, but also opposed what it named the 'church theology' of the mainline multiracial Churches, accusing them of promoting 'cheap reconciliation':

> In our situation in South Africa today it would be totally unChristian to plead for reconciliation and peace before the present injustices have been removed. Any such plea plays into the hands of the oppressor by trying to persuade those of us who are oppressed to accept our oppression and to become reconciled to the intolerable crimes that are committed against

us. That is not Christian reconciliation, it is sin. It is asking us to become accomplices in our own oppression, to become servants of the devil. No reconciliation is possible in South Africa without justice.[36]

Rejecting the liberal rhetoric of reconciliation, the *Kairos Document* called for direct Christian participation in the struggle, including acts of civil disobedience in resistance to government tyranny.

Heated controversy around the meaning of reconciliation once again ensued within the Churches as state repression against Christian activists associated with the *Kairos Document* intensified.[37] Many white Christians and church leaders believed that they could be agents of reconciliation without becoming engaged in the anti-apartheid struggle. But even Churches and church leaders who had rejected apartheid and who were engaged in the struggle to end it, such as Archbishop Tutu, were unhappy about the way in which 'church theology' and reconciliation were, in their terms, caricatured and criticized. Clearly there was hesitation about the ideological abuse of such a key doctrine of Christian faith, whether by those who used it in defence of their supposed neutrality, or those who rejected it as counterproductive to the struggle.

There was sharper criticism of the *Kairos Document* emanating from a circle of black theologians who remained faithful to the more radical concerns of the Black Consciousness movement. For them, the discourse of reconciliation was controlled by the 'ruling class' rather than by those who were alienated from whites, from the land, from the means of production, and thus from power. If reconciliation was to mean anything significant for the poor and oppressed, it had to reverse this alienation. Only then would it become possible to speak of the reconciliation of black and white and enter into negotiation around the 'national question'.[38]

Precisely at this time, while still in prison, Nelson Mandela began secret talks with the National Party leadership in order to explore the possibility of negotiations. In doing so he set in motion a new process of possible reconciliation between white and black.[39] Those who were engaged in the liberation struggle, and who came to know of these talks, were at first concerned that Mandela had sold out and become engaged in an exercise of cheap reconciliation, the very temptation against which the *Kairos Document* warned. But Mandela had not served such a long term in prison for the sake of selling out the birthright of the oppressed. As far as he was concerned there could be no negotiated settlement unless the government was prepared to accept the goal of a non-racial democratic society. There could be no reconciliation without liberation and justice. Until that was accepted in principle he would stay in prison, the armed struggle would continue, and sanctions would remain in place.

Nevertheless, the fact that Mandela initiated the talks, and the way in which he entered into them, indicates that he was committed to pursuing the path of reconciliation as an integral part of the process of achieving the goal of liberation. It had become abundantly clear to him that there was no alternative other than a protracted civil war. Neither the state nor the liberation movement had the capacity to achieve a decisive victory, and the prolonging of the vicious stalemate could only spell disaster for the country. Seeking reconciliation was therefore an instrument in which the revolutionary struggle, political realism and moral integrity combined to produce an almost irresistible force.

Yet, it was also the path of principled compromise for the sake of preventing further bloodshed and opening up space for the transition to democracy, a willingness to give ground on what was not essential for the sake of a greater good. Mandela recognized the need to allow those in power to discover space in which to manoeuvre within their own constituency without loss of face. He helped them catch a vision of a new and just South Africa with its promise not only of the liberation of the oppressed but also of the restoration of their own humanity. Fortunately there were those in the apartheid government who were willing to risk responding positively even if reluctantly to Mandela's overtures.

That there were also moves afoot amongst the Churches in

South Africa to reach out to each other for the sake of a new South Africa was apparent at the Rustenburg Church Leaders' Conference in November 1990.[40] Church leaders from eighty denominations were present for this weeklong event and they spanned virtually the whole of the theological and ecclesiastical spectrum. Tensions ran high at points and full consensus on the burning issues of the day was not reached. But there was remarkable agreement nonetheless considering the past history of relationships around apartheid. For many the highlight of the Conference came when Professor Willie Jonker, speaking both personally and on behalf of the Dutch Reformed Church, confessed guilt for his Church's support for apartheid, and when Archbishop Tutu spontaneously embraced Jonker in an act of vicarious acceptance and forgiveness. Despite some critical observations about that gracious act of reconciliation it set the path for a new era of church relations and a joint commitment to serving the cause of national reconciliation.[41]

Reconciliation as national project

The achievement of a negotiated settlement in South Africa, which reached its symbolic climax in the inauguration of Nelson Mandela as President on 11 May 1994, was internationally hailed as a modern miracle. Political analysts had long anticipated that South Africa would erupt in civil war given the history of colonial oppression and the forty or more years of bitter apartheid repression. Everyone now knows, not least as a result of the TRC, something about the horrific lengths to which apartheid's security agents were prepared to go in countering the revolution. But even at the time anyone engaged in the struggle already knew what had been going on. All the signs of a descent into hell were apparent. The miracle is that within the short space of four years the spiral of violence that threatened to turn the country into an ash-heap was countered.

Violence, it is true, escalated during the negotiations, and hope see-sawed with despair as South Africa staggered on the brink of transition. But the spiral downwards into racial war was halted as politicians and parties clawed their way out of the morass and up the ladder of tough negotiations towards national reconciliation. Even hardened cynics could only marvel when the new South Africa was born amidst global applause. Whether described as a miracle moment in our history, or in the more prosaic terms of political theory and analysis, it was an event of mythic proportions. And the key phrase that lay at its heart was 'national reconciliation', with Nelson Mandela its icon.

Looking back to those heady days that led to the transition to democracy in 1994, it is now evident that the miracle required enormous energy and diplomatic skill on the part of those involved in the process. Even those who believe that God is at work in history, recognize that there is a necessary synergy between divine providence and human activity though the proportions may be debated. To negotiate a revolution, and to set the process of reconciliation in motion, takes enormous effort and considerable skill. Hence the respective negotiating teams worked hard and long to ensure that all parties were drawn into the negotiations. There were many sticky issues needing resolution, but none so problematic as dealing with the past and especially accountability for the crimes of apartheid, though the abuse of human rights within the liberation movement was also a matter of concern. The ANC and other leaders in the struggle against apartheid had come to accept that there would be no South African equivalent of the Nuremberg Trials that followed the defeat of Nazi Germany.[42] But equally the past could not simply be pushed under the carpet as though nothing had happened, nor could the consensus reached through negotiation be adequate in healing the nation.

There were two alternative routes to such reconciliation. The first was to declare a general amnesty, but to allow justice to run its course through the courts in those cases where there was sufficient evidence to try perpetrators of apartheid crimes. For a variety of reasons this was deemed unsatisfactory, though it was accepted that the prosecution and punishment of those guilty remained a possibility and perhaps even a necessity. The second was to institute a process of uncovering the truth outside of the courts that would promote national reconciliation. On the one hand, such truth-telling on certain conditions[43] would provide the basis for granting amnesty to individual perpetrators. On the other hand, it would give victims an opportunity to tell their stories and hear the truth as told by the perpetrators, and therefore, provide the basis for some measure of reparation. This was the path chosen by the new cabinet at its first meeting following the 1994 election when it approved the formation of the TRC. As one of the founding documents of the TRC put it: 'Once we know the truth, we can begin to put the past behind us and move with hope into a peaceful future.'

The Interim Constitution approved late in 1993 as the basis for the election of a new democratic government had a final clause on National Unity and Reconciliation. It included these words:

> The pursuit of national unity, the well-being of all South African citizens and peace require reconciliation between the people of South Africa and the reconstruction of society.
>
> . . . there is a need for understanding but not revenge, a need for reparation but not for retaliation, a need for *ubuntu*[44] but not for victimization.

human solidarity

On Friday 21 October 1994, the South African Parliament approved a Bill establishing a Commission of Truth and Reconciliation to enable the country to pursue these goals. Reflecting on this decision, the South African Council of Churches (SACC) commented at the time:

> The Commission for Truth and Reconciliation is not another Nuremberg. It turns its back on any desire for revenge. It represents an extraordinary act of generosity by a people who only insist that the truth, the whole truth and nothing but the truth be told.[45]

The SACC went on to say that this would create space 'where the deeper processes of forgiveness, confession, repentance, reparation and reconciliation can take place'.

Clearly reconciliation was now seen as part of the process of national reconstruction; equally clearly it was regarded as contingent upon the perpetrators of oppression to 'tell the truth' about their misdeeds, and for the victims to receive reparation. Thus reconciliation through uncovering the truth became the key in speaking about how we should deal with the past and in defining national goals for the future. As Mandela said on receiving the Report of the TRC in February 1999: 'The quest for reconciliation was the spur that gave life to our difficult negotiations process and the agreements that emerged from it.'[46] But this did not mean that there was consensus either on its meaning or on how it could be achieved.

A comparison of similar commissions in various parts of the world has shown that while in South Africa reconciliation was, from the outset, regarded as essential to the process and as necessary to its outcome, most of the others did not understand their task in this way.[47] One major reason for this was the extent to which the TRC vision arose out of religious and specifically Christian conviction and was shaped by the Christian doctrine of reconciliation. The debate about reconciliation within the TRC and the wider South African public would undoubtedly have been different if the Commission had been chaired by a judge rather than an archbishop, by a politician rather than a pastor and father confessor.[48]

But that was not the case. In addition, several of the commissioners were devout Christians, and some were clergy and theologians who had participated in the *Kairos* debate. This certainly made it difficult for those of other faiths, or secularists with a forensic mindset, to reach consensus on several issues related to our theme.[49] For those who belong to other religious traditions, the particular way in which Christians speak about reconciliation may be appropriate within the life of the Church, but it does not necessarily relate to their understanding of the word. And for those who are secular in outlook, and for whom politics is primarily about justice, power relations and economic forces, the use of such a specifically theological term is highly problematic unless its theological meaning and its political usage is clearly distinguished.

During the work of the TRC it soon became clear that, irrespective of its Christian meaning and its specific sense of national reconstruction, the rhetoric of reconciliation had become highly politicized. It even became possible to determine a person's political commitments by examining the way in which he or she used the term. Those who wanted to forget the past spoke of the need for reconciliation as though it was coterminous with moral amnesia, a particular failure of the apartheid ruling class. Hence former state president F. W. de Klerk and others emphasized the importance of letting 'bygones be bygones', which explains in part their opposition to the TRC. Right-wing conservatives spoke of reconciliation as an impossible dream and clung to their apartheid ideals. For them, the TRC was a waste of time and money. On the other side of the political spectrum, some victims or their families were totally opposed to the granting of amnesty to the perpetrators and challenged this in the courts. But there have been other critics whose support of the TRC and commitment to truth, justice and reconciliation is firm, but who have been critical of the way in which the TRC approached its task.[50] Or they have questioned the ability of the TRC to uncover the truth and really promote national reconciliation.[51]

South Africans are well aware that whatever the TRC has done to promote national reconciliation, it could not and did not fulfil the hopes of all those who long for justice and peace in South Africa. That challenge will be with us for generations. Despite the TRC we remain, in President Thabo Mbeki's words, 'two nations, the one white and relatively prosperous, and the other black and poor'.[52] Such rhetoric highlights reality, even if it requires qualification, for the social reality of South Africa is always more complex than can be captured in trenchant phrases no matter how true. But we must not miss Mbeki's point. His comment was a call to action, for the future of South Africa depends on how past enmity and present alienation can be overcome and the 'two nations' find each other and build a new nation on a moral foundation that can endure. That is what rec-onciliation is about, and as such it requires nothing less than continuing the struggle against the legacy of colonialism and apartheid.

Nonetheless, there is a qualitative difference between then and now. In the first place, the achievement of a constitutional state such as we now have it is, as Gerwel put it, 'the single most telling statement of national reconciliation'.[53] And, in the second place, there are many signs of reconciliation to encourage us along the way, not least those that have resulted from the work of the TRC. In sum, both in rhetoric and in reality, reconciliation has become a key word in shaping policy, indicating not only politi-cal allegiance but also religious orientation or lack of it, and in encapsulating the achievements and failures, the fears and hopes of contemporary South Africans.

We have considered some of the reasons why we may hesitate, but must dare to speak about reconciliation, and some of the ways in which we can do so. We have distinguished between, but not separated from each other, primary and secondary expres-sions of reconciliation. We have also considered some of the meanings of this multi-layered word, the core of which has to do with overcoming alienation, but the range of its references being much broader than any one form of enmity and estrangement. And we have examined the way in which understandings of reconciliation, both political and theological were shaped during the struggle against apartheid and how these informed the transition to democracy as well as the establishment of the TRC. The time has now come to turn our attention more specifically to the Christian understandings of reconciliation. How has the Christian doctrine of reconciliation been constructed? Or to put it differently: what do Christians mean when they speak about reconciliation?

2

Reconciliation in Christian Tradition

James Denney, a Scottish divine at the turn of the twentieth century, spoke of the doctrine of reconciliation as 'the inspiration and focus of all' doctrines of the Christian faith.[1] Denney's particular approach to the doctrine may be contested, but not his more general claim. So it is not surprising that reconciliation or *Versöhnung* became the central theme of Karl Barth's *Church Dogmatics*, that massive achievement of twentieth-century Protestant theology. With this doctrine, wrote Barth,

> we enter that sphere of Christian knowledge in which we have to do with the heart of the message received by and laid upon the Christian community, and therefore with the heart of the Church's dogmatics.[2]

If this is the heart of the Christian message, and therefore the heart of Christian doctrine or teaching, what does it mean and what are its implications for the struggle for reconciliation in the social and political arenas of our world? How are we to speak Christianly of reconciliation? If theological discourse has influenced political rhetoric, to what extent has theology been shaped in turn by political ideas and social forces?

Scripture and Christian tradition employ a range of metaphors, symbols and words to express God's saving activity in the world. These reflect the rich and multifaceted character of redemption as experienced and understood by Jewish and Christian believers in a variety of changing historical contexts. 'Reconciliation' is one of the words used in English to describe this experience, though the word 'atonement' has often functioned as its equivalent in theological textbooks. But 'at-one-ment' is a peculiarly English construction coined to describe the reuniting of God and humanity through the sacrifice of Christ on the cross. As such, atonement expresses but does not exhaust, the meaning of reconciliation.[3]

In Christian doctrine, the word 'reconciliation' carries a range of meaning and is used in two fundamental or primary ways. First of all to express the sum total of what Christians believe about God's saving work in Jesus Christ. As such it is the equivalent of the more comprehensive German *Versöhnung*, and is interchangeable with 'salvation', 'redemption', or 'atonement', each of which has been used to describe the doctrine. Partly for this reason we will sometimes use these metaphors in an interchangeable way to describe the doctrine as a whole. Yet each word gives the doctrine a particular emphasis and character, drawing on different biblical traditions and metaphors. Which brings us to the second way in which the word is used, namely as the term derived chiefly from the letters of Paul to explicate the meaning of the doctrine.

For Paul 'reconciliation' is the controlling metaphor for expressing the gospel. This does not exhaust the whole range of possible meanings implicit in the doctrine, for 'reconciliation' is only one of the words used by Paul to describe God's redemptive activity in its different aspects. Apart from 'salvation', 'redemption' and 'deliverance', Paul also speaks frequently of 'justification', which links his understanding of reconciliation directly to God's justice. Taken together all the metaphors form an indissoluble whole.[4] Yet, for Paul, the specific sense captured by reconciliation goes to the heart of the matter. And as he is virtually the only New Testament writer to use the word and its cognates, it is important for us to grasp what he meant by it if we are going to make 'reconciliation' our keyword for understanding the Christian doctrine of salvation.

There are several reasons why reconciliation is the most appropriate, though never the only, metaphor to describe what

God has done for the salvation of the world in Jesus Christ. One is the interpersonal character of the term. This relates well to both what Christians believe about the triune God and our understanding of human and social existence. It also relates to many strands in contemporary thought beyond the borders of theology for which 'relationality', 'alterity' and 'difference' have become keywords for understanding reality and dealing with the human predicament.[5] Hence its use today in every situation where the healing of relationships, whether in the family, in politics, or in religion has become necessary. And, of course, it speaks directly as well as analogically to the discussions that have emerged around the work of the TRC, having a particular significance in a world that has experienced conflict on such a global and devastating scale between divided ethnic and religious communities.

Paul borrowed the word from secular usage, and even though it had lost something of its original sense when he did,[6] it retains the potential for reconstructing the doctrine in relation to politics.[7] To speak of salvation, redemption, or atonement within the political arena does not have the same potential or carry the same sense of relevance as when we speak of reconciliation. But therein also lies the danger facing us as we embark on this task, namely that of allowing culture and context to determine its specifically Christian meaning. Or of confusing the genre in such a way that the differences between the political and the specifically Christian understandings of reconciliation are blurred. The relevance of the Christian doctrine of reconciliation is contingent on it retaining its distinct theological meaning even as we engage in exploring and embodying its political significance. The doctrine of reconciliation will be most relevant to social and political life when it is most true to its own distinct character. How pointless it would be if we were simply to provide religious terms in which the discussion about political reconciliation could be clothed in order to make it more palatable to religious people.

What, then, is the distinctive contribution that the Christian tradition makes to the contemporary debate about reconciliation, its meaning and praxis? In seeking to answer that question we will begin by recalling the 'grand narrative' of redemption that is fundamental to all else. In doing so we recognize that the notion of 'grand' or 'meta-narrative' is problematic, as Jean-François Lyotard and other deconstructionists have shown us, suggesting triumphalist pretension, absolutism and closure. There is no doubt that Christianity has traditionally made claims that evoke such criticism, and it is probably inevitable that it will never be able to escape them. There is, after all, an irreducible core to Christian faith, shaped by a 'grand narrative' without which Christianity loses its identity and relevance.

At the same time, we can and must read the story in ways that take the critique of the deconstructionists seriously even if we do not fully agree with them or agree to relativize Christian claims. Finding ways to do this is very difficult for theological discourse because talk about God invariably slides into a universal mode that suggests a total perspective on things, seeing things, as it were, from God's point of view. But, as Rowan Williams has argued, religious and theological integrity demand that our 'discourse about God *declines the attempt to take God's point of view*'.[8] This is not to say that we should not think theologically in relation to what we believe has been revealed, but that we should not do so in a way that is ideologically closed, uncritical and in protection of our own interests or power. The gospel is itself critical of idolatry, absolutism and human pretension, and therefore critical of a triumphalist Church or of a Christianity which does not respect the 'other'. Read in this way, the Christian 'grand narrative' is open-ended, a story still in the making through the Spirit, a story inclusive of all who wish to participate and respectful of those who do not. But it is a story nonetheless that claims our whole-hearted allegiance, and one that helps us understand reality in a certain way that informs faith and satisfies reason.

The 'grand narrative' of redemption

Even though the doctrine of reconciliation is central to the Christian faith, it was never defined in the ecumenical creeds of the Church and remained relatively undeveloped until the Middle Ages.[9] Since then, and right up to the present day, no one explanation has gained universal or ecumenical approval, though each confessional church family may have its own preferred interpretation. But even though Christians may put the emphasis differently, all Christian traditions have been shaped by a common foundational narrative of redemption. This is confessed in the creeds, and expressed and celebrated in their respective liturgies, hymnody and art. All of which reflects the narrative structure of much of Scripture, and the key place within that structure of story and parable as literary genre. It is in the telling and responding to this narrative that Christian identity is formed and sustained. For the past two millennia this story has also shaped human consciousness wherever Christianity has provided the dominant framework within which reality has been understood, even though it is often misunderstood and no longer has the same controlling power. For our purposes, the story needs little retelling except to remind us of the presuppositions on which the doctrine of reconciliation has been constructed.

Briefly told, the story has its primordial beginnings (Gen. 1–11) in the creation of humankind to be in relation to God as partner in managing the world. This covenantal relationship of trust between God and humanity expressed in faithful stewardship is the first presupposition of the doctrine of reconciliation. Everything else is contingent on the conviction that men and women are created to be in a covenantal relationship of companionship and co-operation with God, with one another, and in harmony with nature. Created 'in the image of God', all of us share a common humanity and are included in the scope of God's love and purpose. The second presupposition is that as a result of human disobedience humanity is alienated from God, experiences enmity in its own ranks, and is estranged from nature. Hence the notion of the fall and the later development of the doctrine of original sin to explain the contradictions of the human condition and its longing for healing and wholeness. Reconciliation would be unnecessary if this were not the case. The third presupposition is that God, out of love and grace, freely chooses to overcome this alienation and redeem humanity from its bondage to sin and its consequences.

Fundamentalist attempts to take this account of creation and fall as historical fact fail to recognize its true character as explanatory myth, and so land us in unnecessary and insurmountable problems. For what we have here is a profound attempt to describe the nature and destiny, misery and grandeur of humankind from the perspective of faith in God as creator and redeemer, and to do so in a way that relates directly to human experience and social reality.[10]

The character of the story shifts from explanatory myth to the sketchy beginnings of history as the vehicle of redemption with God's covenant made with the patriarch Abraham (Gen. 12). As we shall see in Chapter 4, this covenant has a special significance for Jews, Christians and Muslims. Whatever its historical foundations and details of the story, the biblical account is seeking to do something other than simply document history, namely, to witness to God's redemptive activity in history. Abraham's faithful obedience to God's call is both the prototype and the beginning of this process of reconciliation. Subsequently the liberation of the Hebrew slaves from Egypt, the settlement of Canaan, and the subsequent exile and return of Israel to Jerusalem, which would have been understood quite differently by Egyptians, Canaanites, Philistines and Babylonians, became for Jews defining moments in describing God's redemptive power and purpose.

These events also provided the interpretative framework for the Christian understanding of the mission and fate of Jesus of Nazareth as Messiah, that is, as God's anointed mediator of redemption, in and through whose life, death and resurrection the power of evil, sin and death were overcome. For those who shared in the renewal of the covenant in Christ through faith and baptism, reconciliation with God and life in the Spirit became a reality. Salvation was a present experience celebrated in worship and sacrament. But the story of redemption remained incomplete, for evil remained rampant. Salvation had to do with deliverance from God's judgement at the end of the present age. Then

God would finally establish justice and peace on earth that, for the present, remained only a confident hope. In the meantime, believers could be assured of God's forgiveness, experience life in the Spirit as a foretaste of the new age, and live in anticipation of the resurrection of the body and life eternal. The Church as that community in which reconciliation is embodied is taken up into this story through the gift and presence of the Spirit, and thereby becomes an integral part of the narrative. The calling and task of the Church is to tell the story to others and invite them to participate in what God has done and what God is doing in reconciling the world. In doing so the Church lives in expectation of what God will yet do for the redemption and restoration of the whole cosmos.

This brief and perhaps simplistic account of the 'grand narrative' of redemption is, in itself, an interpretation of the story that will be contested by others, not least by people of other faith traditions and by secular critics. Certainly Jewish and Muslim believers and scholars will read the narrative differently and at certain key points will disagree fundamentally with the Christian account.[11] This is why it is important that members of different faiths read, and seek to understand, their sacred texts in dialogue with each other. But the story will also be read and narrated differently by Christians even if the core remains much the same. It was inevitable that in its telling and retelling through the ages people have appropriated and made it their own in a variety of ways appropriate to their existential condition. As a result there are various interpretative layers or trajectories both within Scripture and the history of Christianity that reflect different historical contexts, each with its own experience of alienation and brokenness and therefore its own way of expressing God's redemption. But every Christian who seriously considers the meaning of reconciliation begins, in the words of Rowan Williams, 'from the experience of being reconciled, being accepted, being held (however precariously) in the grace of God'.[12] This was profoundly true of St Paul, to whose teaching on reconciliation we now turn.

The Pauline trajectory of reconciliation

The idea of reconciliation, as Ralph Martin has shown, 'was current and was developed across a broad chronological and cultural spectrum of primitive and later Christianity'.[13] In fact, Paul's use of reconciliation derives from sources in both Jewish and Hellenistic Christianity that precede him, and is then developed by Paul's own disciples as, for example, in the letter to the Ephesians. But Paul is the pivot in the development of this 'trajectory of reconciliation' as he relates God's reconciliation of the world in Christ to a variety of contexts and issues.[14]

The Greek words translated by 'reconciliation' or 'reconcile' only occur 15 times in the New Testament, and almost only in the Pauline letters.[15] Yet they are highly significant for understanding what it is that Christians believe God has accomplished for the salvation of the world. All of them are compounds of the Greek ἀλλασσω, 'to exchange', and this in turn is derived from ἀλλος meaning 'the other'.[16] The words thus carry with them the sense of exchanging places with 'the other', and therefore being in solidarity with rather than against 'the other'. It is important to keep this in mind, for it is fundamental to the Christian understanding of reconciliation, to its process and practice, and to the notion of vicarious representation which lies at the heart of the gospel. Reconciliation literally has to do with the way in which God relates to us, the human 'other', and in turn with our relationship to 'the other', whether understood as an individual person or a group of people. It has to do with the process of overcoming alienation through identification and in solidarity with 'the other', thus making peace and restoring relationships.[17] Reconciliation has to do, if we may put it colloquially, with God making us friends.

This understanding of restored relationships is also reflected in those New Testament texts in which 'reconciliation' is found outside the Pauline literature, namely in the Sermon on the Mount:

> So when you are offering your gift at the altar, if you remember that your brother or sister has something against you,

leave your gift there before the altar and go; first be reconciled (διαλασσομαι) to your brother or sister, and then come and offer your gift. (Matt. 5.23–24 NRSV)

These verses are often used as a preface to the sharing of the peace in the Christian liturgy. They go to the heart of the matter and find resonance in Paul's own writings where 'reconciliation symbolism stresses the contrast between enmity and peace, hate and love (cf. Rom 5.1–12; 8.31–39; 2 Cor. 5.14–21).'[18] Reconciliation in Paul, as in the Sermon on the Mount, always has to do with personal relationships, but Paul's understanding of its meaning is particularly rich in texture and character, and it is from him that we discover both its range of meaning,[19] and the reason for its appeal.

Arguably the most remarkable aspect of Paul's teaching on reconciliation is that in virtually every instance in which he uses the word or its cognates, God is the subject or agent of reconciliation.[20] In speaking of God in this way, Paul becomes the first Greek author to speak of the person offended as the one who initiates the act or process of reconciliation.[21] This not only distinguishes Paul's use of the term 'reconciliation' from other Hellenistic sources, but also from other cultures and languages. For in the latter it is normally the case that reconciliation has to be initiated by the person responsible for the alienation and hostility, hence acknowledgement of guilt becomes the precondition for reconciliation. But, for Paul, the gospel is precisely that God is the one who takes the initiative in seeking an end to hostility.[22] Thus reconciliation in Pauline theology refers to the way in which the love of God in Jesus Christ turns enemies into friends thereby creating peace. Significantly, then, reconciliation tells us something about the personal and relational character of God, namely, that God is love. This understanding is embodied in the way in which Christian tradition understands the triune nature of God in whom difference is not the cause of division but the enrichment of unity.

The varied ways in which Paul's understanding of reconciliation develops can be seen by examining the way in which he uses the term to address different issues and needs in the varied contexts to which his correspondence is addressed. For example, in 2 Corinthians he links the gospel of reconciliation to the new creation in Christ, the righteousness of God and the mission of the Church.[23] But he does so in a way that is deeply personal. The background to Paul's teaching is his own rejection by the Christian community in Corinth who questioned his authority and his motives in writing to them. The language Paul uses is clearly intended to bring about reconciliation. As Erik Doxtader helpfully puts it: 'The words of reconciliation afford Paul the vocabulary needed to invite his audience to enter into the Word of reconciliation.'[24] Thus there is an interaction between the divine act of reconciliation in Christ and human appropriation of that act in relating in a new way to each other. The need for and the dynamics of reconciliation between Paul and the Corinthian Church become the reason as well as the basis for Paul's rhetoric about God's reconciliation.

Reconciliation in Colossians is far less personal than in 2 Corinthians, addressing as it does the challenge of gnosticism. The essential background is Paul's acute sense of cosmic disorder, of a world in captivity to 'the principalities and powers of this world'. But whatever cosmic powers there may be, they have all been brought under God's control and there is now no hostility or dichotomy between the creator and the creation. The world is not at the mercy of fate, a world in cosmic free-fall, but one that has been reconciled to God in Christ. As a result, Christians have no need to engage in vain speculation, but rather to live a life that matches up to their reconciliation in Christ.[25] Not only humanity, but the whole created cosmos is included in God's act of reconciliation in Christ, thereby linking redemption and creation. In that remarkable opening chapter of Paul's letter to the Colossians (1.18–23), God's cosmic reconciling activity precedes and provides the framework within which God's reconciliation of humanity occurs. This has particular implications for our approach to the environment from the perspective of the gospel.

Reconciliation in Romans derives from Christ's work of

expiation as a result of which humanity is justified by faith. Justification is a key metaphor for Paul and especially for those Christian traditions shaped by the Protestant Reformation, but much ink has been used in trying to determine the relationship between justification and reconciliation.[26] One way of doing so is to argue that whereas justification is interpreted 'in terms of the legal character of the Old Testament covenant of God (Rom. 3.2–6)'[27] reconciliation is understood 'in terms of the Old Testament covenant of God as electing love (cf. Rom. 9.11, 13; Col. 3.12)'.[28] Justification is about the expiation of sin; the justification by grace through faith of the sinner before God. But this is not wholly adequate, for reconciliation is God's overcoming estrangement and establishing a new relationship not just with individuals who come to faith, but also with the world in all its complex of relationships. Paul's use of the term 'reconciliation' thus shifts the focus of Christ's redeeming work from a forensic-cultic idiom of individual guilt, justification and acquittal to a universal, personal and inclusive understanding.[29]

More importantly, for Paul the language of justification derives from a special understanding of justice, namely justice as restorative rather than punitive. From this perspective justification and reconciliation belong together, they are inseparable descriptors of God's work in restoring relations. God's justice, in Paul as elsewhere in Scripture, has far less to do with the law-court and much more to do with healing relationships and social justice with a particular bias towards the poor and oppressed. In other words, to say that God was reconciling the world in Christ is another way of saying that God was busy restoring God's reign of justice.[30] One implication of this understanding of the relationship between the gospel of reconciliation and justice is that, for Paul, theology and ethics are inseparably bound together. To be reconciled to God and to do justice are part and parcel of the same process. In sum, for Paul:

> The atonement is an all-encompassing act of justice-making that overthrows oppressive powers (cf. Rom. 8.38–39; 1 Cor. 15.24–26), forgives all those guilty of collaboration with the

enemy (5.6–10), and restores to full covenant-relationship all who believe, Gentiles as well as Jews.[31]

The restoration not only of justice but of God's covenant relationship in Christ through whom Gentiles are now included, finds particular expression in the letter to the Ephesians. Reconciliation with God in this letter means participation in the Church as the covenant community representing the new humanity in which Jew and Gentile are reconciled in Christ as members of one body. This does not mean severing connections with Israel and the faith of the old covenant, but rather an overcoming of the ethnic hostility that has kept Jew and Gentile apart. Reconciled to God, the Church is a multi-ethnic community, the embodiment of a new humanity. As such it is 'a novel entity on the world stage' mirroring in microcosm 'the hope of the world and the universe, at present divided and at odds with its creator'.[32]

Reconciliation, then, is more than a theological code-word for God's work of restoring men and women to himself, it refers to a way of life to which Christians are called in the world, sharing in God's work of reconciliation. Just as Paul anchored reconciliation in the historical events of Jesus' passion, so he tied it to the ethical transformation of historical and material conditions. Reconciliation has to do with the breaking down of the walls of enmity that separate Jews and Gentiles, men and women, masters and slaves, thereby creating the conditions on which harmonious relations can be established. For Paul, the death of Jesus on the cross is understood as a sacrifice for sin, but as Timothy Gorringe rightly notes, Jesus' death does not bring a new *doctrine* into being, 'but a new *movement* in which alienated beings were to be caught up and reconciled'.[33]

The gospel of reconciliation thus leads directly to defining the mission of the Church in the world, namely to proclaim the gospel of reconciliation (2 Cor. 5.11–20) and the eschatological hope of God's restoration and renewal of the whole creation. The Church is God's reconciled and reconciling community, God's new humanity, a sign and witness of God's purpose for the whole inhabited universe or *oikumene*. Reconciliation, in other words, is an open-ended process that occurs through the Spirit and anticipates the coming of God's reign of justice and peace. If reconciliation must be understood sequentially when we speak of it within the context of interpersonal, social and political struggles for healing, then from the perspective of the New Testament and Paul's theology, we need to understand it eschatologically. This means that God's future for the cosmos, a future of humanity and the cosmos restored and fulfilled, is always coming towards us even though we experience its reality through the Spirit in the present. Complete reconciliation is a future hope that shapes the way in which we live our lives.

The Pauline trajectory of reconciliation does not come to an end with the closing of the New Testament canon. On the contrary, the concept is one that expands to embrace new contextual and historical realities, relating the saving work of Christ to them in a way that overcomes alienation and establishes peace. This is because reconciliation is not only a past historical event, but also the present activity of the Spirit of God in the life of the world drawing men and women into its orbit. Through the Spirit we share in God's reconciliation of the world, and through the Spirit God's reconciliation becomes a reality for those who enter into it in a way that transforms their experience. That is why any account of the doctrine of reconciliation from a Pauline perspective is and must remain 'a relatively *open enterprise*'.[34]

All in all, reconciliation in Paul 'covers matters as extensive and far-ranging as human thought can imagine'.[35] But it never loses touch with concrete reality. On the one hand it is always historically grounded in the life, death and resurrection of Jesus Christ, and on the other, in the life and mission of the Church, and the ethical responsibility of the Christian in the world. Thus those who seek to interpret Paul's understanding of reconciliation in Christ for today must of necessity go with but also beyond Paul, not staying in Corinth, Colossae, Rome or Ephesus, in seeking to interpret the heart of the gospel in the contemporary world. But the core message remains constant. How, then, has the doctrine of reconciliation been conceived and constructed in the course of Christian history?

Constructing the doctrine

Theological students of my generation spent a great deal of time trying to understand the various theories of the atonement that developed in the course of the history of Christian doctrine. The names are familiar to many of us even if the details and the debates are not, and I must confess a reluctance to even mention them, let alone examine their content. Read today they appear somewhat sterile, remote from our experience and the realities we face. Whatever their explanatory potency in their own historical context, their interpretation of Scripture and theological reasoning in hindsight often leaves much to be desired. So there is no merit in simply repeating them as though by doing so we are faithfully representing the Christian doctrine of reconciliation. We dare not, as H. A. Hodges put it, fall prey to the 'tyranny of the theories'.[36]

Yet each theory and the debates they engendered represent a serious attempt to interpret the narrative of redemption in a particular historical context. Taken together they provide a legacy of insight and warning that needs to be heeded. We therefore need to understand what they were really getting at, rather than simply discarding them as outdated or even outrageous. Indeed, as I reflected on some of the heated discussions within the South African TRC about guilt and forgiveness, reconciliation and justice, remorse and reparation, I was frequently aware that whatever their current status, the issues have long been debated within Christian circles. I was aware, moreover, that some of the problems of understanding encountered in the TRC process derived from differences of interpretation within the Christian community, and from a lack of understanding of the history of Christian doctrine by Christians and others alike. Last of all, I was aware that reflection on the way in which each theory developed and gained explanatory favour within a particular context could help us better understand how it is that reconciliation has become the preferred metaphor for describing the Christian doctrine of redemption today. Each theory, in fact, reflects the social variants in which it developed, saying perhaps almost as much about the conditions under which it was formulated as it does about the gospel. So in briefly recounting the theories I am really trying to discern the core concern of each in order to see whether it is something that remains important for us.

Of all the theories, those of the first few centuries stayed closest to the narrative of redemption. Earliest amongst these patristic theories was Irenaeus' doctrine of recapitulation, which continues to attract attention.[37] Building on Pauline theology, Irenaeus argued that what was lost in Adam was retrieved in Christ through his obedient redemptive retracing of the human story. Redemption is not about part of human existence, the spiritual separated from the material, but rather the totality of human experience. Every aspect of what it means to be human has been assumed and redeemed by Christ. Gustavo Gutiérrez made the same point in his seminal study on Latin American liberation theology:

> Salvation embraces all persons and the whole person; the liberating action of Christ – made human in this history and not in a history marginal to real human life – is at the heart of the historical current of humanity; the struggle for a just society is in its own right very much part of salvation history.[38]

Patristic sermons and tracts are also full of references to the sacrificial system and images of the Old Testament in order to speak of the death of Jesus as a vicarious sacrifice for sin. Suffering and the shedding of blood are necessary not to appease the deity, as in pagan sacrifices, but for the sake of dealing with guilt and restoring the wholeness of the community. This approach to reconciliation can be abused, especially when it leads to the conclusion that the suffering and death of victims is necessary for the sake of the greater common good. But it is impossible to remain faithful to the New Testament and not recognize the centrality of Jesus' self-giving on the cross, the 'shedding of his blood', as the pivotal moment in the history of salvation. Or in acknowledging Jesus' call to his followers to 'take up their cross' if they are to be his disciples and thus become participants in the work of reconciliation.[39] What we are talking about is nothing other than the vicarious offering of one's life for the sake of others without which Christianity would become a mere moral code.

Another favourite patristic metaphor, that of ransom, recalled Jesus' statement that he would 'give his life as a ransom for many' (Mark 10.45). At a time when the payment of ransom for the release of captives was a widespread social practice this had a special significance. Some theologians spent much time debating the terms of the ransom needed to release human beings from the clutches of the devil or the payment due to God to cancel our debt. In the process the metaphor was abused and the point of Jesus' saying was lost. He was not teaching a theory of atonement, but describing the way of the 'suffering servant' and the implications this has for his disciples as those called to serve others. Nonetheless, the conviction that Christ gave his life to deliver us from the powers of evil is a central part of Christian belief. 'Christus victor!' is therefore the primary Christian confession and the 'classic' understanding of redemption as Gustav Aulén called it,[40] with the resurrection regarded as the decisive redemptive act. In sum, the patristic understanding of reconciliation, which has fundamentally shaped the development of the Christian doctrine of reconciliation, means that God

> refuses to abandon the world of sin and death in all its alienated darkness but, on the contrary becomes involved in it even to its direst consequences, suffers for it, strives for it, and in conquering it liberates it.[41]

St Anselm of Canterbury's famous eleventh-century tract, *Cur Deus Homo*,[42] signals a turning-point in the history of doctrine in the Western Church. It was the first major attempt to provide a rational account of how and why the drama of salvation must be true. Fundamental to Anselm's account was Augustine's doctrine of 'original sin' and the latter's personal struggle with guilt. Within the context of a Roman emphasis on law and feudal society's insistence that injury to honour demands satisfaction,

Anselm stressed the need to satisfy the demands of God's justice. For Anselm, the gravity of sin and guilt could only be overcome through paying the penalty for human disobedience and its consequences. But since we sinful humans are incapable of making such satisfaction, Christ did so on our behalf by satisfying the demands of God's holy justice and imputing God's righteousness to us.[43]

This emphasis on the objective work of God in Christ through which sin is overcome and the world reconciled to God, and the forensic framework in which it was described, became the benchmark of Catholic orthodoxy that found its most obvious expression in 'the sacrifice of the mass'. But Anselm's theory also prepared the way for the Protestant theory of penal substitution.[44] Not only does Christ pay our debts, he is also punished for our faults. Through Christ's death on the cross in our place, the penalty for sin has been fully paid, God's righteousness is imputed to us fully by grace alone, and we are justified by faith alone. This reading of Paul's theology is open to serious criticism and is based on a misreading of Paul's rhetoric. Paul's 'justice' language is not forensic in the Roman legal sense but is, on the contrary, a critical challenge to such an understanding. Paul's 'substitutionary' language is far better understood in terms of representation or vicariousness.[45]

The strengths of the satisfaction theory are also where its weaknesses lie. Anselm rightly stresses the cost of reconciliation, but makes redemption contingent on the Son of God appeasing the anger of God the Father rather than as an event of anguish and pain within the life of the triune God. He rightly stresses the seriousness of sin as the root cause of the human predicament and the need to honour God's justice in the world, but does so in a legalistic way that leads to an unhealthy emphasis on guilt, and misplaces the focus of divine wrath. That God is judge is not at issue here, for God is the God of justice. But the focus of God's justice is on human oppression, not on divine honour. God is not one who stands above us to condemn or acquit in the Roman sense, but in the Hebrew prophetic sense of one who judges everything that oppresses humanity and destroys creation. God therefore stands with us rather than against us.

When we speak of the satisfaction of God's justice with regard to our individual sins, and interpret justification in a Roman forensic way, we change the biblical focus on God's reign and righteousness as primarily the restoration of relationships and social justice. This subverts Jesus' own insistence that 'we seek first God's reign and his justice' (Matt. 6.33–34.) by misreading and spiritualizing both the 'kingdom of heaven' and God's 'righteousness'. In this way the biblical concern for the transformation of the world is reduced to the salvation of the individual soul. This was the context in which Martin Luther's search for a gracious God sparked off the Protestant Reformation. At issue was not the objective work of Christ in satisfying God's justice, nor whether we are saved by God's grace or not, on this all agreed. At issue was the way in which God's saving grace is appropriated in order for the individual to be accepted by a God whose wrath condemns but whose grace saves.

There is a further ambiguity in the theory of satisfaction that needs comment. Timothy Gorringe has persuasively shown that the doctrine of satisfaction 'formed part of the "ideology" of Western Christendom' and, as such, has had a powerful influence on the shaping of Western culture and consciousness.[46] But the influence was ambiguous. Affirming its positive contribution, Gorringe writes that the theory of satisfaction

> addressed the need for order both in society and in the human soul; it addressed the sense of justice and the need to express moral outrage; it gave voice to the experience that suffering might sometimes be redemptive; above all it was a means of dealing with guilt.[47]

But the theory also had dire negative consequences in each respect as well. There is, as Gorringe shows, a strong connection between the theory of satisfaction and the sanctioning of violence against those whom the dominant in society need to exclude for the sake of maintaining order. Hence there is a connection between the satisfaction theory and the justification of retributive justice as well as the death penalty.

Following René Girard, Gorringe argues that making the 'other' a scapegoat was an act of collective violence justified as necessary to save both society and our own souls, as well as the soul – though not the body – of the culprit. So the story of Christ's suffering death on the cross, which was a unique protest against and confrontation with the powers that bring death, whether religious or political, became the source of legitimating that power in punishing others. 'That this could happen', writes Gorringe, 'and not be perceived, was due not just to the ambiguity of the New Testament texts, but to the fact that profound and necessary truths about suffering and vicarious love are concealed within the conventional interpretation.'[48] It is these profound truths about vicarious suffering and love, as well as the costly character of reconciliation and its connection with God's concern for justice, that we need to hold on to while avoiding the tyranny of the theory.

In contrast to Anselm's forensic understanding, Abelard, writing a little later from Paris, proposed an alternative that has had enduring appeal as an alternative reading of the doctrine. Rather than putting the emphasis on atonement for sin that happened objectively beyond us, something that Abelard did not deny, he spoke of the way in which the love of God in the sacrifice of Christ on the cross affects us. In other words, the love of God revealed on the cross calls forth a response of love on our part. Thus, for Abelard, the gospel saves through its power to influence and transform our lives rather than through the forensic satisfying of God's wrath. In his own words:

> our redemption is that supreme love manifested in our case by the passion of Christ, which not only delivers us from the bondage of sin, but also acquires for us the liberty of the sons of God; so that we may fulfil all things from the love rather than fear of him . . . [49]

Abelard's explanation of the work of Christ, sometimes referred to as the 'moral influence' theory, emphasized the existential effect which the death of Christ has on us in making us contrite for our sins, awakening faith, and kindling love for God and one another. This approach later found expression in the Socinian reaction to Protestant and especially Calvinist orthodoxy. Reconciliation derives from the love of God rather than the satisfaction of a wrathful God's justice, the very notion of the latter being repugnant to enlightened reason and morality, as well as theology. Redemption cannot come about through an act that is fundamentally unjust.

But there is another dimension to the Socinian approach to the doctrine of reconciliation that can be traced backwards as well as forwards in those more radical movements, such as Anabaptism or the Quakers, that have always offered an alternative reading of redemption. For them, the message of the cross is not simply about what God might have done in and through the death of Christ, but on the *way* of the cross as the way in which we participate in God's work of reconciliation and redemption. Jesus' servanthood, his teaching about non-violence, his willingness to suffer for the sake of others, the inclusiveness of his embrace, all finding expression in the Sermon on the Mount, provide the basis for our participation in God's reconciling work. This corrective to both Catholic and Protestant orthodoxies remains pertinent and necessary. Yet, important and fundamental as it is, it does not do full justice to the language of the New Testament and the profound mystery to which that language is pointing. However problematic, something happens in the death and resurrection that requires the writers of the New Testament and subsequent generations of Christians to speak of vicarious sacrifice and expiation for sin as they ponder the cry of dereliction on the cross.

Several observations are appropriate and necessary in reflecting on these traditional theories. First is the awareness that there can be no adequate, fully satisfying, rational account of how it is that God has reconciled the world. What we have, rather, is a series of bold attempts to weave together a rich range of biblical images and metaphors into a coherent whole that seeks to interpret the grand narrative of redemption, helps faith and experience understand themselves, and informs both worship and witness. Yet it

is no more possible, as Hans Küng comments, to 'commit ourselves now than in New Testament and patristic times to a
particular conceptual framework – whether juridical, cultic,
metaphysical, or even scientific, technical, psychological, sociological – for the interpretation of the highly complex event of the
redemption'.[50]

Second is the awareness that each theory has emerged and
found particular significance within different historical contexts.
This indicates that while each theory can claim some biblical
sanction, the way in which the theory developed was also shaped
by the social conditions prevailing at the time. This implies the
need for us to develop our own contemporary understanding of
the doctrine, drawing on Scripture in a way that speaks to our
situation. Christian tradition does not stand still, it is the handing on and interpreting of that which has been received. The fact
that reconciliation is such a dominant concern and need in the
contemporary world is a major reason why the doctrine has been
reconstructed using that term. The point is well made by Shailer
Mathews, a representative of the so-called 'Chicago School' in
the 1930s, in his classic study on *The Atonement and the Social
Process*. The permanent value in the theories, Mathews argued,
is seen when we ask 'what function they have had in satisfying
human need' in successive periods. He writes:

> In general they may be said to be those (needs) which on the
> plane of political life were caused and met by those institutions
> and practices utilized as patterns in the doctrines of atone-
> ment. As the political elements operated in the actual social life
> of the community, so they functioned analogically in the
> doctrines.[51]

Whatever other substantive connections there might be in
relating the Christian doctrine of reconciliation to political reconciliation in our time, there is surely an analogous relationship
that makes the doctrine of particular relevance.

Yet none of this implies that we cannot learn from earlier
theories in developing our own approach to reconciliation. For

while it is true that each theory of the atonement developed and found analogical resonance within a particular historical context, it does not mean that they have no explanatory power at other times and places. A few examples must suffice to make the point. The traditional African practices of animal sacrifice and the veneration of ancestors undoubtedly influences the way in which many African Christians today understand the biblical story of redemption just as it may play a role in social and political reconciliation. This was frequently the case in response to the work of the TRC. Reconciliation between the living and the 'living dead', in which sacrifice played a key role, was important for the cleansing of the notorious Vlakplaas headquarters of the death squads of the apartheid regime. In a world where there has been an upsurge of terror and hijacking, the idea of a ransom as means to freedom has fresh significance. Irenaeus' doctrine of recapitulation can speak anew to those who conceive of salvation in terms of the restoration of human wholeness.[52] The notion of vicarious sacrifice is by no means foreign to a world in which people give their lives for the sake of saving others.

However true it may be that each theory developed in relation to a particular social need, the assumption that there is one dominant social or political characteristic of each age and culture that informs our understanding of the need for redemption is surely not valid. Just as it was not true during the period in which the New Testament was written, so it is not true in today's world. Take South Africa as an example where liberation was the key metaphor during the struggle against apartheid and where, today, alongside the need for national reconciliation, there are many other needs reflected in the diverse range of cultural and social contexts, as well as current experience. Victims of rape, abuse and HIV/AIDS cry out for justice, dignity and healing. Wealthy citizens go in search of spiritual enlightenment and enrichment, while those trapped in their poverty cry out for liberation and land. Disadvantaged communities seek education, acknowledgement of their cultural identity and language, as well as access to resources. The truth is that human need is diverse, even if there is a basic need for grace, forgiveness and wholeness.

A third observation about the theories of atonement is that even if the metaphors employed derive from social and political needs, they were rarely used in a way that related to those needs. They become analogous for personal and individual redemption. Drawing heavily on a particular forensic reading of Pauline theology, they seldom if ever do justice to the prophetic trajectory in the Synoptic Gospels and Jesus' teaching on the reign of God. Likewise, they fail to recognize that the message of the cross is not one that provides legitimacy for power and the maintenance of social order, but a radical critique of power and a potential source for social transformation. In Christ the victim of injustice, God identifies with other victims. Thus for many Christians struggling against poverty, injustice and oppression in our own day, reconciliation has become suspect because of its association with privatized religion, or because it is understood as something that awaits us in the future beyond this vale of tears.

Finally, we must recognize that the doctrine of reconciliation cannot be understood in isolation from the rest of what the Church believes and practises. Consider, for example, Barth's treatment of the doctrine of reconciliation in his *Church Dogmatics*, an account from within the Reformed tradition. While there is undoubtedly fresh and developing insight in his exposition, what he says about reconciliation is the culmination and refining of everything that has gone before. The doctrine of the triune God, creation, covenant and election, the incarnation and life in the Spirit, all major themes in the previous volumes of the *Church Dogmatics*, laid the foundation for those in which the work comes to its climax. Hence we need to see the doctrine of reconciliation within the framework of the witness of Scripture as a whole. To wrench the doctrine of reconciliation from its foundations, or to separate out its different parts in order to build a theory of atonement, must inevitably lead to distortion and misunderstanding. Reconciliation then becomes a label that can more or less mean whatever we wish it to mean. But reconciliation as proclaimed in the New Testament is dependent upon God's covenant with humanity and the family of Abraham; on the totality of God's saving revelation in Jesus Christ; and on the work of the Spirit in the renewal of human life, the restoration of human community and the renewal of the cosmos. Each of these is important, and each must inform our discussion of reconciliation if it is to do justice to the doctrine and to contribute to its critical reconstruction.

Elsewhere I have described the development of public theology in South Africa from the early days of the struggle against apartheid to the present post-apartheid era.[53] This development may be described as a movement from a more liberal theology of reconciliation, evident in *The Message to the People of South Africa*, through a period of liberation theology, evident in the *Kairos Document*, to present attempts to develop a public theology of democratic reconstruction and transformation. This development, I suggest, mirrors a broader movement in the development of the doctrine of reconciliation which takes it beyond the historic theories of atonement into the realm of politics and public life. In many respects it begins with the publication in 1888 of Albrecht Ritschl's three-volume study entitled *Reconciliation and Justification*.[54]

A public theology of reconciliation

Albrecht Ritschl's *Reconciliation and Justification* was the first major modern attempt to critically reconstruct the doctrine of reconciliation in a way that tried to avoid the inadequacies of both Anselm and Abelard. Ritschl, whose dislike of pietism was as strong as his dislike of the theory of penal substitution, did not replace an objective understanding of atonement with one wholly subjective. Christ's work is to forgive us our sins (justification) whereby communion with God is restored (reconciliation). Thus part of Ritschl's contribution to the reconstructing of the doctrine was his attempt to overcome the split between the objective and the subjective. But his major contribution was to recast the doctrine in terms of moral values and to see reconciliation as extending the kingdom or reign of God. Reconciliation has to do with the moral transformation of the world.

Reconciliation, from this perspective, is more than deliverance from guilt. It is a calling to emulate God's character, which means that love of one's enemies, or forgiveness of one's debtors, 'is not dependent on their rendering satisfaction'.[55] As a result of God's reconciliation 'we come to cherish a different estimate of self, and are changed in disposition'.[56] In this way we are brought into the fellowship of the kingdom of God through which Christ's moral influence makes an impact on the world. This insight was Ritschl's great contribution, and its effect can be seen most notably on those theologians in the United States who pioneered the 'social gospel'. Whatever Ritschl's shortcomings, Walter Rauschenbusch's attempt to recast Christian doctrine in terms of Jesus' prophetic witness to the social demands of the reign of God remains a constant challenge to theological endeavour, and not least when it comes to the doctrine of reconciliation.[57]

Many Protestant theologians at the turn of the twentieth century came under Ritschl's influence in this regard, including Barth who was later to treat him with such disdain.[58] In his lectures on *The Work of Christ*, published in 1910, the Scottish theologian P. T. Forsyth confessed that many of his insights on 'reconciliation' were stolen from Ritschl,[59] especially the need to recover the moral core of the doctrine. However, Ritschl's liberal theology proved inadequate in enabling the German Church to address the cataclysm of 1914–18. Neither did it completely capture the loyalty of theologians like Forsyth who were wary of reducing reconciliation to the spreading of liberal moral values in society under the pretext of extending the kingdom of God.

In implied criticism of Ritschl yet building on his influence, Forsyth set out the essential elements of the doctrine of reconciliation by returning to Paul's theology. Reconciliation, he argued, 'meant the total result of Christ's life-work in the fundamental, permanent, final changing of the relation between man and God, altering it from a relation of hostility to one of confidence and peace'.[60] This presupposed atonement, that is, it required more than the revelation of God's love; it required that sin be overcome through the death of Jesus Christ.[61] In other words, although it is God who reconciles the world in Christ, it is also in Christ that God is reconciled to the world.[62] Moreover, again following

Paul, Forsyth emphasized the interpersonal character of reconciliation, but refused to reduce it to a matter of individual salvation. Reconciliation is cosmic, 'not a person here and another
there, snatched as brands from the burning; not a group here and
a group there; but the reconciliation of the whole world'. And,

> it is a reconciliation *final in Jesus Christ and his cross*, done
> once for all; really effected in the spiritual world in such a way
> that in history the great victory is not still to be won; it has
> been won in reality, and has only to be followed up and
> secured in actuality.[63]

This recovery of the historical reality of reconciliation achieved
through the incarnation, death and resurrection of Christ also
lies at the heart of Barth's doctrine of reconciliation, for Barth –
like Forsyth – also draws deeply on Paul's theology. According to
Barth, the covenant God makes with humanity provides the
framework within which the message of reconciliation is to be
understood. The covenant refers to God's graceful decision and
purpose to restore relations with humankind and, indeed, to
restore the cosmos itself to its full created glory. In other words,
Barth locates reconciliation on a much broader canvas than is
sometimes done, ensuring that creation and redemption are not
separated but are considered as a whole. This means that nothing
remains outside the redemptive and reconciling purposes of God,
for while the covenant made with Abraham refers to the calling
of a people to witness to God's purposes, that covenant presupposes God's redemptive will for the whole created order. In
Christ, the mediator between God and humanity, God has
renewed his covenant in a new initiative 'to reconcile all things to
himself'. From the perspective of faith, this event radically
changes human history and provides the objective basis both for
our present experience of reconciliation and the hope that we
have for the future of the world. In Jesus Christ the human
situation has been fundamentally changed. What remains is for
Christians

to welcome the divine verdict, to take it seriously with full responsibility, not to keep their knowledge of it to themselves, but by the witness of their existence and proclamation to make known to the world which is still blind and deaf to this verdict the alteration which has in fact taken place by it.[64]

Although Barth was highly critical of Ritschl, there is a close connection between his doctrine of reconciliation and his political ethics.[65] In his lectures on ethics (1928/29) Barth declares that on 'the basis of accomplished reconciliation' citizens are called to serve their neighbour, and live for others on the basis of mutual forgiveness.[66] Which leads him to go even further and assert that the state is 'an order of reconciliation', whose goal parallels that of the Church. Barth gave these lectures on ethics before the rise of Nazism. But this did not radically alter his understanding of the role of the state as he expressed it 10 years later on the eve of the Second World War, for the Third Reich had rejected its divine mandate and therefore had to be resisted.[67] The role of the Church and that of the state have to be distinguished and each respected, but they serve the same end, namely God's reconciling will for humanity. What is proclaimed in the narrative of reconciliation is neither a utopian dream nor a programme of action, but the claim that the future of the world, its ultimate reconciliation with God, has already begun.

Alongside the recovery of the objective reality of reconciliation and its ethical significance in twentieth-century Protestant theology, came a renewed emphasis on the vicarious suffering of Christ as our representative on the cross. The humble self-emptying of God in Christ, and the humiliation and suffering of Christ as our representative on the cross at the hands of political and religious power, was God's chosen way of achieving reconciliation. Thus, for Barth, the grand narrative of reconciliation is woven around the 'journey of the Son of God into the far country' of human alienation in order to redeem and set us free.[68] Through vicarious suffering on our behalf, God in Christ reveals his love for the world, pronounces forgiveness, struggles against and overcomes dehumanizing powers and idolatries, judges and condemns everything that is unjust, sets us free from oppression, and restores both our humanity and our relationships. The logic of representation in Barth's doctrine of reconciliation is, however, quite different from that of traditional notions of substitution or propitiation.[69] God in Christ stands in solidarity with us in our sin, speaking for and acting on our behalf, judging our sin yet embracing us as prodigals drawn by the love of the Father to a new status of friendship and freedom. With this understanding we reach 'the final, solid core of our salvation', declared Hendrikus Berkhof, and 'it is very much a question whether this core can be further split or elucidated'.[70]

The idea of Christ as our representative and of his vicarious expiation is not alien to our modern world.[71] We are all familiar with the role of scapegoats who bear the brunt of oppressive power, though not always, as in the case, of Christ, in a way that brings about liberation and moral transformation. We are also familiar with the courageous example of many aid workers and others whose daily lot often requires taking risks on behalf of those whom they serve. How many people in our own time have suffered and died on behalf of the liberation of others! All South Africans have been liberated vicariously by those who, like Steve Biko, Beyers Naudé or Nelson Mandela, have given themselves so fully for the sake of others in the struggle against apartheid. Indeed, the victims of injustice, and those who have resisted victimization, have redefined the meaning of vicarious suffering.

Already in his doctoral dissertation, *Sanctorum Communio*, published in 1927, Bonhoeffer wrote of 'vicarious action' as the life-principle of the new humanity that Christ has brought into being.[72] 'God does not "overlook" sin', wrote Bonhoeffer, for 'that would mean not taking human beings seriously as personal beings in their very culpability; and that would mean no re-creation of the person, and therefore no creation of community'.[73] In other words, the way of reconciliation is the way of struggle against a world that has rejected the way of Christ, and Christ as our representative (*Stellvertretung*). There is nothing cheap about God's reconciliation. Yet, despite the world's rejection of Christ and his way, the reality of reconciliation remains:

> The reality of the world has been marked once and for all by the cross of Christ, but the cross of Christ is the cross of the reconciliation of the world with God, and for this reason the godless world bears at the same time the mark of reconciliation as the free ordinance of God.[74]

This understanding of the reconciliation of God and the world in Christ became foundational for Bonhoeffer's ethics, providing him with the basis for his participation in the conspiracy against Hitler. For Bonhoeffer it meant that it is no longer possible to think in terms of two spheres, the one religious and the other secular. There is 'only one reality, and that is the reality of God, which has become manifest in Christ in the reality of the world'.[75] As a result, Christian ethics must be directly involved in the life of the world, not in a separate religious sphere, for there is no part of the world that God has abandoned or not reconciled. What distinguishes the Church from the world is not that it inhabits a separate sphere, but the fact that the Church 'affirms in faith the reality of God's acceptance of humanity, a reality which is the property of the whole world'.[76]

The reality of the world reconciled by God in Christ does not mean that the world has become good, that all evil has been eradicated, or that the reign of God has come. Quite the contrary, for the 'world remains the world because it is the world which is loved, condemned and reconciled in Christ'. For that reason neither the Christian nor any other social reformer has the mandate to 'overleap the world and to make it into the kingdom of God'. But the opposite is also unacceptable. To believe that in Christ God has reconciled the world does not mean that we can abandon the wicked world to its fate.[77] The reality of the world as he experienced it was, according to Bonhoeffer, 'always already sustained, accepted and reconciled in the reality of God'.[78]

Given the situation in which he was living, with evil, death and destruction on every side, this was a remarkable confession of faith. But Bonhoeffer was adamant. The central message proclaimed in the New Testament was that 'God loved the world and reconciled it with himself in Christ', a confession that assumes 'that the world stands in need of reconciliation with God but that it is not capable of achieving it by itself'.[79] But it is the will of God, already fulfilled in the coming of Christ, that the world be reconciled to God. So it is that the 'figure of the Reconciler, of the God-Man Jesus Christ, comes between God and the world and fills the centre of all history'.[80] And since God's will for reconciliation has thus been fulfilled, Christian ethics can have no other purpose but to ensure 'participation in the reality of the fulfilled will of God':[81]

> Not man's falling apart from God, from men, from things and from himself, but rather the rediscovered unity, reconciliation, is now the basis of the discussion and the 'point of decision of the specifically ethical experience'.[82]

The point of departure for ethics, in other words, cannot be 'the conflict between the good and the real', but only 'the reconciliation, already accomplished, of the world with God and the man Jesus Christ and the acceptance of the real man by God'.[83] Thus it is that Christian action 'springs from joy in the accomplishment of the reconciliation of the world with God'.[84] We can celebrate because a new creation has been brought into being.

Bonhoeffer's rejection of any attempt to 'think in two spheres' was very influential in shaping the debates about theological social ethics which erupted within the Churches in the 1960s. It was the time of the Civil Rights Movement in the United Sates, the war in Vietnam, the intensification of the struggle against apartheid, the WCC Programme to Combat Racism, and much more. These debates profoundly affected the life of the Churches, opening up new lines of division and, at the same time, forcing a redefinition of the Church's identity and mission.

In reading afresh Jan Milic Lochman's study on *Reconciliation and Liberation*, published at that time, I was reminded of those debates and of Lochman's able rejection of a 'one-dimensional view of salvation'.[85] Such views of salvation were widely held in South Africa at the time when the *Message to the People of South Africa* was published, hence the strong reaction to its attack on apartheid as a 'false gospel'. Salvation, it was vociferously argued by its critics, was a personal and spiritual matter, unrelated to politics. The 'social gospel' was the false gospel! Yes, indeed, the central theological issue, as Lochman perceived, was precisely around the meaning of reconciliation. But reconciliation with the 'other', Lochman argued to the contrary, is the condition of true worship of God and it is 'characterised by a hopeful and inventive realism'. It has to do with conditions and systems, or power relations, both in the Church and in the world.[86]

Lochman wrote his book at a time when liberation theology was beginning to make considerable impact on the life of the Church. 'Liberation' had become the new key theological metaphor for understanding the doctrine of reconciliation in many contexts of oppression. As such it was necessary to rethink the connection between reconciliation and liberation, the very task that Lochman took upon himself:

> The message of reconciliation can and must . . . be transposed into political terms; not in the form of 'law' or 'utopianism', of course, but certainly as a binding Gospel, as an initiative for peace and reconciliation, as an encouragement to 'concrete utopias,'[87] to the analysis, exposure and dismantling of ways of thinking and social structures which reflect wilful intransigence and injustice, to the patient search for possibilities of establishing genuine reconciliation and peace, to the extension and development of such possibilities at every political level.[88]

Such an understanding of the Christian doctrine of reconciliation was powerfully expressed in an address given by Emilio Castro, the then General Secretary of the World Council of Churches, when he visited South Africa in 1992. Given the history of colonialism and apartheid, Castro acknowledged that it needed courage to speak about reconciliation at all. But as Christians we have no other alternative, because 'all currents of Christian spirituality coincide in seeing the cross as God's ultimate attempt to overcome human alienation'.[89] But Castro recognized a serious dilemma, namely the problem of bridging the gap between 'a reality that makes reconciliation impossible and a vision, a conviction, a promise and an obligation that makes reconciliation available'.[90]

Bridging the gap between the Christian vision of reconciliation and the realities that confront us on the social and political stage is, at the primary level of doctrine, trying to develop a public theology related to the politics of democratic transformation. But at the level of secondary expressions of Christian faith, that is, the erecting of signposts of reconciliation in the world that signify the reality of God's gift, it is a challenge facing the Christian Church as God's agent of reconciliation. This challenge takes us beyond discourse and speech to agency and embodiment. As we indicated at the outset, reconciliation is an event, an action, a praxis, a process and celebration, before it becomes a doctrine or theory.

The gap between the eschatological vision of reconciliation and the realities of social and political life cannot be bridged by words alone, but only by words that take on flesh and concreteness. What the doctrine of reconciliation points to is an *'event of transformation'* in which we participate, an event that occurs in the liturgy of the Church as well as 'in all the relationships of the human community from the personal to the political'.[91] For that reason, it is a vision and a hope that must, and continually does, seek to develop structures that enable it to become a reality amidst the brokenness and alienation of life in the world. Only in this way will it truly become a public theology of reconciliation informed both by vision and praxis, a theology able to contribute to political discourse and inform public action. In sum, Christian reconciliation, as defined by Liechty and Clegg in their study of sectarianism in Northern Ireland, refers to

the processes and structures necessary to bring all the elements of the cosmos into positive and life-giving relationship with

God and one another. It is a vision of both an ongoing process to establish a community of love in which conflict and injustice, though still present, are actively being addressed, and the eschatological goal of cosmic communion in love being definitely achieved.[92]

In this chapter we have considered the Christian doctrine of reconciliation based on the 'grand narrative' of redemption and explicated in the Pauline trajectory in the New Testament. We have seen how the doctrine has developed over the centuries in a variety of theories of atonement, each of them building on particular metaphors within the biblical canon. We have also considered how the doctrine has been reconstructed through a retrieval of the Pauline trajectory and especially in more recent times in relation to public life, beginning with liberal theology in nineteenth-century Protestantism through to liberation theology and theologies of social transformation. All of this has to do with primary expressions of the doctrine of reconciliation. But this is not unrelated to the secondary signs of reconciliation erected amidst the enmities and alienations of the world. How these secondary expressions become embodied in the life of the world as signs of God's gift of reconciliation, thus bridging the gap between Christian vision and political reality, is the question that now demands our attention.

Part Two

Agency

3

Reconciliation Embodied

Mozambique was liberated from Portuguese colonial rule in 1974. This event had enormous ramifications for the whole of southern Africa, setting in motion a process that would eventually lead to the liberation of Zimbabwe and Namibia, and the ending of apartheid in South Africa. But soon after Mozambique gained its independence it was torn apart by a civil war between its ruling party Frelimo, which had led the liberation struggle, and Renamo, a movement sponsored by the then UDI Rhodesian government of Ian Smith and South Africa. This bloody war lasted for almost two decades until it was finally brought to an end in 1992. I was fairly well informed about what was happening in Mozambique during those years, but one crucial part of the story had escaped my attention and, I suspect, the attention of many others who were following the unfolding events.

The story has to do with a remarkable Christian community based in Rome called the Community of Sant'Engidio. Comprised of lay Catholics, many of whom also pursue professional careers, the community was formed in the late 1960s to pursue an ecumenical vocation of reconciliation both within the Church and in society. Located in the old Carmelite monastery of Sant'Engidio in the Trasteverre quarter of the city, traditionally the home to those on the periphery of Roman society, the community meets daily for worship, for meals and for planning its projects. On a visit to the community in August 2001 I discovered to my surprise that members of the community had played a vital role in helping to bring the civil war in Mozambique to an end.[1] Sharing a meal in the community house where

Mozambiquean President Joaquim Chissano and Renamo leader Alfonso Dhlakama signed an agreement to end the civil war, was a moving experience for a South African visitor. It was a good reminder that whatever its failures, there are many stories to be told that restore our faith in the Church as an agent of reconciliation in the world.

Reflecting on my visit to the Community of Sant'Engidio, I recalled the role that Churches, congregations and individual Christians played in the struggle against apartheid in South Africa, in the transition to democracy, and now in the task of national reconciliation and transformation. Similar accounts could be given of the role of the Church in many other places around the world, amply correcting the balance of its obvious failures. What is striking about most of these stories, as in the case of the Community of Sant'Engidio's role in Mozambique[2], or the Corrymeela Community in Northern Ireland,[3] or the International Centre for Reconciliation and the Community of the Cross of Nails at Coventry Cathedral,[4] is the way in which the Church has functioned vicariously as an agent of reconciliation. This is one of the distinguishing features of the Church when it truly fulfils its reconciling role both as a mediator of reconciliation and as a community seeking to embody and express reconciliation in its own life.

This understanding of the Church as the embodiment of reconciliation immediately brings to mind another Christian community that has served as a model and inspiration to many others, including the Community of Sant'Engidio. The story of the Taizé Community near Cluny in France is well known.[5] Founded during the Second World war by Roger Schutz as an ecumenical monastic community espousing the traditional vows of 'poverty, chastity, and obedience' and the Rule of Taizé,[6] the Community has been a remarkable ecumenical witness to God's reconciliation of the world in Jesus Christ. Many people around the world, especially young people, share in acts of worship modelled on the Taizé liturgy, or journey to Taizé to experience a spirituality in which prayer and political action are blended in witnessing to the reconciling power of the gospel.

In 1980 a large group of young South Africans, at the invitation of Desmond Tutu, went to Taizé on a Pilgrimage of Hope. Taizé not only provided an ideal environment for reflecting on the need for justice and reconciliation in South Africa, but for some it was also a life changing experience. When I first visited Taizé in 1964 it was not so widely known. But its large modern Church, the Church of Reconciliation, built by young German volunteers between 1960 and 1962 as a sign of post-war reconciliation, was already standing on the hillside beyond the old farm and chapel in which the community began. Near the main entrance to that imposing new building, the Community placed a large noticeboard, no longer there, which if my memory serves me correctly read:

> The Church of Reconciliation
> for the reconciliation
> of God and humanity
> of husbands and wives
> of parents and children
> of separated churches
> of Christians and Jews

This reconciliation is all-embracing, whether between groups and nations torn apart by conflict, or between divided Churches, or within the lives of individuals. Schutz, one biographer writes:

> always thought that Christians would be reconciled by broadening their horizons, by going out to those who differed from themselves, by being open to non-believers, by carrying the preoccupations of those who were in difficulty and by being attentive to the poorest of the poor. It was the vision of reconciliation of the whole of humanity which made the effort of striving for reconciliation between Christians worthwhile.[7]

The Taizé community makes no claims about being a model for others to follow; rather it seeks to be a parable of reconciliation, embodying the word in deed. The sign now in front of the

Church, written in many languages, reads: 'You who enter here, be reconciled and discover in the Gospel the spirit of the Beatitudes: joy, simplicity and mercy.'[8]

The Communities of Sant'Engidio, Taizé, Corrymeela, the Cross of Nails at Coventry and many other ecumenical communities along with parishes and congregations in many places,[9] have sought to give substance to Bonhoeffer's hope that the word 'reconciliation' would become embodied in a new language born out of prayer and the struggle for justice. Implicit in Bonhoeffer's words was also the need for Christians to overcome the barriers that kept them apart, preventing them from speaking and acting as peace-makers between warring factions and nations. Schutz spoke to this when he wrote that the Church had to take two steps in order to recover its role as the community of reconciliation in the modern world. The first was 'to seek for an equitable distribution of the wealth of the earth'. That is at the heart of the struggle for justice. The second was to work for Christian unity, a task that required 'a heart big enough, an imagination broad enough' and 'a love passionate enough' to break the chains that have locked Christians into separate denominations.[10]

The struggle for justice, the rebirth of an authentic spirituality, and the search for Christian unity are essential and inseparable elements of the ecumenical vision which underlies the Christian understanding of reconciliation. We discovered the truth of this relationship in the early days of the Church Unity Commission in South Africa, a commission established in 1968 to work for the union of the Anglican, Congregational, Methodist and Presbyterian Churches. Even though at first the focus was purely on matters of faith and order, it soon became apparent that we could not seek Church union unless we were at the same time engaged together in the struggle against apartheid. We also discovered, as have ecumenically committed Christians elsewhere, that Church unity is not simply or chiefly about the uniting of divided denominations into a new institutional framework, but the overcoming of ethnic and class divisions, or as in the case of Northern Ireland, sectarianism.[11] That, too, was the starting-point for Paul's understanding of the Church as the embodiment of the new humanity in which God had reconciled Jew and Gentile.

Treasure in clay jars

Christianity is premised on the incarnation. God did not simply speak the word of reconciliation through a prophet, but 'the Word became flesh and dwelt amongst us' (John 1.14). Reconciliation became embodied; it was expressed in a life that could be seen, touched and handled (1 John 1.1). For the writers of the New Testament, God's reconciliation of the world was not an idea, an abstract doctrine or utopian thinking, but a historical reality, something embodied in the life of the world. It had to do with the historical fate of Jesus, a Jew living in first-century Palestine, crucified in Jerusalem at the hands of the political and religious leadership of the day. And for those who believed that God had raised Jesus from the dead, it had to do with a new history and the birth of a new humanity in anticipation of the 'new heaven and new earth' envisaged by the Hebrew prophets (Mic. 4.1–5.5; Rev. 21). Thus God's act of reconciliation in the death and resurrection of Jesus led directly to the formation of a new messianic community within Judaism born on the day of Pentecost that embodied and witnessed to the good news of what God had done. Devoted to prayer and to the word of the witnesses of the resurrection, this community held everything in common, attracting many others into its life together (Acts 2.42–47).

Within a very short period, this community of Jewish believers began to include Gentiles – that is, people from beyond the boundaries of Judaism. At first there was a reluctance to move in this direction, but failure to do so would have fatally compromised the good news of reconciliation, and prevented its embodiment as a world-transforming reality. Hence, pushed and pulled by the Spirit, there came a dramatic reaching out to embrace 'the other' or 'outsider', the first moment of which was nothing less than a second Pentecost (Acts 10). If the first Pentecost was an outpouring of the Spirit on Jewish believers whether in Jerusalem

or the *diaspora*, the second attested to God's acceptance of
people from every ethnic background and to God's will to incor-
porate them into a new community. Through baptism into
Christ and thereby incorporation into the Church as the 'body of
Christ', anyone irrespective of origin, class or gender could now
enter the covenant and become a child of Abraham and thereby
an inheritor of God's promise of redemption. Nowhere is this
expressed more clearly than in the letter to the Ephesians, written
by one of Paul's disciples:

> Remember that at one time you Gentiles by birth . . . were
> without Christ, being aliens from the commonwealth of Israel,
> and strangers to the covenants of promise, having no hope and
> without God in the world. But now in Christ Jesus you who
> once were far off have been brought near by the blood of
> Christ. For he is our peace; in his flesh he has made both
> groups into one and has broken down the dividing wall, that
> is, the hostility between us. He has abolished the law with
> its commandments and ordinances, that he might create in
> himself one new humanity in place of the two, thus making
> peace, and might reconcile both groups to God in one body
> through the cross, thus putting to death that hostility through
> it . . . (Eph. 2.11–16 NRSV)

For Paul and those influenced by his theology, the good news of
reconciliation meant nothing less than that Jew and Gentile had
been reconciled 'in Christ', and this was embodied in the Church
as the community of reconciliation. This was not the doing of the
Church, though it had the responsibility of bearing witness to the
gift of reconciliation, it was something brought about by God
through the Spirit. Thus it was that the early Christian community expanded its horizons, spreading the good news and seeking
to bring the Gentile world into the household of faith.

Documented in the Acts of the Apostles this story is a continu-
ation of the 'grand narrative' of redemption, and thus an integral
part of the embodiment of reconciliation in deed. The Church,
from the perspective of the New Testament then, was not an

addendum to God's reconciling work accomplished in Jesus Christ, it was an essential element within it. But in the same way as God's reconciliation of the world in Christ is not something you can prove by reason, so too, understanding the Church as the embodiment of God's new humanity is an article of faith. In the young Bonhoeffer's words:

> The concept of the Church is conceivable only in the sphere of reality established by God; this means that it cannot be deduced. *The reality of the Church is a reality of revelation, a reality that essentially must be* either believed or denied.[12]

But just as the gospel of reconciliation is contested, so too is the narrative of its embodiment in the Church. You do not have to read between the lines of the story in order to discover that alongside the claims made by Paul and others for the Church, there were less salubrious dimensions to its life and witness that severely compromised its witness to reconciliation. The treasure was, as Paul painfully acknowledged with regard to his own ministry, embodied in clay jars (2 Cor. 4.7).

The idea that the Church was, for the first few centuries at least, a model community and only then, following the Constantinian settlement, began to decline, is questionable though it contains more than an element of truth. Certainly once the Church became the established religion of the Empire it was adversely affected in ways that undermined its claims to embody the reconciled new humanity. But from the beginning there was dissension, as is evident in the New Testament. Paul's teaching on reconciliation in his Corinthian correspondence was not just the exposition of doctrine but an attempt to heal the rift between himself and the Corinthian Church. But it was also addressed to serious divisions in the community itself that had to do with disagreements about leadership, worship, ethical behaviour and belief. Such causes of division have dogged the history of the Church ever since.

More serious than even the divisions in Corinth was the fact that despite the breathtaking declaration that in Christ, Jew and Gentile were reconciled, the early Christian community was torn apart by the controversy that erupted between Jewish and Gentile believers. In essence it had to do with the ritual conditions Gentiles had to fulfil in order to become part of the 'new Israel' as the embodiment of God's new humanity. Such controversies may seem far away from the contemporary world, but that is an illusion. Reconciliation invariably has to do with the conditions of inclusion and exclusion, the grounds on which we relate to and accept 'the other'. Questions of ritual purity continue to divide contemporary societies across the religious and ethnic spectrum. Consider the extent to which the implementation of *Shari'ah* has become divisive in many Muslim societies, or the exclusion of the 'untouchable' Dalits from the social mainstream in India, or apartheid in South Africa. Racial prejudice and xenophobia is based on questions of 'ethnic' and 'ritual' purity as much as it is on social and economic factors. The declaration by some Churches in South Africa that 'apartheid is a heresy' had to do precisely with the fact that those Churches supporting segregation excluded people from their fellowship on the grounds of racial impurity, and thereby gave theological legitimation to the policy itself.[13] But the ethnic captivity of the Church, leading to sectarianism and worse, has undermined its witness to reconciliation in many other places as well.

The Judaizers in the early Church lost the battle, if not the war, over the conditions for Church membership. Paul's message of 'grace alone', and his insistence on freedom for Gentile believers, so powerfully articulated in the letter to the Galatians, became the basis for inclusion. God's grace, not obedience to Jewish law, thus became the core of Paul's gospel and of his mission to reconcile Jews and Gentiles. This recognition of God's gracious inclusion of people from every nation into the household of Abraham is fundamental to Paul's conviction that in Christ, God was reconciling the world and had given to the Church 'the ministry of reconciliation' as its primary task (2 Cor. 5.16–21). At the same time, what made it possible for Gentiles to be included in the household of Abraham made it increasingly problematic for Jews who wished to believe. However, once the inclusive nature of God's grace was acknowledged, then it was not only

Jew and Gentile who were reconciled in Christ but also men and women, masters and slaves (Gal. 3.28). By inference, as Beyers Naudé, the celebrated leader of the Church struggle in South Africa, declared in a sermon on Acts 10 that marked his break with the Dutch Reformed Church in 1962, God had accepted all races on equal terms into the new humanity.[14] Nothing God had created should be regarded as unclean.

The writers of the New Testament were fully aware, then, of the spirit of division within the early Christian communities and of the conflict between Church and synagogue. They all acknowledged in one way or another that the treasure embodied in the Church is contained in fragile clay jars. Given the past two thousand years of Christianity, we are even more conscious of failures that have compromised the claims made by faith for the Church, and led to consequences quite contrary to the gospel. Ironically, chief amongst them has been a glorying in the status of being the embodiment of God's new humanity. This triumphalist pretension has manifested itself in different ways, but chiefly in claiming a power that only belongs to God, and in attitudes towards and actions against the 'other' and 'outsider' that have repelled them from rather than attracted them to the Church. So we do not have to be secular cynics to recognize the chasm that has often separated what Christians declare in the creed, 'one, holy and apostolic Church', from the reality we experience on the ground.

Over the centuries theologians have developed several ways to handle this contradiction, distinguishing, for example, between the Church visible and invisible, or the true and the false Church. Often such rhetoric has led to even further divisions as some, claiming to be the *true* Church broke away from those they regarded as the *false*. In certain circumstances this might have had some justification, as when the Confessing Church in Germany broke its ties with the official *Reichskirche*. But whatever might be appropriate in such emergency situations where a clear-cut break became necessary, the struggle for the true Church is something which recurs again and again in the life of the Church as a whole, and therefore within rather than between what we now refer to as denominations. The Church, for this reason amongst others, is only the Church when it is being constantly renewed by the Spirit. What is obvious to us, as it was to the writers of the New Testament, is that we cannot simply equate the Church as God's community of reconciliation with any or every empirical ecclesial structure claiming to be the Church. The reality of the Church as the embodiment of God's reconciled new humanity is always something of a mystery, a third dimension, a treasure that cannot be encapsulated. There is, as Paul recognized, good reason for this. The fact that the treasure is in clay jars is to remind us, and to demonstrate to others, that the extraordinary power of the gospel of reconciliation does not belong to the Church but to God.

The truth of the matter is that Church is a social construction and human institution, whatever else we may claim it to be. The way in which the Church has historically developed, the forms in which it has become structured, and the kind of struggles that it has been engaged in provide ample evidence to show this to be the case. At the same time, if there is no connection, no visibility or earthing of the message of God's reconciliation in a community that believes it to be true, reconciliation as Christians understand it would remain a disembodied ideal. Both reconciliation and restorative justice are relational concepts and require embodiment in a community of restored relations. This is of the essence of the Church; if it were not so, the Church would simply be an association of religiously inclined people. Such an association might well engage in acts of reconciliation, as do many people who do not belong to the Church, as a matter of choice. But there is an essential difference between a voluntary association of people engaged in reconciliation, and a community founded on God's gift of reconciliation and called to embody and witness to that gift.

The issues we are exploring here are helpfully dealt with by James Gustafson in his book on the Church entitled *Treasure in Earthen Vessels*. Gustafson's starting-point is, however, different to that of Bonhoeffer's. Whereas Bonhoeffer starts with revelation and speaks of 'Christ existing as church community',

Gustafson begins with the Church as a human community, a social institution amongst others. Yet, as Gustafson acknowledges, the conclusion he reaches about the identity and relevance of the Church in the world is not that different from Bonhoeffer's position and aptly sums up much of what I am trying to say. He writes:

> The Church shares in common with other communities a natural and political character. The common characteristics, however, do not end here. It shares the processes that make any community identifiable through time and across space. Its differentiation does not lie in the fact that it has a language, but in its *particular* language; it does not lie in the processes of interpretation, and subjective understanding, but in that which it interprets and understands.[15]

The consequences of this are far-reaching for locating the Church within society and the political arena, and in discerning the connection between theological and political language. 'At every point', Gustafson says, 'one might consider the meaning of the social and historical processes in the light of Christian belief about divine action through Jesus Christ and the work of the Holy Spirit.'[16]

Whatever its faults and failures, for Christians the Church is something more than the sum total of its members, and something more than what and who they are. Hence, alongside decrying the members of the Church for arrogance, sectarianism and the like, Paul can still speak of the Church as 'the body of Christ', that is, the embodiment of God's gift of reconciliation. And it is precisely on this issue that the Spirit of Christ continually challenges the empirical Church to break free from its captivities to denominational, class, race, ethnic and gender divisions, and become what it confesses to be in the power of the Spirit. The confession that 'we believe in the Church' is an article of faith that acknowledges the ambiguities that beset the Church in every age and context. Yet it is a faith that is regularly surprised and confirmed as the gift of reconciliation becomes a reality in its midst and through its ministry. Reflecting back on the TRC, Tutu expressed this conviction with a passion commensurate with his own ministry of reconciliation:

> There is a movement, not easily discernible, at the heart of things to reverse the awful centrifugal force of alienation, brokenness, division, hostility and disharmony. God has set in motion a centripetal process, a moving towards the Centre, towards unity, harmony, goodness, peace and justice; one that removes barriers. Jesus says, 'And when I am lifted up from the earth I shall draw everyone to myself,' as he hangs from His cross with out-flung arms, thrown out to clasp all, everyone and everything, in cosmic embrace, so that all, everyone, everything, belongs. None is an outsider, all are insiders, all belong. There are no aliens, all belong in one family, God's family, the human family.[17]

The Church, then, is committed to a particular vision of the world, it is a witness to that movement 'at the heart of things to reverse the awful centrifugal force of alienation' which is expressed in exercising love, enabling forgiveness, and seeking justice. The Church may be *in* the world with all that that implies but, as Paul insisted, it is not meant to conform to values and strategies that conflict with the gospel (Rom. 12.1–2). In Jesus' words, the Church is called to be 'salt' of the world, and it can only really make a different to the world if it does not lose its savour (Matt. 5.13–14). This points us towards those constitutive elements in the life of the Church that enable it to be the embodiment of the new humanity, though never in its own unaided wisdom or power. In exploring what these are and what they mean I wish to draw on insights from Bonhoeffer's thoughts on the Church that have inspired many who have been engaged in seeking to be communities of reconciliation and justice in the world. They have also been influential in shaping my own thinking about the Church.

Sociality, solidarity and vicarious action

If we trace the development of Bonhoeffer's theology and, more specifically, his understanding of the Church, from *Sanctorum Communio* to his prison writings, it soon becomes evident that there are at least three major inter-connected trajectories. The first has to do with his understanding of the human person and what has been called the 'sociality of humanity'.[18] The second concerns the intimate relationship between Christ and the Church, encapsulated in Bonhoeffer's celebrated formula: 'Christ existing as Church-community' (*Christus als Gemeinde existierend*).[19] How we answer the question, 'Who is Jesus Christ, for us, today?' will determine how we understand the Church. The third trajectory is the inseparable relationship between theology and ethics, and therefore between faith and praxis, between our life together in the Church and responsible action in the struggle for justice and peace in the world.

The Christian doctrine of reconciliation presupposes a particular understanding of what it means to be a human person, and this in turn is fundamental to what is meant by the Church as the community of reconciliation. The sociality of humanity means that we only exist in relation to others, something also expressed in the word *ubuntu* that is repeatedly used in South Africa, including in the founding documents of the TRC, to describe the process of reconciliation. This means that we come into being as persons through encountering and embracing the 'other', whether neighbour or enemy. In this encounter, God confronts us with an ethical choice that determines whether or not we become truly responsible human beings. This, in turn, becomes a precondition of genuinely human relationships and the building of a sustainable community. For only within such a relationship is there a genuine reciprocity of wills.[20] The alternatives are the alienation that comes with atomistic individualism or absorption into an undifferentiated mass.[21] In both instances there is no true recognition of the 'other' as person, or respect for the differences that distinguish the 'other' from ourselves. On the contrary, for Bonhoeffer,

God does not desire a history of individual human beings, but the history of human *community*. However, God does not want a community that absorbs the individual into itself, but a community of *human beings*.[22]

God's primary concern, then, is the establishment of human community in which the uniqueness of the individual person is not lost in the mass but discovered in relationship to the 'other'.

The truth is, nonetheless, that humanity is fallen, basic human relationships have been broken, and genuine community has become impossible. 'Humanity-in-Adam' is united, but only in its sinfulness and alienation. There is an 'ethical solidarity', but it is one of ethical failure. It is the 'I–You' relation actualized in a sinful way through domination.[23] Such unity or solidarity is not genuine community, but individualistic and fragmented. It is *peccatorum communio*.[24] But if God's reconciliation of the world in Christ is a reality rather than an idea or an ideal, it implies the establishment of a new humanity, *sanctorum communio*, as part of that act of reconciliation. Hence Bonhoeffer's declaration: 'God established the reality of the church, of humanity pardoned in Jesus Christ – not religion, but revelation, *not religious community, but church*.'[25] This brings us to the key question: On what basis is the Church constituted, or better, how does it come into being as the new humanity?

The way in which the new humanity is realized is, for Bonhoeffer, through the 'vicarious representative action' (*Stellvertretung*) of Christ,[26] this is 'the sum and substance of Christology'.[27] Through Christ's vicarious representative action, rather than through its own moral striving, the new humanity is made whole and sustained. Belief in the vicarious redemptive action and role of Christ thus goes to the heart of the Christian understanding of reconciliation and, as such provides the basis for the Church's very existence and therefore the model for the way in which it exists in the world. Precisely because 'vicarious representative action' is the basis of the Church's life and existence, it becomes possible for a community of human beings to live in love for each other.[28] That is, to be a community of reconciliation. In this sense, the Church as a gift of revelation becomes actualized in an empirical religious community whose chief reason for existence is to be the community of God's reconciling love, forgiveness and grace.

The social acts that constitute this community of love determine the character of its action in the life of the world. Church members are structurally 'with-each-other' (*Miteinander*), and active in 'being-for-each-other' (*Füreinander*), which is precisely what is meant by the principle of vicarious representative action.[29] This implies acts of love, namely 'self-renouncing, active work for the neighbour, intercessory prayer and the mutual forgiveness of sins in God's name'. These imply further self-giving on behalf of the neighbour, and significantly in anticipation of Bonhoeffer's own fate, a

> readiness to do and bear everything in the neighbour's place, indeed, if necessary, to sacrifice myself, standing as a *substitute* for my neighbour. Even if a purely vicarious action is rarely actualized, it is intended in every genuine act of love.[30]

The 'vicarious representative action' of the members of the Church not only gives the Church its specific sociological character as a 'community of love' (*Liebesgemeinschaft*)[31] but also points to the concrete reality of God's revelation, that is, to the gift of reconciliation in Christ. And because it is already established in Christ prior to any human willing or doing, the vicarious representative structure of the Church is real not an ideal, ethical and not metaphysical.[32] God in Christ, being 'with' and 'for' the human other, enables the members of the body to be 'with' and 'for' each other through the power of the Holy Spirit.[33] Hence the fact that soon after its foundation, the Church was impelled by the Spirit to embrace and unite in one body Jew and Gentile, male and female, slave and master. As Bonhoeffer once described it in a sermon, the Church is the cell or spore (*Keimzelle*) of reconciliation in the world.[34]

What it means to be a human person, who Jesus Christ is 'for us', and the relationship between faith and ethical responsibility are, as intimated, interconnected. So it is that the Church which presupposes the sociality of humanity and is brought into being and sustained by the vicarious action of Christ, exists vicariously in the world, that is, for the sake of the 'other'. This means that the Church exists for the sake of restoring justice, reconciliation and peace. Christ who is, as Bonhoeffer put it at the end of his life, 'the man for others' thus implies a 'Church for others', a Church that comes into being and exists through embracing the 'other' and the 'outsider'. In other words, *when true to its given nature*, the Church cannot but be a community of reconciliation whatever its failures. As such it is what God wills for humanity as an end, but it is also a means to enable the realization of that goal.[35]

In order to be true to its christological nature as the vicarious representative of the new humanity, the Church is not an entity separate and aloof from the world, but deeply embedded in its life. As such, it is in solidarity with the world in its sin, its suffering, its struggles and its hopes. The Church does not approach its task from outside the framework of a fallen world in search of justice and peace; it is part of that world. As an institution comprised of men and women who are in the world, the Church shares in its sin and suffering, its struggles and its hopes. It cannot be otherwise. This explains in part the ambiguities that surround its witness. Vast sections of the Church in South Africa, for example, were the victims of apartheid, suffering its oppression, struggling for liberation, and hoping for the day of democratic change. But there were many others who were members of the Church and yet part of the apartheid machine. Perpetrators of crimes against humanity, or guilty bystanders and beneficiaries co-inhabit the Church alongside victims, a phenomenon that both compromises the Church and yet at the same time opens up possibilities for reconciliation.

In order to overcome this contradiction and pursue its reconciling vocation, the Church is called to identify primarily with victims even while it seeks also to minister to those who perpetrate injustice. Much of the failure of the Church can be attributed to the fact that the Church has too often sided with the powerful, with oppressors, with conquistadors and colonial powers. The ministry that the Church must exercise to those with power (whatever the nature of that power), or their beneficiaries, must however be exercised from the perspective of those who are its victims, those who suffer and are oppressed.

Our discussion is beginning to lead us inexorably to the point at which the theology of reconciliation and political reality begin to connect, where what it means to be the Church begins to make an impact on the life of society. That is, to the connection between theology and social ethics, faith and action, the third element we have noted in Bonhoeffer's ecclesiology. This brings us back to the debates engendered by the TRC and other attempts to bring about reconciliation in the world. We will delay discussion of these themes, however, because there remains one other aspect of the life of the Church that needs to be considered before we do so, both because of its own significance for the Church and because of its potential significance for the process of reconciliation.

Another way to speak of the Church as the embodiment of the new humanity, is to speak of it as a sacramental community. Before Protestant readers become too jittery about this proposal, it is important to reflect on what I mean by it. Thinking sacramentally about the Church means that we understand its empirical, material existence as that which God transforms and uses, rather than positing an invisible ideal as distinct from a real and visible Church. In other words, the treasure of the gospel of reconciliation is embodied in clay jars, to return to that metaphor. It is through the mediation of human beings, fallen and fallible, but also seeking to be a community of vicarious love in the world, that reconciliation becomes a reality. With this in mind we turn to consider the importance of the sacraments in the life of the Church, not as additional things we do in worship, but as expressing the very essence of what it means to be the Church. And, by analogy we can also begin to think of the TRC as a 'civic sacrament',[36] a subject to which we will return in Chapters 5 and 6.

Sacraments of reconciliation

In Christian tradition, though practised and understood in different ways, the sacraments are communal acts of remembering and representing the gospel narrative through dramatic actions, using material signs and symbols – water, bread and wine and, I would add for reasons that will become evident, acts of peace-making and reparation. The sacraments rightly understood and practised within the worship life of the Church play a central role in shaping Christian community and its witness to God's reconciliation.[37]

Each sacramental act is interpersonal and communal in which the covenant relationship with God and each other is either established, as in baptism, or renewed, as in the Eucharist, or worked out in the world of material relationships, as in the sacrament of penance. Each sacramental event is also profoundly material, uniting the spiritual and the material, thus signifying the overcoming of the separation of reality into different spheres and pointing to the reconciliation of the world in Christ. Each sacrament is the liturgical embodiment and enactment of speech about reconciliation; events in the life of Christian community where reconciliation is celebrated and visibly portrayed. As such, the sacraments are an essential part of the primary expression of faith in God's gift. But as John Howard Yoder once suggested, even 'people who do not share the faith or join the community can learn from them', for they can 'function as paradigms for ways in which other social groups might operate'.[38] The sacraments connect Christian doctrine and social ethics at a primary level of expression, but as such they also provide models of and insight into the process of reconciliation in all spheres of personal and social life.

'All Christian community', Bonhoeffer wrote in *Discipleship*, 'exists between word and sacrament.'[39] Too often, however, that interaction between word and sacrament, between the gospel preached and the gospel enacted and embodied, has been lost due to confessional controversies, most notably during the Protestant Reformation. In their reaction to Catholic abuses of the sacramental system, the Protestant Reformers spoke of the need to administer the sacraments 'rightly' in order for them to be the means of grace. This included, above all else, reconnecting them with the preaching of the word. The reuniting of word and sacrament was a necessary step for the renewal of the Church, for speech and action belong together, the one informing the other. But tragically, the attempt to recover the sacraments in this way often led to the loss of sacramental life in the Church. Not only did the Protestant sacraments become too didactic, but sometimes they even became a sign of division and a source of abuse. Nowhere has this been more evident than in the history of the Church in South Africa.

In the earliest times of colonial settlement at the Cape of Good Hope, people were classified not on the basis of race but of religion. Baptism was the rite of passage not only into the Church but also into European society, leading on some occasions, albeit rare, to racial intermarriage. This was the basis of a new identity, a fact symbolized by indigenous people assuming Christian names, which often simply meant taking European ones, thus confusing conversion and deculturalization. As racial prejudice became entrenched and ethnicity became determinative for social stratification, baptism remained the basis upon which people of different races participated together in Holy Communion, but blacks were usually required to sit at the back of the Church and communicate last of all. However, Holy Communion itself became the critical testing ground within the dominant Dutch Reformed Church in the mid nineteenth century when, because of the 'weakness of some' white members, it became permissible to allow segregation at the sacrament.[40] This eventually led to the segregation of the Dutch Reformed Church itself and provided theological support for what later became the policy of apartheid.

South African social history, and that of other countries as in Latin America where the Roman Catholic Church was dominant, might have been very different if the sacraments had been 'rightly administered' and truly represented the reconciling power of the gospel. But these brief comments on the social role of the sacraments at the Cape also illustrate something more

broadly about their significance for either preventing or enabling
the birth and maintenance of a community of reconciliation. In
this regard we should keep in mind the controversy over both
baptism and the Lord's Supper in the Church at Corinth where,
instead of them being sacraments of unity they became sources
of division around questions of leadership and relations between
rich and poor (1 Cor. 1.10–31; 11.2–34). How baptism and the
Eucharist are understood and celebrated in the life of the Church
in terms of social relations and not simply individual piety is, in
fact, indicative of the health of the Church as a community of
reconciliation.

Though generally omitted by Protestants in speaking about
the sacraments, the sacrament of penance – or reconciliation as it
has been called since Vatican II – is nonetheless important both
for the life of the Church and for the subject at hand. Community
does not only happen in the interaction between word and sacrament, but in the act of being accountable and reconciled to God
and one another. That is why Bonhoeffer writes in *Life Together*
that it is in confession that 'there takes place a breakthrough to
community'.[41] Acknowledging accountability for faults and
dealing with alienation and estrangement is fundamental to the
creation of a reconciled and reconciling community. Of course,
the sacrament of penance can be and has been abused, especially
by manipulating a false sense of guilt in ways that become
destructive. But the Protestant rejection of the sacrament by no
means overcame that problem. Penitential piety penetrated
Protestantism, not least through Luther, and made the awakening of a sense of guilt a priority in preaching and its acknowledgement a prerequisite for receiving the gospel.[42] Awakening a
sense of guilt is often necessary, as we shall later insist, but very
often this has had consequences contrary to the gospel. Instead
of the gospel setting people free from guilt, such preaching too
often evokes self-condemnation; instead of the gospel awakening
genuine shame, repentance and creating community, such preaching makes conscience an individual burden, turning people
inward in self-hatred rather than outward in joyful embrace of
the 'other'.

The intention of all the sacraments, however, is to be a means of grace for healing and transformation, for creating community and engendering communion. Consider, then, the following aspects of what the Christian sacraments of baptism, Eucharist, and penance actually mean when rightly understood and rightly practised as sacraments of reconciliation. That is, as means to the embodiment of reconciliation concretely within the life of the Christian community with all the wider implications that has for society as a whole.

First of all, through the water of baptism, people of every race, gender and class are incorporated into the 'body of Christ'. Through confession and penance believers become reconciled to God and one another, liturgically embracing each other with the 'kiss of peace'. And through sharing the eucharistic meal, believers are bonded together 'in Christ' in a fellowship that overcomes human alienation. The altar-table is symbolic of the place of both presence and meeting. The presence of Christ through the Spirit as welcoming host and the meeting of the family of God around the table in fellowship with one another involves reaching out to bring others to the 'messianic banquet'. The significance of the table as the space around which the new community meets and is formed is also a sign of the reconciliation God wills for society as a whole. It points beyond the liturgy of the 'upper room' to the family meal, the sharing of goods with the poor, and the round table of political negotiation.

Second, to take the last observation further, the sacraments have far-reaching social and political implications. Baptism should fundamentally change relationships within the community in a way that directly affects the structures of both Church and society. This is poignantly illustrated in Paul's letter to Philemon. Confession and penance not only require that we become reconciled to our fellow believers, but demand that we recognize our accountability and pursue justice and peace in the world. The Eucharist is not only a sharing in the 'breaking of bread' at communion, but a commitment to share our lives and goods with those in need, that is to become 'bread for the world'. That means building human community in such a way that the chasm between rich and poor is bridged through restorative justice. This is one reason why the recovery of the centrality of the Eucharist in contemporary liturgical renewal has such revolutionary possibilities for society.

Third, the sacraments link remembrance of the past with hope for the future in such a way that they enable the embodiment and practice of reconciliation now. That is, they become means of grace for healing and renewal. As we well know, the process of reconciliation depends a great deal on how we remember the past. Memories can return with a vengeance unless they are redeemed and become a way of transforming the future. So in baptism we are grafted into the death of Christ in order to participate in his risen life through the Spirit. Past sins and guilt are washed away so that we might live in the newness of life, open to God's future for us. Baptism thus becomes not just initiation into the Church but into the ministry of reconciliation in the world. In confession we recall and acknowledge past sins in order to be set free to live our lives more faithfully, more accountable, reconciled with and open to the future claims of our neighbour. The sacrament of penance not only provides a means whereby we can confess our sins and be reconciled to both God and our fellows, but also sends us forth to make reparation. In the Eucharist we remember the Lord's death in anticipation of the coming of God's reign in its fullness, so that our lives may be renewed for service in the world today. The sacrament helps us grasp the significance of both the gift that has been given in Christ and the fulfilment of that gift in the future, and thus to live faithfully between memory and hope. For just as baptism initiates us into the ministry of reconciliation, the Eucharist reaches its climax when the community is sent into the world to serve its needs. The sacraments rightly understood, then, enable us to remember rightly, that is, to remember the past in such a way that we can live rightly and share in the task of building a more just society in anticipation of God's future.

Let us now consider more fully the significance and practice of penance as the sacrament of reconciliation, aware of its widespread neglect and yet its potential for reawakening accountability within social and political life. I introduce this not in expectation that penance as traditionally practised will become widely adopted beyond those Churches where it is a normal part of Christian life. But I do so in the hope that its significance for our theme will be recognized and that its purpose and practice may be recovered in ways that are appropriate for both Church and society today. In this regard the sacrament of penance provides an important analogy for what is required in overcoming social and political alienation and fostering national reconciliation. Indeed, I would suggest that the sacrament of penance is the sacrament of restorative justice. Let us then gather some perspective on this sacrament in Christian tradition.

There is a great deal in the Hebrew Scriptures, not least in the penitential psalms,[43] that provides the foundation for the New Testament teaching on accountability, repentance, forgiveness, reparation and reconciliation. This in turn anticipated the development of what eventually became the sacrament of penance. The early history of this sacrament is not entirely clear, though it was clearly influenced by the rigorous teaching of the African Latin theologian Tertullian in the second century, especially in the aftermath of persecution and the consequent failure of many Christians to keep the faith. By the third century public penance, often referred to as a 'second baptism', was required for serious sins. This had to do with discipline in the life of the Church. The issue was whether a member who had grievously sinned, as in denying the faith under persecution, could remain part of the fellowship and participate in the Eucharist. Just as baptism was the sacrament of initiation into the Church, penance was the way whereby sinners were held accountable and could be readmitted. But like baptism itself, the sacrament of penance could only be administered once, and was a slow, painful and laborious process befitting the gravity of the sin. This led many to postpone both baptism and confession until they could be absolved of all their sins in anticipation of death. Such public penance, whether strictly observed or not, continued until well into the sixth century.[44]

Gradually, however, chiefly as a result of the influence of

Celtic Christianity in Western Europe, the practice of private confession became the norm. Indeed, Celtic practice, with its well-developed discipline, became 'firmly rooted in the social and cultural life' of the people.[45] Confessing sins, albeit in private, but then doing public penance, was part of what it meant to belong to society if the violated norms of belonging were to be repaired. Similar rituals and rites have been practised in most cultures, not least in ancient Israel, in order to protect the life and integrity of society through isolating offenders and then, when appropriate, reintegrating them into the community.[46] These anticipate the TRC and similar institutions and processes, such as granting amnesty, through which contemporary societies have dealt with transgressors or perpetrators of crimes against humanity.

Celtic penitential practice included three elements: confession of sin, absolution or the pronouncement of God's forgiveness over the penitent, and the need to do penance. The disciplines governing this practice were arduous, not least the demands made upon the forgiven penitent. These provided the basis for the rules formally adopted by the Roman Catholic Church at the Fourth Lateran Council in 1215, which also mandated that at least an annual confession of sin was obligatory. Rather than only being administered once like baptism, the sacrament of penance was necessary whenever serious (or mortal) sins were committed. Failure to observe this requirement carried serious penalties, chiefly excommunication and therefore also the denial of ecclesiastical burial.[47] In this way the sacrament of penance could be, and on occasion was, put to political use not as a means of reconciliation but as an instrument of domination and control. After all, in Catholic teaching, the penalty of excommunication and the possibility of absolution resided in the apostolic successor of St Peter in Rome, to whom Jesus Christ had given the 'power of the keys' to the kingdom of heaven (Matt.16.19). Excommunication within the context of Christendom was, in effect, banishment from society.

The theology of the sacrament of penance was systematically developed by Thomas Aquinas in the Middle Ages. Thomas distinguished between the *material substance* of the sacrament – 'contrition of the heart', 'spoken confession' and 'satisfaction' or acts of reparation – and its *form*, namely the pronunciation of absolution by the priest.[48] This distinction was the subject of considerable critique in the medieval Church, and later by the Protestant Reformers who questioned whether something that lacked 'matter' (water, bread and wine) could be a sacrament. For Thomas, however, the 'matter' in penance was those very specific and concrete acts which penitents were required to do. But also at issue in the medieval and Reformation debates were questions about the connection between God's forgiveness and our response. Does God only forgive conditionally? Do penitents have to show contrition? In other words, to what extent is absolution contingent upon what we do? In case we think that such questions are remote from our present enquiry, we should recall that similar questions abounded during the work of the TRC, even though they were usually expressed differently. On what conditions are forgiveness and amnesty dependent? Is it sufficient for perpetrators to tell the truth, or is it also necessary that they show remorse for their criminal deeds?

The question raised during the Middle Ages was, however, largely religious, for it had to do with eternal life. What must we do in order to be right with God? The threat was not so much imprisonment but damnation; the solution was not political amnesty but divine forgiveness. Whatever the social and political reasons for the Protestant Reformation in the sixteenth century, it was an overwhelming sense of guilt and the search for a gracious God that triggered off Luther's personal struggle. He attacked the system of indulgences because it made mockery of both the gospel of God's free grace and the gravity of the sacrament of penance, undermining genuine repentance and obedient discipleship. But his critique soon became an attack on ecclesiastical authority and the 'power of the keys' whereby Rome exercised control over society. So what was, for Luther, primarily a matter of saving his soul, became the source of political controversy. Protestant princes, who came to share Luther's understanding of salvation, relished their newly found freedom from papal hegemony. Within a short period of time the power of the confessional was broken in Protestant Europe, but the demise of the practice also deprived large sections of society of an institution intended for its well-being and seriously affected the integrity of the Church.

Luther did not reject the sacrament of penance. He objected to its abuse, to the notion that doing acts of penance was the basis for absolution, and to the danger that instead of the sacrament empowering discipleship it actually could lead to the reverse.[49] But the forgiveness promised by Jesus depended neither on 'the sincerity of the contrition, nor on the completeness of the confession, much less on satisfaction, however strictly accomplished – but on the promise of God alone, received by supernatural faith'.[50] Trust in God's promise of forgiveness was the only essential requirement in appropriating God's saving grace. If that evangelical understanding of confession was upheld then, for Calvin as much as for Luther, private confession to a pastor was to be encouraged. The confessor, whether pastor or another Christian, was not to be regarded as a mediator of God's grace but a minister proclaiming God's word of forgiveness.[51] In this way the Reformers provided an alternative to the confessional that recovered the central part of its original intention. For Protestants, however, the norm became a general confession of sins in the liturgy, or a personal confession in private devotions, or maybe in more recent times, during a time of pastoral counselling despite attempts to recover the more traditional practice within some Protestant circles.[52]

The European Enlightenment's rejection of the notion of original sin and its belief in the inherent goodness of humanity, coupled with the growing secularization of Western society, further eroded the practice of confession in parts of European society, thus completing what the Reformation had unwittingly begun. If you do not have a sense of guilt, you do not see any need to confess sin; and if society has lost its religious cohesion and its sense of communal values, then the Church's sacraments no longer fulfil a social need, however much they might serve individual piety. Of course, the sacrament of penance can be abused in ways that are unhealthy for both the individual and society. But there are also negative consequences and social costs that have accompanied its demise.

The widespread absence of the confessional in Protestantism, as Carl Jung noted in his classic comparison of the role of psychotherapists and clergy, has had serious negative consequences for human health and spiritual well-being.[53] People not only need to acknowledge their guilt but also to accept that they have been forgiven. For Jung, psychotherapy was an alternative that appealed especially to those who had lost their religious faith. But such therapy could not deal with some of the deeper, spiritual problems that people face. Psychotherapy and confession are similar, even complementary in certain respects, but they are distinct and sometimes at odds with each other.[54] Perpetrators of crimes who appeared before the TRC in South Africa required more than counselling; they required forgiveness and the assurance of being forgiven. Of course, if guilt is denied, whether by the perpetrator who is unable to recognize the criminal nature of his or her actions, or by a psychotherapist for whom guilt must be explained away, then the need for grace and forgiveness is not seen to be necessary. Victor White, a Dominican priest and a psychoanalyst, summed up this difference very simply:

> Confession presupposes the power to sin and to turn from sin and seek forgiveness; analysis usually presupposes necessity and impotence and seeks liberation and freedom. If the confessional deals with 'wilful misdeeds', analysis deals with 'involuntary misfortune'.[55]

Years ago, as a student in Chicago, I was challenged by the work of a psychiatrist at the University of Illinois, O. Hobart Mowrer. He was concerned about the need for the recovery of a true practice of Christian confession and for a psychotherapy that, contrary to Freud, took guilt seriously.[56] 'We have tried to believe', Mowrer wrote, 'that personality disorder is basically an *illness* – *mental* illness; but we are now increasingly persuaded that the problem is fundamentally *moral*, that the guilt which is so obviously central in psychopathology is *real* rather than false.'[57]

The sacrament of penance, Karl Rahner once wrote, is 'the liturgy of the prodigal son'.[58] It is a liturgy that begins the moment we prodigals acknowledge our sin and guilt and accept responsibility for what we have done. From this perspective reconciliation is far more than an idealist concept open for debate and logical clarification. It is a story to be lived and a story to be told. Given the narrative structure of reconciliation, it is thus not surprising that the most potent accounts of the work of the TRC were not those that engaged in philosophical or political analysis, but those that told their story of what happened or did not happen during the process.[59] By reflecting on such stories we begin to discern what reconciliation might concretely mean within a particular context, and we are able to relate them to the paradigmatic story of God's reconciliation of the world in Jesus Christ. Through retracing the journey of the prodigal son, the Son of God recapitulates and so redeems what went wrong in the fall of humanity. But the journey of the Son of God also provides the path along which humanity returns to the parental welcome and warm embrace:

> I will get up and go to my father, and I will say to him, 'Father, I have sinned against heaven and before you; I am no longer worthy to be called your son . . .' But the father said . . . 'let us eat and celebrate; for this son of mine was dead and is alive again; he was lost and is found!' (Luke 15.18–24)

Although written with the sacrament of penance in mind, the following comment surely sums up what many a perpetrator experienced after telling the truth to the TRC: 'Through confession, we throw ourselves into the arms of humanity again, freed at last from the burden of moral exile.'[60]

If the Reformers were worried about the negative moral consequences of the sacrament of penance, its absence from Protestantism has not just had negative consequences for personal well-being, but also with regard to moral values and social responsibility. There has often been a failure to name specific sins; to recognize that sins and the attached guilt vary in terms of moral seriousness; and therefore that putting things right needs to be appropriate and concrete.[61] Perhaps one of the reasons why some perpetrators of apartheid crimes were unable to confess their guilt and see the value in doing so was related to the lack of any spiritual formation or liturgical practice informed by the sacrament of penance or its equivalents. Reflecting on the moral consequences of the absence of the sacrament of penance in Protestantism, Bonhoeffer observed:

> the Protestant Church ceased to possess a concrete ethic when the minister no longer found himself constantly confronted by the problems and responsibilities of the confessional. With a fallacious appeal to Christian liberty, he evaded his responsibility of concrete proclamation of the divine commandment. It is, therefore, only by rediscovering the divine office of confession that the Protestant Church can find its way back to a concrete ethic such as it possessed at the time of the Reformation.[62]

That concluding comment is a remarkable statement coming from one whose ethics of responsibility has such relevance for today.

Within the Roman Catholic Church, the danger has been different. The practice of confession for many became so perfunctory, so much a matter of duty, so privatized, that it lost its real significance as a sacrament of social accountability and reconciliation. The danger here, as Bonhoeffer observed, was that of 'reducing the divine commandment to a mere code of laws'. This, he argued, could only be overcome through a rediscovery of the 'office of preaching', that is, the ministry of the word of grace and forgiveness that calls men and women into discipleship. The Second Vatican Council responded positively to such criticisms and, in doing so, gave fresh ecumenical significance to penance as *the* sacrament of reconciliation.[63]

A further development spurred on by Vatican II, and one of

particular interest for our discussion has been the way in which, under the influence of Latin American Catholic liberation theology, the sacrament of penance has been interpreted in respect of structural sin and the creation of community.[64] Communal confessions of sin with regard to injustice and oppression require corporate penitence and commitment to joint acts of reparation.[65] This linking of confession to social issues has become quite common in many Christian denominations in South Africa, bringing confession back into the public domain in relation to the struggle for justice and reconciliation.[66] In this way the practice of the sacrament of penance has to do with social accountability, peace-making, reparations and the restoration of justice. It is also related to the need for the Church itself to recognize its own guilt and accountability, and to fulfil its ministry of reconciliation vicariously within the social and political arena. To that theme we now turn, in anticipation of a further discussion in Chapter 6 on guilt and accountability.

Vicarious confession of guilt

At a time when the defeat of Germany and the Treaty of Versailles were recent memories, and still a matter of deep resentment, Bonhoeffer courageously penned these words:

> There is not only the culpability of individual Germans and individual Christians, but also the culpability of Germany and the Church. It is not enough for individuals to repent and be justified; Germany and the Church must likewise repent and be justified.[67]

For Bonhoeffer, both the German nation and the Church were guilty, they were bound together in a solidarity of sin, just as they were bound together in the suffering they had endured in the conflagration. But neither was willing to confess their guilt, and certainly the victorious powers saw no need to do so.

The situation was somewhat different after the Second World War, especially given the Holocaust. Thus it was that in October

1945 the German Confessing Church published the Stuttgart Confession of Guilt:

> we accuse ourselves for not witnessing more courageously, for not praying more faithfully, for not believing more joyously and for not loving more ardently. Now a new beginning is to be made in our churches.[68]

This has been referred to as 'one of the most remarkable events in Church history'[69] because many of the confessors had opposed Nazism and suffered greatly as a result. It was also remarkable because it was made so soon after the defeat of Germany, with the country lying in ruins. Not unexpectedly, the Stuttgart confessors soon came under attack. For their many critics, to acknowledge guilt in this way seemed to provide a good pretext for another 'Versailles', for Germany to suffer not only devastation and disgrace but also to be prevented from any meaningful post-war recovery.[70] But there was more disquieting criticism, that from within the German Church itself, as Willem Visser 't Hooft, General Secretary of the World Council of Churches and a guest at Stuttgart, commented later.[71]

Several things need to be noted about the Stuttgart Confession. It was, first of all, an expression of solidarity with the nation in its sin and suffering. The confessors were not standing in judgement over against a guilty nation that had been brought to its knees; they were experiencing the pain of the nation, and acknowledging their part in its guilt. They did not make excuses. At the same time, and second, they did not have a false sense of guilt. They stated that they had opposed the Nazi regime and suffered as a consequence. But this did not take away from their share in the guilt of the nation. In the third place, their sense of guilt did not drive them to despair but to fresh commitment. They committed themselves to a new beginning. Repentance, they discerned, should lead to real change and a commitment to action. Each of these illustrates what we have called the vicarious nature of the Church's agency in reconciliation.

Nations or ethnic groups seldom repent of their sins; they are too proud and self-willed. They blame others or else they glory in what they have done, exalting those who committed war crimes to the status of heroes. Indeed, it is seldom the case that those who perpetrate violence and evil are prepared to confess their guilt. Certainly they did not hasten to do so at Nuremberg, nor have they done so at the many modern day truth commissions. That is one reason why the Church has to act vicariously on behalf of the nation under such circumstances. It is not that the Church is lacking in culpability, but rather that it is called to accept its vicarious responsibility. As in Abraham's plea to God on behalf of Sodom and Gomorrah, those who pursue righteousness in a society, no matter how few, can make a vital difference.[72] Indeed, the moment the Church fails to acknowledge its guilt, and its responsibility for the guilt of others and the nation, it stops being the Church.[73] As such it surrenders its role as God's community of reconciliation in the world.

The Stuttgart Confession of Guilt opened up the way for reconciliation between Christians in Germany and those in other parts of Europe who had suffered at the hands of Germany. But there is a sense in which it came too late. What was required, as Bonhoeffer perceived already in 1927, was a confession of guilt that could pre-empt the eruption of evil and destruction and not just one expressing penitence and sorrow afterwards. This was also understood by at least some of the leaders within the Confessing Church who, in 1937, developed a liturgy of penitence in which they confessed the sins of the nation, though it was never used. A few years later, in 1942 in the midst of the War, Bonhoeffer wrote a remarkable essay on 'Guilt, Justification and Renewal' in which he himself vicariously made a confession of guilt on behalf of the Church that had so disillusioned him:

> She has been silent when she should have cried out because the blood of the innocent was crying aloud to heaven. She failed to speak the right word in the right way at the right time. She has not resisted to the uttermost the apostasy of faith, and she has brought upon herself the guilt of the godlessness of the masses.[74]

Needless to say, both the Confessing Church leaders and Bonhoeffer were accused of treason, of undermining the national will, of injecting a spirit of defeatism into the life of the people. But imagine if in 1927 the Churches in Germany and in the rest of Europe as well, had confessed their guilt for what had happened in the First World War, and really meant it. Imagine if in 1937 the Church in Germany had come to its senses, and with those perceptive leaders in the Confessing Church and amongst the Allied nations had acknowledged their past and present guilt and sought to work out the implications in practice.

There is no guarantee that a confession of guilt will alter the course of history or restrain the forces of evil. There is no guarantee that those who confess their guilt will, in fact, follow through with actions that indicate they are truly repentant for the wrong for which they are responsible. But at the same time, it can surely be said that without such repentance, the possibility of breaking through the log-jam of hatred and bitterness caused by oppression, violence and war becomes virtually impossible. Imagine if the Churches in Northern Ireland had done so at the time before the Troubles began, or the Churches in South Africa before the advent of apartheid. The course of history might have been very different.

The TRC hearing devoted to the 'Faith Communities', held in East London in November 1997, was in some respects a public confessional for the Churches. During the hearings we were reminded yet again of the very ambiguous role that the Churches played during the apartheid years.[75] In their submissions all the so-called mainline Churches in South Africa acknowledged that whatever their criticisms of the ideology and its implementation, they had not done as much as they should have to combat it. Church leaders confessed that too many of their members had connived with apartheid, and some had been amongst those who had perpetrated atrocious crimes. Hence a major emphasis in their statements was that of penitence for past failure, and a commitment to work for national reconciliation and justice in the future. Of course it is widely recognized that certain Churches, Church leaders, and many Christians played major roles in the liberation struggle. Moreover, in so far as the majority of Christians in South Africa are black, many of the victims of apartheid were Christian, and many local Church communities suffered at the hands of the regime. This connection between the victims and Christianity was often evident during the TRC when those present, encouraged by Desmond Tutu, sang hymns or offered prayers – a matter of some concern to those of other faiths who were also present. But the representations made to the TRC highlight the extent to which, more than any other faith community, the Christian Churches represent the broad spectrum of South African society. Victims, benefactors and perpetrators were members together in the Churches, an indication of both the failure of the Church to be a community of reconciliation, but also of its potential to help bring about national reconciliation in this post-apartheid period.

But what about the role of the other faith communities who appeared before the TRC and who, along with the Churches acknowledged their faults and committed themselves to national reconciliation? How do they, and especially those of the family of Abraham, relate to the Church in its calling to embody reconciliation? Indeed, what about their relationship to each other at a time of international tension and terror that has its roots at least partly in historic conflicts between them? These are the questions to which we must now turn.

4

Reconciliation and the Household of Abraham

The events of 11 September 2001, followed by the ferocious unleashing of the 'war against terror', sent shock waves of horror, anger and fear throughout the world.[1] Previous claims that the movement towards a new world order of democracy and peace was irreversible were blown apart by the unfolding cycle of violence and vengeance. These events have reshaped the political contours of the new millennium and reinforced apocalyptic speculation that we are witnessing a clash of civilizations, simplistically depicted as a struggle between the Christian West and resurgent Islamic fundamentalism,[2] or between 'the domain of Islam' (*dar al-Islam*) and the 'domain of war' (*dar al-harb*). The thesis is misleading and potentially dangerous. Yet it has an element of truth in that it indicates the extent to which relationships between the West, with its largely Christian heritage, and the Arab and Islamic world, have reached a critical point in world history at the centre of which lies the Palestinian–Israeli conflict.

The impact of resurgent Islam has been felt in many local and regional contexts where conflict between Christians and Muslims has erupted during the past decades. Nigeria, the Sudan, Bosnia and Indonesia immediately come to mind. But tensions have also been experienced in many European cities,[3] as well as post-apartheid Cape Town.[4] At the same time as the TRC was setting about its task of enabling national reconciliation, there was a series of urban terror bombings in the Western Cape attributed to PAGAD. This community organization emerged in the post-apartheid era ostensibly to combat drug trafficking and gang related crime, but was soon taken over by militant Muslims.[5] Hence suspicions have long been rife that the notorious bombing of the Planet Hollywood restaurant, part of an American franchise, at the Waterfront in Cape Town in November 1998, was related to the bombings of United States' embassies in Nairobi and elsewhere.

Already in 1994, when the 'clash of civilizations' thesis was first being propounded, an editorial in the ecumenical journal *Concilium* firmly rejected any easy or fatalistic acceptance of this notion. Instead, the editors Hans Küng and Jürgen Moltmann argued that Christianity and Islam present a challenge to each other that has the potential to provide the necessary ferment for worldwide peace and reconciliation.[6] That same year Karl-Josef Kuschel published his study on *Abraham: Sign of Hope for Jews, Christians, and Muslims.* In his conclusion he stated that the 'future of Europe and the Middle East in the third millennium may well depend on whether or not Jews, Christians and Muslims' achieve an 'Abrahamic brotherhood and sisterhood'. He went on to say that if they together practised an Abrahamic ecumenicity, Jews, Christians and Muslims could become a blessing to all humankind making the world 'that much richer in friendliness, righteousness and humanity'.[7] That was a tall order prior to the events of 11 September, now it is even more problematic, but also more necessary and urgent. As such it presents a major challenge to the Christian Church and its commitment to the ministry of reconciliation.

In seeking to understand this challenge we will explore the relationship between Judaism, Christianity and Islam as alienated members of the household of Abraham in order to discern how they may both be more reconciled to each other and work together for the sake of reconciliation and justice and peace. This is not to suggest that other religious traditions are unimportant or have little to contribute to this task, but to acknowledge the special character of the family of Abraham and its particular covenantal obligations today. Our focus will be especially on Islam for obvious reasons, but in the awareness that relations between the three Abraham faiths must, today, be considered as a whole.

Alienating memories and present realities

The original Pauline conviction that, in Christ, Jew and Gentile would be reconciled in one body soon became an eschatological hope rather than a present reality (Rom. 9–11). Following the destruction of Jerusalem in 70 CE, relations between rabbinic Judaism and the Jesus messianic movement became increasingly strained. However, the separation between synagogue and the emerging Church became a reality only after the Roman crushing of the Bar Kochba revolt in 135 CE. In the process the Church turned its back on Jewish forms of Christianity, lost its character as a Jewish Messianic movement, and gained a new, catholic identity, embracing people of many ethnic communities, but few Jews. The Constantinian settlement ushered in a new era of deteriorating relations. Jews were persecuted on the pretext of being responsible for the death of Jesus, and Judaism, having been superseded by Christianity, it was argued, had no reason or right to exist. The only path open was for Jews to renounce their faith and be baptized. Thus began a tragic history of anti-Judaism and anti-Semitism that eventually led to the expulsion of the Jews from Spain in the fifteenth century, their exclusion from mainstream society in the ghettos of Europe, and eventually the Shoah.[8]

The roots of Islam are deeply embedded in both Judaism and Christianity as is evident from the life of the prophet Muhammed and from the Qur'an itself. When it first emerged, some Christian theologians regarded Islam as a Christian heresy.[9] This is unhelpful, even though there are similarities between Islam and Syrian Christianity, a tradition that remained apart from the mainstream of Roman and Byzantine Christianity.[10] While the prophet Muhammed taught his followers to respect Judaism and Christianity as 'religions of the Book', both were regarded as superseded by Islam and neither met the needs that Muhammed discerned in his own context. The rise of Islam was partly due to the inability of both Judaism and Christianity to bring cohesion to the various warring Arabic factions. Islam blamed the failure of Christianity on its reversion to paganism (the doctrine of the Trinity being the chief culprit), and its attitude towards God's law, and therefore of compromising their status as the spiritual heirs of Abraham. Even though Islam allowed Jews and Christians to continue in their respective faiths, Islam regarded its own calling or task (*Da'wa*) as bringing the world back to obedience and submission to God's law or *Shari'ah*. This was the only way to establish a social order of justice and peace between warring clans, tribes and peoples.

The story of the conquests and expansion of Islam across the Mediterranean world requires no repeating. Well known, too, is the remarkable contribution of Islamic scholars to the life and culture of Medieval Europe and the story of Muslim rule in Spain where the 'Umma evinced a spirit of tolerance towards other faiths and cultures that has been rare in history'.[11] We often speak of the Judaeo-Christian tradition of the West, but the Jewish scholar Bernard Lewis reminds us of the long tradition of Judaeo-Islamic symbiosis.[12] Islam, along with Christianity and Judaism, has contributed significantly to the cultural inheritance of Europe and the shaping of the Western world.[13] But in spite of times and places of dialogue, collaboration and mutual enrichment, suspicion and hostility have mostly shaped the relationship, whether defined by conquest, inquisition or crusade.

The modern period of the relationship between Christianity and Islam may be traced back to Napoleon's invasion of Egypt in 1798.[14] This led to the European colonization of Arab lands, the formation of nation states in political and economic dependence on Europe, and to the gradual decline in the influence of Islam as a factor on the world scene. At the same time, much of the Christian West, under the influence of the Enlightenment, the French and industrial revolutions, succumbed to the forces of secularization. This has long been of concern to Islam, as well as to all other religious traditions for whom secularism and modernity are regarded as inimical to religious faith and practice, and therefore to the well-being of humanity. The First World War and the Russian Revolution signalled the final collapse of Christendom and demonstrated the spiritual and moral bankruptcy of the West.

The relationship between Christianity and Islam is now indelibly marked and disfigured not only by the Crusades of the distant past, but also by the extent to which Christianity has been identified with European colonization, modernization and global control. In addition, Western arrogance and assertiveness, to which the Church has contributed, has cast a long and dark shadow over Christian–Muslim relations. The sad truth is, as Elizabeth Scantlebury says, that 'negative examples of theological, historical and political interaction have lived longest in the collective memory and have, therefore, been the prime motivation for continued mistrust'.[15] As those engaged in Christian–Muslim dialogue testify, historical memory of conflict invariably overshadows more positive and peaceful experiences.[16] I recall a Muslim student in one of my classes on Christian history, expressing amazement that I had been so critical of the Crusades. Baffled, I asked for some explanation. 'Why', he responded, 'we Muslims have always believed that Christians regard the Crusades with pride!'

While the past provides the point of reference for those who are disillusioned and alienated, the struggle for what has been called 're-Ismalization "from below"',[17] or 'the moral explosion of the masses' has the material future as its goal.[18] This is true in Palestine as it is in every part of the Middle East; it is also true in South Africa and elsewhere where Islam is a minority shaped by years of oppression and discrimination. Even though the dramatic change in the oil prices in the 1970s brought enormous wealth to some Arab nations, this did not change the feudal character of Arabic society or overcome widespread poverty. Western support for Israel and corrupt Arab leaders, together with the effects of the Cold War further alienated many Muslims from the West and its Christian affiliations, producing the consequences with which we are now familiar.

Almost exactly two centuries after Napoleon captured Cairo, with the collapse of the Shah's rule in Iran in 1979, Shi'ite Islam provided a leader, the Ayatollah Khomeini, under whose influence Islam began to reshape world politics.[19] If the escalation in value of the petro-dollar changed the balance of global economic power, the Iranian revolution gave disenchanted Muslims around the world an Islamicist ideology and spiritual direction that spoke to their condition and awakened their hopes. Even so, it did not fundamentally change their material condition. Times have rarely been as bad, as stressful, or as disorientating for many Muslims, as they are now. This fact goes a long way to explain the militancy which characterizes Muslim politics today.[20] The way in which large sections of the Muslim world relate to global as well as local issues is not determined by some international Islamic council that has final authority, nor by liberal Muslim scholars, but by social and material conditions. It is these that foster a particular reading of the Qur'an and shape political action.

In some respects, the resurgence of militant forms of Islam during the latter decades of the twentieth century is a postmodern phenomenon.[21] But postmodern in the sense that it is a strident rejection of modernity, the code word for the fruits of Western technology and secularism, and a decisive shift to affirming Islamic identity over against global conformity. Also characteristically postmodern is the extent to which this identity has been shaped by the media, leading to vitriolic fury at the West and Israel,[22] and to a dangerous stereotyping of Islam and of Muslims. What the image too often hides is Islamic pluralism, its diversity and even division, thereby 'conveying the impression that there is a unity in Muslim perception and a totality in Muslim endeavour' which 'is manifestly not so'.[23] One sad result of this is that the rich 'mosaic of Muslim cultures'[24] tends to be forgotten. There are, in fact, other Muslim interpretations of the Qur'an and *Shari'ah* that stand in strong contrast to that of militant Islam with its isolationist and exclusive views, and its particular interpretation of *jihad*.[25] Indeed, what is meant by *jihad* provides a very useful way of discerning the plurality in the Muslim juridical tradition.[26]

The origin of *jihad* is the need to establish an egalitarian and just political order on earth according to the *Shar'iah*. *Jihad* is not a 'holy war' but the struggle to do justice in society. Within the South African context *jihad* was sometimes understood as synonymous with the liberation struggle from a Muslim perspective. Even when the Qur'an is most explicit in its encouragement of Muslims to act decisively against idolaters, even by taking up arms, it speaks against committing excesses (Sura 2.190–1). The majority of Muslims decry those who advocate violence and hatred, along with the strident propaganda that drowns out 'Muslim voices of learning and balance'. But the propaganda is powerful and persuasive, thus confronting Islam with a critical choice as to the meaning and implications of *jihad*. 'In the long term,' Akbar Ahmed asks, 'would Muslims replace the central Quranic concepts of *adl* and *ahsan*, balance and compassion, of *ilm*, knowledge, and *sabr*, patience, with the bullet and the bomb?'[27] For Ahmed, 'Islam is essentially the religion of equilibrium and tolerance; suggesting and encouraging breadth of vision, global positions and the fulfilment of human destiny in the universe'.[28] *Jihad* is thus also, as the Sufis teach, the inner struggle to overcome the passions and not to sin. To quote from the Qur'an:

> The good action and the bad are not alike. Repel the evil one by one which is better! And behold! He between whom and you there was enmity, shall be as if he were a fervent friend. (Sura 41.34)

The Abraham to whom all three faiths look as the rock from which they are hewn was 'not an apocalyptic fighter, a fanatical exclusivist, or a raging iconoclast'.[29]

If Christians have often misrepresented Islam, similar dangers attend the Muslim stereotyping of Christianity and Judaism. Many Muslims continue to regard Christianity simplistically as the religion of the West, the religious arm of colonialism, imperialism and capitalism, and propagate views about Christianity that are often mischievous. Even the demand of Church leaders 'to evoke the UN's Declaration of Human Rights in favour of Christian minorities has been seen by Muslims as the Church "siding with" and in "favour of" Western secular advancement in the Muslim world'.[30] Just as we must condemn the atrocities committed against Palestinians by the State of Israel, so too we must deplore militant Islam's continuing vitriolic attack on Jews

and Judaism. There is today a frightening escalation in anti-
Semitic rhetoric and Holocaust denial on the part of certain Arab
leaders and Islamic fundamentalist groups that rival that of Nazi
propaganda. Just as not all Muslims agree with or support
Islamic fundamentalism or revivalism, so not all Jews are fundamentalists or militant Zionists, or agree with the politics of the
West.

Given the history of alienation and aggression, the collective
memory that sustains it, along with the daily media reinforcing
of stereotypes, it is essential that the past be healed if the family
of Abraham is to contribute to peace and justice. For this to happen each side needs to engage the other in dialogue, exercise self-
criticism, and take responsibility for past actions of alienation
and betrayal of social responsibility. Although addressed
specifically to Christian–Muslim relations, the words of David
Kerr have relevance for the family of Abraham as a whole:

> there can be no movement towards reconciliation without
> mutual repentance, no reconstruction without the sacrifice of
> vested institutional interests, and no peace but through com-
> mon commitment to God as the source of all peace, Al-Salam.[31]

This implies that the use of any of the faiths to legitimate the
political ambitions of the nations in which they are dominant, or
to exclude or prejudice the 'other', means that they are guilty of
betraying their founding covenant and its vision of the world
as belonging to God. It also implies the need to counter the mis-
representation of the 'other' within our own communities. If
religious leaders are really committed to the truth they have to
oppose the dangerous and often vitriolic stereotyping of other
faith communities. Furthermore, as Kuschel says: 'After the
holocaust and in light of the pluralism of the postmodern
world, Christianity and Islam will have to reject their own
claims to supersede Judaism. And Jews will, more clearly than
before, recognise these religions as outgrowths of the original
covenant.'[32]

Whatever understanding might be achieved at a scholarly level does not easily percolate down to the grass-roots where communities engage one another, or to the enraged masses on the streets of Palestine, Teheran, Karachi or, for that matter, Cape Town. Yet Christians, Muslims and Jews did stand shoulder to shoulder in the struggle against apartheid, and they are likewise involved at many levels in working together today to make democratic transformation a reality. It is appropriate then that we now consider the relationships between the members of the family of Abraham in South Africa, the way in which they responded to the TRC, and to the challenge to work for national reconciliation.

The household of Abraham and national reconciliation

The role of Christianity in shaping the social fabric of South Africa over the past 350 years has been widely documented, discussed and contested. Christianity, in its many and varied forms, is the dominant global religious tradition, with Church affiliation numbering about two thirds of the total population.[33] Christianity took root in South Africa as the religion of both the European settler community and, as a result of European missions, of the indigenous population. But its role as the embodiment and an agent of reconciliation was seriously compromised by colonial interests and by the denominational divisions that were planted in South Africa. Converts often complained that the coming of Christianity introduced new divisions into African society, reinforcing ethnic divisions as a result of missionary strategy, and dividing communities along traditional and Christian lines. Paradoxically, however, Christianity also served to unite Africans from various ethnic groups, preparing the way for the emergence of African nationalism. This highlights the ambiguous role that Christianity has played, an ambiguity most in evidence during the apartheid era and the struggle for liberation.

The Jewish community in South Africa is very different to that of the Christian, not only because of its ethnic character and religious life, but also because it is a very small minority, less than 0.5 per cent of the total population.[34] The community largely stems from two waves of immigration, the first from Britain and Germany in the nineteenth century; the second, as a result of persecution, from Eastern Europe at the turn of the twentieth century. Over the years the community has experienced considerable prejudice, initially in terms of immigration laws, but especially during the 1930s and 1940s when there was a surge of anti-Semitism fuelled by Nazi ideas.[35] But as part of the white community Jews have also been beneficiaries of apartheid, even though a significant number were deeply involved in the anti-apartheid struggle. One Jewish social activist notes that 'the history of Jewish leadership, including rabbinic leadership, from 1948 until about 1991, was completely accommodationist of apartheid and white supremacy'.[36] During the past few decades the Jewish population has shrunk considerably through emigration, but it remains an influential minority in the country.

Shortly after the TRC began its work, a symposium to discuss Jewish Perspectives on Justice and Forgiveness was held in Johannesburg.[37] Several themes emerged that relate to our discussion. For Jews, the TRC and the discussions surrounding it had, as one Jewish educationist put it, a 'parallel sub-text running through their psyches that calls to mind the Holocaust and the Nuremberg Trials'.[38] While Jews would not equate the Holocaust and apartheid, it is significant that the Holocaust Museum in Cape Town draws striking parallels between them. 'We have been there' aptly summed up this sentiment.[39] This meant that Jews should have a greater sensitivity to crimes against humanity, even though many Jews, as part of white South Africa, failed to resist apartheid. These themes were eloquently presented by Chief Rabbi Cyril K. Harris and by the Gesher Movement in their submissions to the TRC.

The Torah and Talmud insist on justice and truth as the basis for peace and reconciliation in the world, a view shared with Christians and Muslims, and fundamental to the work of the TRC. Reconciliation is only possible after repentance, and it demands reparation,[40] though how to deal with guilt and repentance if full reparation is no longer possible is an issue that remains unresolved.[41] Here some divergence from Christianity is detected, and the basis for criticism of the TRC as being too dominated by Christian views becomes evident. For Judaism there can be no vicarious repentance and there are circumstances where forgiveness is not possible.[42] Quoting Emmanuel Levinas, a Jewish political analyst declared: 'Yes, Judaism believes in compassion, but Judaism holds out the proposition that to posit infinite pardon is to posit an infinite temptation to evil'.[43] What is fundamentally necessary is the pursuit of social justice, the only antidote to vengeance and the only basis for reconciliation. This is not unlike the criticism made by the progressive Muslim theologian Faried Esack regarding the 'Christianization' of the TRC process, and his expressed hope that the process would not fail through the 'unbounded grace' of its chair. Reconciliation, Esack declared, 'is premised on truth, but reconciliation is not only premised on truth, reconciliation is also premised on justice'.[44]

The Islamic community is larger than the Jewish yet still small, numbering around 1.5 per cent of the total population. But in recent years the community has taken on significance far greater than its numbers because of the global resurgence of Islam. Islam came to South Africa in two major waves.[45] The first Muslims came from the Dutch East Indies in the seventeenth century as slaves, amongst whom were distinguished leaders of resistance against Dutch conquest in the East. The public practice of Islam was prohibited at the Cape on pain of death from 1642 until 1804, when religious freedom was promulgated.[46] But racial and religious oppression in the name of Christianity continued.[47] The second wave, which came from India and what is now Pakistan, started in 1860 during the British Raj and settled first in Natal and then in the Transvaal. While some were indentured labourers, most became traders. Differences between the two groups, relating both to their origins and to their social location and experience in South Africa have, over the years, been reinforced by differences in theology,[48] political ideology and involvement. In more recent years they have also been shaped by the ways in which they have responded to the global resurgence of Islam.[49] These differences were reflected in the various responses made at the Faith Community hearings of the TRC.

Both the Council of Transvaal Muslim Theologians (Jamiatul Ulama Transvaal), and the Muslim Judicial Council (MJC) based in Cape Town, acknowledged in their submissions to the TRC that some Muslims collaborated with the apartheid regime.[50] The Muslim Youth Movement (MYM) was more outspoken and referred to Muslims who were 'silent accomplices to National Party rule',[51] while Faried Esack, in a personal submission, declared that Muslims had been privileged by apartheid and sometimes guilty of oppressing Africans.[52] But all the submissions detailed the extent to which Muslims were engaged in the struggle for liberation, many of them playing key roles and some giving their lives for the cause. The MJC having been formed in 1945 to serve Muslim unity and to 'protest against oppressive laws and governmental policies'. Already in 1961, it had rejected apartheid as *haram*, the equivalent of the later Christian declaration of apartheid as a heresy,[53] and in 1985, while still in prison, Nelson Mandela praised the Council for its role in the liberation struggle.[54]

In its concluding statement on the role of Muslims in the continued struggle, the submission of the Muslim Youth Movement identified itself with the position adopted by the *Kairos Document* insisting that reconciliation demands repentance on the part of oppressors and a fundamental redistribution of wealth and power. 'It is our conviction', the submission declared, 'that this is exactly what Islam would demand for reconciliation (*sulh*) between perpetrator and victim.'[55] Reconciliation is founded on economic justice, and implemented with mercy and compassion, a task in which religious people should engage but, the MYM warned, if 'we fail in this responsibility, God forbid, it might well be administered with vengeance'.[56]

Not all Muslims who joined the liberation struggle agreed on the way in which they should participate. The MYM, which had emerged in the 1970s under the influence of the Iranian revolution, was committed to working for change in South Africa on the basis of the *Shari'ah* and therefore through the propagation of Islam.[57] However, two other movements inspired by resurgent global Islam that emerged from the MYM were more directly involved in the political struggle. Qibla, established in 1981, aligned itself with the Black Consciousness Movement and the Pan Africanist Congress, while the Call of Islam, founded in 1984, was aligned with the Mass Democratic Movement, which represented the banned African National Congress.[58] Whereas the latter willingly embraced people of other faiths in the struggle for liberation, the fundamentalist Qibla tended to stand aloof as an exclusive Islamic political movement.

These differences have continued into the new democratic era, with Qibla highly critical of the new democratic Constitution and wary of religious pluralism, while those who came out of, or who were influenced by the more progressive Call of Islam, were committed to the new government and its democratic objectives. Many of the latter are now involved in local and national government structures, and co-operate with people of other faiths in pursuit of national reconciliation just as they participated together in the struggle against apartheid 'deeply inspired by' Islam.[59] The South African minister of justice who was responsible for establishing the TRC, Abdullah Omar, is a prominent Muslim, as were several others in key positions in the structures of the TRC, including Justice Hassen Mall, the chairperson of the Amnesty Committee.[60] In its submission to the TRC, the Muslim Judicial Council stressed its own commitment to its work and emphasized the need to lay a 'foundation for a new morality based on a culture of human rights'.[61] Likewise the Council of Transvaal Muslim Theologians called for religious and political tolerance, respect for the rights of others, social justice and equality for all, 'some of the core principles for national reconciliation and nation building'.[62]

The South African chapter of the World Conference on Religion and Peace (WCRP) played a vital role in bringing together the family of Abraham and other faith communities in preparing the way for the first democratic elections and the building of the new nation.[63] A National Interfaith Conference, held in Pretoria in November 1992, expressed the conviction that just as people of religious commitment had shared together in the struggle against apartheid, so they could together contribute to the reconstruction of society. Fundamentalists of all traditions held aloof from this process, with Qibla denouncing it as a Zionist and Communist plot![64] Yet many Muslims were there from a variety of organizations, sharing together with people of other faiths in a common commitment to doing justice and achieving national reconciliation.

But if this common commitment to justice and reconciliation united people of different faiths, the question of what precisely it meant was also divisive. For example, fundamental to the new Constitution in South Africa, and therefore to what is understood as defining the parameters of nation building are a series of progressive views on human rights. Gender equity is at the forefront of the government's agenda and institutionalized in the work of both the Human Rights Commission and the Gender Commission. This is a major challenge to the synagogue, the Church, and especially the mosque, and one that requires positive response if the family of Abraham is concerned at all about justice.

The progressive elements within the family of Abraham faith communities were dominant during the early 1990s, as South Africa entered its new found freedom. Yet, as the 'honeymoon' period began to wane and South Africa struggled with the realities of grinding poverty, unemployment, HIV/AIDS and the many other issues facing the country, conservative and fundamentalist sectors in each religion began to regroup. In some ways their reactions were the same, for fundamentalists in all three traditions were outspoken in their criticism of the abolition of the death penalty, the new laws permitting abortion, and religious education school policies. At the same time, the situation in the Middle East and the war in Afghanistan polarized these groups in ways that run counter to their participation in nation building in South Africa. This tension between global affiliation and local participation is one that has considerable potential for exacerbating national divisions, but it also has the possibility of breaking open the boundaries of a misguided nationalism that prevents participation in efforts to bring about global justice and peace. It is therefore of the utmost importance that alongside the global tensions and conflicts that divide the family of Abraham we also recognize the history of dialogue that has taken place during the past several decades.

Dialogue, commonality and difference

The extent to which the relationship between Christianity and Judaism has developed since the end of the Second World War is evident in the fact that dialogue between them is not dealt with in the Vatican's Pontifical Council for Inter-religious Dialogue, but that for Promoting Christian Unity. This not only signals recognition of the Jewish roots of Christianity, but also of the ecumenical vision of the New Testament. Under this and other ecumenical auspices, conversations between Jews and Christians have been conducted in many places, though invariably limited to theologians and scholars in the West.[65] There has been little dialogue in countries that were largely unaffected by the Holocaust or where the Jewish presence is relatively small, a factor which must inevitably shape our discussion.

The formation of the State of Israel in 1948, and the general though not unqualified alignment of the West with Israel, has significantly altered the parameters of the relationships between the three faith communities. So alienation in the family of Abraham cannot be dealt with in a bilateral way, as though Jews and Christians could talk to each other apart from Muslims, or Christians and Muslims without Jews. This denies both the historical and religious connections, but also present political realities. After all, the situation in the Middle East is a core issue and central to the debate. Nonetheless, the relationship between Christianity and Islam is particularly urgent and challenging both globally and in many local contexts, hence the special focus of attention.

The famous World Missionary Conference held in Edinburgh in 1910 identified Islam as one of 'the storm centres of interest and urgency and anxiety in the ecumenical crusade today'.[66] The choice of the word 'crusade' was unfortunate, but it is indicative of the fact that less than 100 years ago this was the mindset of

Christianity in its outreach to Muslims. There was even talk about opening a mission in Mecca and Medina![67] Such an idea is now almost unthinkable, and its execution would be politically impossible. Ironically today more Islamic missions it seems are being planted in traditionally Christian countries rather than vice versa. But alongside these developments especially since the 1960s, there has been a remarkable growth in dialogue between Christian and Muslim scholars in search of mutual understanding and ways of co-operating in serving the interests of world peace and justice. Much of this has been sponsored by the World Council of Churches and the Pontifical Council for Interreligious Dialogue, and much can be learnt by reflecting on its development.[68]

Ataullah Siddiqui's study of this process in his book *Christian–Muslim Dialogue in the Twentieth Century*, provides a useful point of departure for our discussion in drawing our attention to issues on which there is considerable consensus amongst the six leading Muslim scholars he discusses.[69] Alienation or reconciliation between Christians and Muslims, they insist, will depend on how the two communities address 'the nature of dialogue, *Shari'ah*, human rights, religious pluralism, and Islam and the West in general'.[70] We begin, then, with some comments on dialogue, paying special attention to what has been learnt by way of guidelines for meaningful conversation.

For Christians, the Church is a key element in the doctrine of reconciliation, providing the embodiment of the new humanity as reconciled in Christ. In Islam the *umma* fulfils a similar role. Comprised of all believers, the *umma* is the community that ideally binds them together irrespective of ethnic origin and culture. I say 'ideally' because divisions within Islam compromise the *umma* just as they do the Church. Nonetheless, the *umma*, according to the Qur'an, has been appointed 'a middle nation' to witness against the sins of the nation and to call them to true faith in the One God (Sura 2.143; cf. 22.78). The *umma* is God's agent for executing judgement and justice in the world. The problem for dialogue is, however, that the *umma* is not structured or institutionalized in the same way as the Christian

Churches, and especially those Churches that have a clearly defined hierarchy. This means that while the *umma* represents Islam globally, there is no official entity that can enter into formal discussions in a way that will have the support of the global Muslim constituency. Islam is essentially a lay movement with a clearly defined sense of identity, but not an institution in the same sense as the Christian Church. Participation in dialogue is therefore largely a matter of individual involvement and personal commitment.

Many Muslim participants have been wary of inter-faith dialogue because they are usually the guests of Christian Churches and often uncertain about their intention. Clearly sensitivity towards the perceptions of 'the other' is essential for any meaningful dialogue, and the process itself must not be a subterfuge for proselytism. At the same time, genuine dialogue not only requires the input of dispassionate scholars but of believers, people committed to the truth of their respective traditions. In the case of both Christians and Muslims, part of that commitment is to spread the gospel or the *Shari'ah*. If Muslims did not believe that God's will for the establishment of a just social order is embodied in the teachings of the Qur'an, and if Christians did not believe in the good news of God's reign and reconciliation in Jesus Christ, there would be little point to the discussion. Hence it is important at the outset to acknowledge, with the delegates to the World Conference on Mission and Evangelism in San Antonio in 1989:

> We do not water down our commitment if we engage in dialogue; as a matter of fact, dialogue between people of different faiths is spurious unless it proceeds from the acceptance and expression of faith commitment.[71]

Not only does the Qur'an decree that 'there shall be no compulsion in religion' (Sura 2.256), but it also enjoins Jews to be faithful to the Law and the Prophets, and Christians to the gospel:

> Let the People of the Gospel
> Judge by what God hath revealed therein. (Sura 5.50)

For Christians this requires that we exercise our judgement on the basis of the gospel, but also respect the judgement of our co-religionists on the basis of their own faith convictions. Muslim scholars and theologians, like Christians and Jews, have a particular responsibility to expound their own tradition, drawing from it those insights that both sustain their communities and yet also contribute to the welfare of society as a whole.

Dialogue is about more than dealing with the past or the process of meaningful conversation; it also has to deal with substantive issues that perplex, confuse and divide. That is why it must be far more than a superficial 'getting to know you' exercise. Hence Kuschel's description of an 'Abrahamic ecumene' as 'an ecumene of learning, studying, of spiritual exploration of one another's religion, culture and civilization'.[72] This implies trying to understand each other's Scriptures, if possible through reading them together.[73] In engaging in such an exploration it is important to recognize at the outset those things which actually unite. As the description 'family of Abraham' indicates, there is considerable commonality between Judaism, Christianity and Islam, a sense in which they belong to each other and are mutually responsible for the justice and peace in the world.

Abraham is, for each, 'the primal image of faith' and 'Torah, Gospel and Qur'an are concretions of the faith of Abraham'.[74] Moreover, Abraham's quest for true faith in God and his humility in depending on God alone provide the basis for each religion's self-critique.[75] Christians know, though we often forget, that our roots are in the Hebrew Scriptures and that we have become, according to the New Testament, the spiritual heirs of Abraham. But we also need to learn to appreciate the truth in Islam, hewn as it is from the same Abrahamic rock. As Kenneth Cragg indicated in his *Muhammed and the Christian*: 'Loyalty to Islamic essentials brings us more vitally into Christian fields of meaning than anything else could – and more hopefully'.[76] Cragg was referring in particular to the questions of transcendence, of law and of salvation, for each of these takes us directly to the heart of the matter at stake, highlighting both areas of agreement and disagreement.

For Christians, as for Jews and Muslims, there is only one God to whom the prophets bear faithful witness, and this God is both compassionate and a God of justice. Seyyed Hossein Nasr, one of the great Islamic scholars of the twentieth century, has spoken of the way in which each of the Abrahamic faiths contribute to our understanding of God and what it means to live faithfully in the world. In the opening chapter of his *Ideals and Realities of Islam*, despite his claim that Islam fulfils the others, he shows how they complement each other in representing aspects of the Abrahamic tradition. He writes:

> In a sense Judaism is essentially based on the fear of God, Christianity on the love of Him and Islam on the knowledge of Him, although this is only a matter of emphasis, each integral religion containing of necessity all these three fundamental aspects of the relation between man and God.[77]

Nasr's insights here reflect those of the French Catholic scholar, Louis Massignon, who in the first half of the twentieth century did so much to promote Christian–Muslim dialogue, stressing their complementary character. But even though each of the faiths may trace their origins to Abraham, whether through Isaac (Israel), Ishmael, or only spiritually as in the teaching of Paul, each is a distinct religion with a long tradition. This means that dialogue between Judaism, Christianity and Islam has to be based not only on an acknowledgement of commonality and agreement, but also on a respect for difference.

Difference becomes apparent when it comes to discerning the way in which God is known, and how God's law is to be appropriated and implemented. Abraham cannot replace Moses and the Torah, Jesus and the Gospel, or Muhammad and the Qur'an. As Kuschel puts it:

> In important theological and anthropological questions Jews, Christians and Muslims are so far removed from one another that there can be no question of a unity in confession, praxis and community structure.[78]

Of particular significance in this regard is that from a Jewish and Christian perspective the way in which Christianity and Judaism are portrayed in the Qur'an is problematic, especially given the fact that the Qur'an is, for Muslims, the Word of God and therefore infallible in such matters.[79]

All three Abrahamic faiths put emphasis on the importance of interpersonal relations within the broader framework of our relationship to God. Abdulaziz Sachedina reminds us that 'according to the famous Prophetic tradition, nine-tenths of faith in Islam deals with interpersonal relations'.[80] On the basis of this, he argues that 'the validity of religious faith in Islam is objectively determined by the way Muslims handle inter-human relationships'.[81] Religious faith implies relationships:

> The moment I, as an individual, begin to deal with the other individual, my sense of relationship comes into focus, requiring me to be aware of my duties as well as my rights. And it is only then that my action is open to scrutiny, ethical reflection, and moral judgement.[82]

While there is no equivalent word in the Qur'an for the New Testament καταλλαγη, there is a great deal that corresponds to the teaching of the Bible.[83] Islam means, after all, surrendering to God's will, and God's will is justice and peace for the world. Indeed, Islam's insistence on the unity of the One God (Allah) has, as its corollary, the unity of humankind. This is the whole point of Abraham's call to obey God and of Abraham's surrender to God's will in destroying pagan idols. Idolatry (*shirk*) is that which brings dissension and disharmony into the world and thus destroys human relations. Hence the need to struggle (*jihad*) against the power of Satan, the agent of sin. The Qur'an nevertheless proclaims God's mercy and forgiveness to those who believe in him and repent of their sins. For Muslims, God is both the beneficient and the merciful. And while the Qur'an allows for vengeance and retaliation on our part when wronged by another, it recommends forgiveness as the way to please God. The validity of repentance requires genuine sorrow for the sin committed and the resolve not to commit it again. It also requires due reparation for any injustice involved.

On this Jews, Christians and Muslims agree, even if the emphasis may vary considerably at times. There is also, as Samuel Schimmel reminds us, some ambiguity on the relationship within the New Testament itself and certainly beyond its pages in Christian tradition. Not 'all Christian spiritual mentors teach that forgiveness should be granted in the absence of repentance and not all Jewish ones teach that repentance must always be a pre-requisite to forgiveness'.[84] This is an important warning to be aware of trying to impose a schema on Jewish, Muslim and Christian teaching on the subject which hardens what is a dynamic relationship into a dogmatic system. It may be true that Christianity generally has a more radical doctrine of forgiveness than the other Abrahamic faiths, but this does not mean that repentance is unnecessary, or that there is no similar dialetic relationship between the two in Islam and Judaism. The real point of divergence between the three faiths lies elsewhere. Nowhere is this more apparent than in the way in which Jesus speaks about the Law.[85] In Hans Küng's words:

> Despite what the Qur'an says, he did not uphold the Law. Rather (as the evidence in the Gospels has compelled us to argue), he opposed every kind of legalism with his radical love (which embraces even the enemy), and for this reason was executed. But this is precisely what the Qur'an, flying in the face of history, will not admit.[86]

For Paul, as for other New Testament writers, this did not mean that Jesus rejected the Torah as such, for that expressed God's will for God's people. Rather, the Torah is understood from a different perspective, finding its fulfilment not its annulment in Jesus and the gospel. This means that for Christians the gospel of God's grace, forgiveness and reconciliation takes precedence and becomes non-negotiable. Obedience to the Torah as such does not bring salvation, but reconciliation to God requires showing gratitude to God through obedience to God's demands.

While it may be true, as the great Muslim scholar Mahmoud Ayoub put it, that 'the Christ of the Gospel often speaks through the austere, human Jesus of Muslim piety',[87] he is still not the Jesus of Nazareth portrayed in the New Testament. From a Christian perspective, Jesus is more than the prophet acknowledged by the Qur'an; he is the Word, that is, the equivalent of what Muslims claim for the Qur'an, in whom God is revealed and through whom the will of God is made known and accomplished. Central to this revelation and redemption is Jesus' death on the cross as the suffering servant and vicarious sacrifice for the sins of the world, something rejected quite explicitly by Islam. For Muslims it is inconceivable that God, in any sense, could suffer on behalf of sinful humanity. This is the major stumbling-block between Christianity on the one hand, and Judaism and Islam on the other. To declare that 'God was in Christ reconciling the world', Barth wrote, is such a bold statement, so potentially blasphemous, that it must not be uttered without considerable care. 'We must', he wrote, 'be able to show that God is honoured and not dishonoured by this confession.'[88] How to maintain the unity *of* God while acknowledging the plurality *in* God is precisely why the doctrine of the Trinity is so essential and cannot be avoided in the dialogic conversation.[89] Yet any hint of tri-theism is unacceptable not only to Jews and Muslims, but also to Christians. Reconciliation in Christ is the action of the one God revealed to Abraham, Moses and Muhammed.

For Jews there is no debate about the historicity of Jesus' crucifixion, only its significance; for Muslims Jesus the prophet could not possibly die such a death. As Paul recognized, this is the scandal that separates Christians from their Abrahamic partners, and yet it is the heart of the gospel, the very power of God for the reconciliation of the world. And the corollary that the Church is called to live beneath the cross not in power but in weakness, 'is barely conceivable in Muslim categories'.[90] Is there any way that this central Christian claim can be communicated in a way that at least makes understanding, if not agreement, possible?

According to René Girard, the cross is a scandal 'not because on it divine majesty succumbs to the most inglorious punishment' but something more radical. The cross 'discredits and deconstructs the gods of violence, since it reveals the true God, who has not the slightest violence in him'.[91] Girard's account may not satisfy all the canons of Christian orthodoxy, but his insight is profound. The cross is the ultimate act of iconoclasm, the destruction of the idols that destroy humanity and dishonour the name of God. In this way, Jesus' death on the cross completes Abraham's rejection of idols, but idolatry itself is redefined. Idolatry is no longer simply the artifacts which pagans make and worship, but human greed, nationalism, xenophobia, racism, sexism, and above all bad religion. All of these dehumanize and destroy what God has created and seeks to redeem. The reconciliation of the world becomes possible through the death of Christ precisely because it signifies the ultimate defeat of the principalities and powers of this world and, at the same time, declares the power of God's love and grace in overcoming sin and alienation. This has immediate implications for the way in which we understand law and the exercise of justice in the world.

The differences between the way in which Christians, Jews and Muslims understand God's way of reconciling the world, need not compromise their sharing together in working for justice and peace in the world. But how to hold on to faith convictions in a world of religious pluralism and secularization, and to fulfil their mutual covenant obligations is an enormous challenge facing the household of Abraham.

Conviction, pluralism and covenantal obligations

Arguably, the prophet Muhammed's greatest social achievement was his success in Medina in uniting warring tribes on the basis of the *Shari'ah*.[92] The *Shari'ah* is the historical and theological foundation on which Islam is built, and the basis for the reconciliation of peoples. Obedience to the *Shari'ah* is the only way to bring about social integration, or unity (*tawhïd*). The *Shari'ah* is, in the words of Seyyed Hossein Nasr:

the divine Law by virtue of accepting which a person becomes a Muslim. Only he who accepts the injunctions of the *Shari'ah* as binding upon him is a Muslim although he may not be able to realize all of its teachings or follow all of its commands in life.[93]

Thus, precisely what makes a Muslim a Muslim is that which unites people and sustains their common life. Despite varieties of opinion, there is a shared sense of supranational identity based on belief, historical consciousness, and shared values that derive from the *Shari'ah*, and these are inherently political.[94] The *Shari'ah* spans the totality of life, regulating all Muslim social relationships, whether these concern property rights, business transactions, marriages or public morals.[95] Even though the *Shari'ah* has to be applied anew in different contexts, and is therefore open to interpretation, it is divinely given and transcends time and history. Allah, not 'the people', is sovereign. A truly Muslim society is therefore one in which attitudes and institutions are brought into harmony with the *Shari'ah*. There can be no separation of religion and politics, the sacred and the secular, for everything falls under and is contingent upon the will of God. Thus, how to relate the *Shari'ah* to the South African Constitution, which is remarkably liberal in its ethos, has become a major issue in the process of achieving national reconciliation. And the same applies more generally in all countries where democratic pluralism is the accepted norm.

While some Muslim political scientists argue that this means that Western liberal democracy cannot be the norm for Muslim countries, they also claim that Islam is not necessarily anti-democratic.[96] As Ahmad comments, 'Islamic resurgence and popular participation in political decision-making are two aspects of the same phenomenon'.[97] The rise of militant Islam has been both a popular reaction to despotic rule, and an attempt to reinstate the *Shari'ah* as the basis of social and political life. But this is precisely where the problem lies, both for predominantly Muslim societies and for other countries where Islam is a significant force. Disagreement on the implementation of the

Shariʿah is not just a matter of scholarly debate, it is also a source of political conflict that often turns violent. Ironically, what is the cornerstone of Muslim unity is also the source of Muslim division.

The implications of the traditional understanding and implementation of *Shariʿah* law are obviously problematic for those societies which have embraced liberal democracy, are religiously plural, and whose legal system is based on social consensus. If the ideal society is one in which the *Shariʿah* governs all of life, the predominantly Western secularized understanding of law as a social construct is unacceptable. For this reason some Muslims question whether it is possible to live a truly Islamic life in the West, while others have come to terms with religious pluralism and a secular environment while still seeking to be faithful to the *Shariʿah*.[98] One way of doing this is to limit the scope of *Shariʿah* to personal life.[99] But however done, the fact of the matter is that many Muslims find it increasingly difficult to implement strictly the traditional understanding of the *Shariʿah*, just as non-Muslims find it unacceptable when they try to impose it on them.

The issues are not unfamiliar to both Jews and Christians. This is evident in the tension between conservative religious Jews and the broader society in contemporary Israel. The history of Christendom is littered with attempts to build the 'new Jerusalem'. Some Christian groups today would still like society to be based directly on the literal teachings of the Bible. Historical experience has shown that none of these experiments has proved successful. But whereas Jews and Christians have generally turned away from a theocratic vision of the state and, on the whole, embraced democracy,[100] for many Muslims a social order governed by the *Shariʿah* remains the ideal that needs to be historically realized. The question is stark: is the reduction of the *Shariʿah* to personal life, and therefore the inevitable privatization of Islam, possible without undermining the very essence of Islam as a total way of life?

The privatization of religion is a recent phenomenon in the history of religions. In many respects it is also uniquely Western, developing out of the European Enlightenment, finding expression in democratic theory and constitutions, and being reinforced by the process of secularization. Yet even in the United States, a country that so strongly insists on the separation of Church and state, religion plays a very significant role in politics and the public square. The fact that prayer might be excluded from the school classroom is but a minor matter when compared to the way in which politicians are beholden to religious pressure groups, and Presidents use their Christian connections. It is not for nothing that the Arab and Muslim world regards the United States as the dominant Christian nation, even though for many of the rest of us this is, at times, somewhat embarrassing.

For much of its history, Christianity has had a dualistic understanding of the world, separating the sacred from the secular and, in theory at any rate, keeping religion and politics apart in two spheres. This dualism is not, however, the dominant worldview of the Bible and is one that few Christian theologians today would defend. Yet it is generally accepted that Christianity does not subscribe to any particular political order as God-given, even if democracy is regarded as the best available option. This does not mean a lack of concern about political issues. Quite the contrary, for Christians are called to witness to the 'reign of God' over the whole of life. Therefore even if they accept democracy as a good system, Christians do not, or should not, do so uncritically. The gradual and general acceptance of democratic and religious pluralism by Jews and Christians implies a recognition that they cannot impose their religious claims on others, even if they are free to convince them of their truth.

Indeed, no religious tradition that insists on everyone adopting or living under the control of its creed or moral code can really contribute practically to the establishment of a peaceful and just society in a global and pluralist world. This implies one further step, perhaps the most difficult of all for all three faiths, but one which needs serious consideration. Can there really be peace within the household of Abraham if Christians believe that Christianity has superseded Judaism? If Muslims believe that Islam has superseded both Judaism and Christianity? And if Jews do not recognize both Christians and Muslims as part of the family of Abraham with a shared responsibility towards pursuing justice and peace in the world?[101]

Even though governing society on the basis of the *Shari'ah* may work in some countries where Islam is the predominant religion, it does not work in all and cannot work in a society that is not predominantly Muslim. But even within the latter the implementation of *Shari'ah* often leads to the abuse of human rights and injustice towards minority religious and ethnic groups. Putting the *Shari'ah* into practice within the political realm in traditional hegemonic terms must impact negatively on the functioning of civil society. In the words of Sachidena: 'In a world of nations trying to live together without hostility and ensuing warfare, insistence on agreement in matters of belief as a precondition for lasting peace is highly problematic'.[102] While not all Muslims would agree with Sachedina's inclusive interpretation of the Qur'an, or his affirmation of the Islamic roots of democratic pluralism,[103] the fact that the *Shari'ah* makes a claim on the whole of life need not imply that the state and religion can or should be conflated. There is a constant need for a compromise between the ideal and historical realities,[104] but even more, a constant need to work out a way of relating whereby Muslim concerns about justice and peace may contribute to the common good. This was clearly acknowledged by Muslim representations to the TRC.

Muslim engagement in political life within a multicultural democratic context requires, then, an interpretation of the *Shari'ah* that enables inter-faith relations to be respectful, peaceful and, where possible, co-operative. Hence the recognition by many Muslim scholars that the classical juridical texts need to be freshly interpreted in terms of changing historical circumstances.[105] Faried Esack's attempt to develop such an approach within the South African context, given both the struggle for liberation and democracy and the realities of religious pluralism, is a remarkable achievement in this regard. In a way that resonates with the various forms of Christian liberation theology, Esack's Islamic theology of liberation is premised on a hermeneutic in which tradition, context and praxis informed each other in interpreting the Qur'an from the perspective of the oppressed and in company with the 'religious Other'.[106]

But the debate must obviously go further than matters of inter-faith relations and the 'religious Other', and engage matters of human rights. The feminist challenge to established patriarchal religion was one of the most significant developments in the final decades of the twentieth century, and the issues surrounding gender and sexuality confront the family of Abraham in a way that is inescapable despite the defences raised and widespread resistance. The issue may be posed in the form of a question: 'What about Sarah and Hagar?' That is, the status and challenge of two women, one Abraham's wife and the mother of Isaac, the other Abraham's concubine and mother of Ishmael.

Fundamentalists of all three traditions reject gender equality, with Muslims in particular regarding it as an attempt to under-mine traditional Muslim values on the part of a decadent Western secularism. Yet it is surely noteworthy that within the context of the struggle against apartheid, as Jews, Christians and Muslims stood with each other in solidarity, it became evident that genuine liberation from oppression had to do not just with racism but also sexism. This was part of the argument put forward by progressive Muslims associated with the Call of Islam in their critique of traditionalist interpretations of the role of women in Islam. Once again, Esack, by no means representa-tive of all Muslims and yet at that time an undoubted leader amongst progressive Muslims as founder of the Call of Islam, even spoke of 'The Gender *Jihad*'.[107]

Already in 1984, the Call of Islam declared: 'We believe that our country will never be free until its women are also free from oppressive social norms'.[108] One of the tracts of the Call even had the remarkable title: *Women Arise! The Qur'an Liberates You!*[109] It is surely noteworthy that one of the few instances of a women 'preaching' in a mosque at Friday prayers occurred in the Claremont Mosque in Cape Town in August 1994.[110] This caused considerable controversy within the Cape Town Muslim community, but it also indicated the extent to which some

Muslims are prepared to retrieve the Qur'anic tradition in terms of the demands of both their social context and comprehensive justice. It also reflects the way in which openness to the plight and the concerns of the 'other', whether the other is defined by race, gender or religion, has a transformative influence on traditional ways of expressing one's faith.

At the heart of the debate between traditionalists of all three faiths and those who seek to retrieve their tradition in terms of human rights issues is the question of modernity and secularism. The Muslim concern about the West's captivity to secular norms is nothing new, and it raises critical issues that Christians have to take seriously. In his provocative essay entitled 'Inheritance and Decay', Bonhoeffer quotes the Muslim leader Ibn Saud with telling effect: 'Europe is full of hatred and will destroy itself with its own weapons'. This is why, says Bonhoeffer, Ibn Saud insisted that while Islam may learn from the West it must never allow the West to destroy 'the Arab soul' or undermine obedience to 'the will of God'.[111] For good reason, many Christians today, not least those in the 'third world', share this concern and are therefore unhappy about the identification of Christianity with the West and its captivity to secularism. In an article in the *New York Times* shortly after the terrorist attacks of 11 September 2001, Lamin Sanneh, a Christian convert from Islam, addressed the question why this happened to America. His main conclusion was encapsulated in these words:

> Oddly enough, what most inflames anti-American passion amongst fundamentalist Muslims may be the American government's *lack* of religious zeal. By separating Church and state, the West – and America in particular – has effectively privatized belief, making religion a matter of individual faith.[112]

Sanneh went on to say that from the perspective of fundamentalist Muslims, 'secular states drained Islam of its vitality'. In the light of this he called for compromises between the West and Muslim leaders. The latter need to 'embark on programs of

democratic renewal', but the former need to recognize the legitimate role which religion can and should play in public life. This
would enable people with religious convictions regarding public
life to participate fully without endorsing secularism.

Standing up for human rights is not falling prey to secularism,
on the contrary, it is retrieving the best in the Abrahamic traditions, and it is essential if the members of the household are to
fulfil their covenantal obligations to the world. Of course, many
secularists would prefer it if religion was kept out of the political
process because of its bad track record in spawning or legitimating conflict. For them the privatization of religion is the only way
forward. This is understandable yet short-sighted. It is certainly
short-sighted to ignore religions if they are part of the reason
for conflict, for that surely requires dealing with them. But
there is a much more positive reason for taking religion into
account. Religious communities and traditions provide significant resources for reducing conflict and enabling reconciliation.
As Kuschel comments in his discussion of the role of Anwar
el-Sadat in brokering peace negotiations in the Middle East:
'a peace policy built on a religious conviction can shape con-
sciences, seize hearts and move former enemies to repent in quite
different ways'.[113]

One of the most famous Christian missionary institutions that
was specifically established with a view to converting Muslims to
Christianity was the Henry Martyn Institute established in 1930
in Hyderabad, India. Gradually over succeeding years there was
a shift of emphasis away from proselytism to dialogue. The
emergence of liberation theology in the 1960s led to a discerning
together of the liberating elements within their respective traditions and, moreover to sharing together in the struggle for
justice.[114] An upsurge of violence between the Muslim and Hindu
communities in Hyderabad in 1990, led the then Associate
Director to the Henry Martyn Institute, Andreas D'Souza, to
state:

Those of us who yearn for better relations between people of
different traditions cannot ignore the cry for a healing touch;

in the midst of the conflict we find the new and necessary frontier for inter-religious encounter.[115]

The staff at the Institute now comprises not only Christians but also Muslims and Hindus, working together to explore what it means to be jointly engaged in the struggle for justice and reconciliation in the Indian subcontinent.

The pursuit of national reconciliation by people of different faiths is not the same as reconciliation within one faith community as envisaged by the New Testament, but it is not unrelated, especially in its commitment to doing justice in society for the sake of humanity as a whole. This is not merely the reduction of religious tradition and faith to the pragmatic and functional, but rather an awareness on the part of Abrahamic believers that faith is inseparable from doing justice.[116] All three faiths when faithful to their prophetic impulse are religions that seek to serve the just cause of the oppressed and to be critical of the powerful who oppress them. The distinguished Muslim scholar Mahmoud Ayoub put this eloquently:

Islam may be able to help humanity in its quest for a way out of its predicament of destruction and alienation, but only when Muslims live equally seriously the piety of their faith and its social, political, ethical and economic demands. In the end, the challenge of Islam as an institutionalized religion is the inner Islam, or surrender of all things to God. It is the courage to let God be God in our individual lives, society and world affairs. This is a challenge not for Muslims alone, but for all the people of God. If domestic politics and foreign policy in the West could be truly Christianized and the world of Islam in all its aspects Islamized, then 'Dar al-Islam' could include the Church, and the Church would see the entire world as the 'mystical body of Christ'. Then will the righteous servant of God and the meek 'inherit the earth.'[117]

Part Three

Process and Goal

5

The Art of Reconciliation

The TRC was neither a Christian confessional nor a court of law, but its chair acted as the nation's father confessor and its amnesty committee was presided over by a judge of the Supreme Court. Much of the debate about its effectiveness resulted precisely from this ambiguity. Some argue that it fell between two stools, achieving neither a comprehensive or genuine confession of guilt from the perpetrators and beneficiaries of apartheid's crimes, nor furthering the cause of justice for the victims. Many critics have contended that justice was sacrificed on the altar of forgiveness and reconciliation. There are sufficient grounds to take this criticism seriously. But it fails to recognize the extent to which the TRC was successful both as an agent of healing and as a catalyst for promoting a more just society. Truth commissions around the world are, as Priscilla Hayner reminds us, 'of a fundamentally different nature from courtroom trials, and function with different goals in mind'.[1]

Truth commissions, as their name indicates, try to get at the truth about the past. That goal determines how they are structured and how they tackle their task. In some instances, as in South Africa, their goal is more than getting at the truth and dealing with the past; it is fostering national reconciliation. For this reason, the TRC was structured in such a way that the telling of the truth was an essential means to a greater end. As such it became 'a forum that provided a platform for story-telling, for revealing the truth, for holding the perpetrator accountable, for reparations, remorse, and forgiveness'.[2] What the TRC did was to create space in which victims, perpetrators and benefactors could encounter one another around the truth for the sake of personal and national healing.[3]

Creating space for interfacing

Creating space is critical, irrespective of the nature of the reconciliation we seek. The space may be defined as 'sacred', a confessional, an altar or sanctuary, perhaps. Or it may be mundane, the kitchen table where estranged spouses talk, or political, a Round Table, as during the process of change in Eastern European countries, or the TRC meeting hall. The fact is, reconciliation cannot be pursued without the alienated parties facing each other. For only then can they speak to, and hopefully hear each other. What happens in that space between them then becomes the critical issue.

The Cape Town artist Sue Williamson, who documented the role of art in the struggle against apartheid and the transition to democracy,[4] has produced a remarkable exhibition entitled 'Truth Games' in which she explores the dynamics of reconciliation within the TRC. Williamson writes:

> In my work I attempt to re-contextualize issues of contemporary South African history. By mediating through art the myriad images and information offered for public consumption in the mass media, I try to give dispassionate readings and offer a focus of new opportunities for engagement. Art can provide a distance and a space for such considerations.[5]

Each of Williamson's pictures is divided into three vertical panels. In the left-hand and right-hand panels Williamson has captured the photographic images of a victim and the perpetrator of the crime against that victim. They are looking, as it were, at each other face-to-face, but over or through the middle space. This space is filled with images of the crime committed. One painting, for example, shows Winnie Madikazela Mandela in the right-hand panel, the abducted and murdered young black activist Stompie Sepai in the middle, and Stompie's mother in the left-hand panel.

There are several wooden rails fixed across each painting. Each rail has a groove along which a narrow board can be drawn by the observer from one side of the picture to the other and placed at any point. A pertinent quotation from the TRC hearing made by either the victim or perpetrator is written on each board. So by moving the boards from one side to the other you have the sense of a conversation that is taking place over and about the person or event on the panel between the two. 'How could another mother do such a thing?' asks Stompie's mother. 'It was a horrible mistake', confesses Winnie Mandela. It is not obvious or clear whether the two hear each other, or actually respond to one another. But the observer is drawn into the middle space, and thus into the conversation as he or she moves the sentences from one side to the other, identifying with victim on the one hand and with perpetrator on the other.

It is there, in the middle between the two, that the real interfacing and interaction occurs, for it is the murdered Stompie himself who becomes the one that draws his mother and Winnie Mandela into confrontation and conversation, and opens up the possibility of healing and reconciliation. But it is also there, in the space between victim and perpetrator that those of us who view the painting have to struggle with our own experience as victim, perpetrator or bystander as we recall those people and events. The opening up of the space in between, drawing us into the confrontation and conversation, is the art of reconciliation at work, the taking of the first step if you like. It makes it possible for us to both see ourselves and to see the other, to recall and remember that which brought about destruction, alienation and dehumanization, and to explore the possibilities of overcoming and transforming the past. The raw material for Williamson's art of reconciliation is the TRC process, but the process she draws us into would apply to other forms and levels of reconciliation as well.

Consider another portrayal of the art of reconciliation in creating space for interfacing. Mike Leigh's film *Secrets and Lies,* first screened in 1996, tells the story of a young black London optometrist called Hortense. An adopted child, Hortense has made a success of her life and career, but she is at a critical moment in her life. Her adoptive mother has recently died and, without any family, she now wants to find her biological mother. To do this she approaches the relevant social agency, but is strongly advised not to pursue the matter. Disregarding this advice, she goes in search of her mother only to discover that she is white. Her mother, Cynthia, gave birth when she was fifteen after a casual sexual encounter with a black man, but had never seen her baby daughter so had no idea of her pigmentation.

Cynthia's life along with that of another daughter, Roxanne, has been something of a disaster, in strong contrast to what Hortense has achieved. The contrast is reinforced by their respective living conditions, with Hortense comfortably located in an affluent suburb while Cynthia and Roxanne live in a semi-detached house in a run-down working class neighbourhood. Damian Cannon, the film critic, describes the relationship between Cynthia and Roxanne as fractious, with the latter 'showering her mother with poisonous epithets whenever the conversation passes beyond the mundane'. Cynthia 'seems beaten down by a harsh life of factory work punctuated with teenage pregnancy, caring for her younger brother Maurice and love-hate life with Roxanne'. Cannon continues:

> Maurice, a successful portrait photographer, has managed to escape the grind of the backstreets through hard work and determination. His wife, Monica, is consumed by the desire to create a perfect home, forever cleaning and stencilling. Whatever affection she has for Maurice lies buried beneath a thick blanket of compulsion, only able to emerge in twisted form. He stoically bears such abuse though, even when it means estrangement from Cynthia and Roxanne.
>
> Eventually Maurice makes the effort to visit Cynthia, hiding his motives beneath the external screen of dropping by casually. Cynthia is almost painfully happy to see her little brother, gently chiding him on his tardiness in calling her (it's at least half her fault though, since she refuses to phone him). As it's Roxanne's 21st birthday soon, Maurice gets around to the real

reason for his appearance by suggesting that he and Monica host a party for their niece.

At much the same time Hortense manages to contact Cynthia, unintentionally crushing her real mother with just a few words. Cynthia is initially repelled at coming face-to-face with her past, scared that she could lose what fragile family she already has. Curiosity wins out though and soon they meet as strangers, parting as friends. With this simple event a fuse has been lit, one which will annihilate and regenerate the family.[6]

Secrets and Lies is a funny, yet deeply moving story of hostile and estranged family relationships woven into the racial and class tapestry of any English city. As the story unfolds it becomes clear that Hortense is a mediator or agent of reconciliation and healing, however inadvertent, within that broader context of social relations. Three extracts from Cannon's commentary highlight key aspects of the process. Cynthia was 'initially repelled at coming face-to-face with her past'; Hortense and Cynthia 'meet as strangers, parting as friends'; and, with reference to the birthday party, 'With this simple event a fuse has been lit, one which will annihilate and regenerate the family.' Each of these points to a crucial aspect in the process of reconciliation which, at the same time, is remarkably mundane and everyday, and yet profoundly theological, even though there is no reference at all to religion or the Church except by way of expletive. 'For God's sake, listen to me!'

Martin Buber spoke of 'the basic movement of the life of dialogue' as 'a turning towards the other'.[7] Without meeting face-to-face and entering into a conversation with an adversary on equal terms – subject to subject – the process of reconciliation is impossible. Meeting the other in this way is still some distance from the embrace of reconciliation, but at least a critical first stage in the process has been reached. How sad it was, then, that some years ago the conflicting parties from Northern Ireland who came to South Africa to learn about the work of the TRC refused to meet each other, even though they were staying in the same conference centre.

The process of reconciliation begins through the taking of what might appear to be small and often tentative steps such as meeting and listening to the estranged 'other'. But it is a critical first step involving both parties. The 'other' is initially experienced as a barrier, someone who stands in the way of us getting our own way. Are we going to regard the 'other' as a conversation partner, a fellow human being struggling with us to find a way beyond the impasse in which opposing claims are countered in an endless cycle? Thus the 'other' makes an ethical demand on us, challenging not only our claims but also our self-understanding and identity. Who do we think we are, and what are we trying to become? What are our interests and values, and how do they serve the common good? In the process we are also forced to see ourselves not as the initiating and dominating 'I', but as one who is also an-other. We discover the identity of the 'other' as a person, and one who may be quite different from what our prior assumptions told us.[8] If there is the will to pursue the conversation for the sake of reconciliation, we will not presume to know the 'other', but be willing to come to know. This implies a respect for the 'other' as a human being no matter how much we may disagree. Whether we see the 'other' as a threat or as a partner in the search for reconciliation, our response will determine whether we are able to make the second choice.

For the next essential step in the process is the willingness to listen to the other side of the story even if we remain unconvinced, a willingness to continue the conversation even when it seems to be breaking down. Even more demanding and threatening, this requires that we learn to relinquish our control of the encounter, to become vulnerable to the 'other', so that the relationship may develop its own momentum and direction. In this way further spaces for dialogue begin to open up as the 'other' presents us with a fresh series of choices that determine how the process might unfold.

On reflection, we might say that the critical step in the process of reconciliation is that of learning to put ourselves in the place of the 'other' who addresses us. To see both the 'other' and the 'other's' claims from a different point of view. We recall here the literal meaning of the New Testament Greek word for reconciliation (ἀλλασσω), 'to exchange', derived from ἀλλος meaning the 'other'. For Christians this is a profoundly christological moment in the process of reconciliation as Paul indicates in 2 Corinthians. Having spoken of Christ's vicarious redemption on behalf of all of us, he then writes: 'so from now on we regard no one from a worldly point of view' (2 Cor. 5.16). Reconciliation begins to become a reality when, without surrendering our identity, who we are, but opening up ourselves to the 'other', we enter into the space between, exchanging places with the other in a conversation that takes us beyond ourselves. In doing so we find ourselves in vicarious solidarity with rather than against the 'other', willing to do to the 'other' only what we would want them to do to us. Furthermore, in the process our self-understanding begins to change.

We have spoken of steps that can and must be taken, and choices that must be made, in the process of reconciliation. The aim of each step is to break through the barriers of the past, discern common interests, and so break open new possibilities that can take the process further. As in any art, to do this suggests that there is a discipline that must be mastered, skills that need to be developed, and decisions that must be made. Yet it is important to recognize that there is no formula that if implemented will automatically bring success. The simple reason for this is that there is no such thing as reconciliation in the abstract. If and when it occurs, reconciliation always does so within a particular context and with regard to a particular set of interpersonal or social relations. The dynamics of the process will therefore vary, even though there will also be constants and, while similar it will be different, depending on whether it is at the level of interpersonal or social relations. Telling the truth within the context and confines of marriage counselling is not the same as telling the truth in public at the TRC, and the same is true in acknowledging guilt, offering forgiveness or making reparation.

If there is no guaranteed formula for success, there is also no precise mechanism for deciding when the goal of reconciliation has been achieved. In the full sense of the word it always lies beyond us. Yet there comes a point in the process when reconciliation becomes a reality, when the conversation reaches a new level of commitment, embrace and shared hope. At this point marriage partners are able to heal their failing relationship, and a country decisively breaks with its oppressive and divisive past and embarks on building a new future. For even though reconciliation as a process never ends, there are moments when the goal is experienced despite the long journey that still lies ahead.

In what follows in this and the next chapter we will explore more fully this process and the goal it seeks to achieve. We will do so by focusing especially on the interaction between victims and perpetrators as they encounter each other face to face, but also on the response of bystanders and beneficiaries to the truth that is told and uncovered in the process.

Telling the truth

The notion that 'the truth, the whole truth, and nothing but the truth' could or would be told or uncovered during the work of the TRC was far more problematic than was recognized at the time of its institution. Moreover, the relationship between discovering the truth and the possibility of achieving reconciliation through its telling was by no means self-evident even though the TRC slogan 'Truth, the Road to Reconciliation' was boldly emblazoned above its hearings. For some critics such notions were 'based on sentimental theological assumptions that very often bear no relation to reality'.[9] This criticism did not imply a lack of concern for discovering the truth about the past, nor did it suggest any lack of commitment to the process of reconciliation. It reflected the not inconsiderable disquiet both within government circles and opposition groups, as to whether the TRC could, in fact, deliver what was needed.

But what was the alternative? General amnesty was ruled out, so too was the possibility of long and drawn-out costly legal trials. In any case, would the latter really promote national reconciliation even if they might get at the truth? The courts would have been log-jammed by trials and appeals and, given the application of due process, convictions would have been very difficult to obtain. Would the law courts get at the truth any more than the proposed TRC and would justice be done and be seen to be done? And, in the end, would we be any nearer to national reconciliation?

Such questions raise further even more fundamental issues that we must now consider. First amongst these is determining the nature of the truth that the TRC sought to uncover. The second has to do with the difficulty of arriving at this kind of truth, given the nature of the truth being elicited and the problems of subjectivity. A third and the most critical of all the issues concerns what we do with the truth uncovered in the pursuit of reconciliation. Although we will try and consider these issues in turn, they are actually so interrelated that it is difficult to separate them from each other.

There are obviously various forms of truth and truth-telling. Several immediately come to mind: the scientific truth sought in the laboratory or observatory; the truth of a value-judgement on morality or aesthetics; the truth claims of a religious tradition; truth as existential commitment and action; and the truth about historical events and their reporting including forensic evidence. The final Report of the TRC differentiates in a similar way between four kinds of truth, largely in terms of how each is sought and uncovered: objective, factual or forensic truth; personal or narrative truth; dialogical truth; healing and restorative truth.[10] Undoubtedly there are connections between these and other understandings of truth, hence the use of the term to describe them all. But each is distinct, and each requires an appropriate method for arriving at and verifying its claims.

Given our human limitations, not least the partiality of our perspectives shaped by social location, past experience, loyalties, values and interests, as well as the nature of truth itself, we can never arrive at or grasp the whole truth. There is an inevitable discrepancy between what happened, and how we perceive and narrate what happened. This does not necessarily imply or lead to scepticism or relativism. In some instances it is possible to know a great deal of the truth, and certainly sufficient to achieve certain goals.

The work of the TRC in uncovering the truth had to do, in the first place, with the truth about historical events and their reporting. Its stated objective was 'to establish as complete a picture as possible of the causes, nature and extent of the gross violations of human rights which were committed during the period from 1 March 1964 to the cut-off date', namely the day of the first general election in 1994.[11] The purpose of the TRC was to promote national reconciliation through unearthing the truth, quite literally at times through the exhumation of the bodies of murder victims, so that the past could be remembered and dealt with in appropriate ways.

In hindsight the TRC by its very constitution and in terms of its mandate was incapable of uncovering the whole truth as experienced by the majority of apartheid's victims. The resultant danger was that of diminishing the truth by focusing on the accounts of perpetrators and of political activists who became victims.[12] In its attempt to uncover the gross violations of human rights by perpetrators the TRC let the vast array of beneficiaries of apartheid off the hook, and equally left the vast array of victims in the same condition as before. In effect, say the critics, the political compromise of 1994 was reinforced by a compromised truth that obscured the whole truth. The end result, they argue, was the suffocation of the debate about how to go beyond political compromise and deal with national reconciliation at a deeper and much broader level.[13] The banality of the fact is revealed in the ironical comment made by many blacks that there are very few whites today who supported apartheid! How apartheid was sustained through the years boggles the mind.

At one level the truth concerning beneficiaries, who were also invariably bystanders,[14] is self-evident in the infinitely better schools, homes, salaries, health care and much else we all had or received. Yet, how does one get at the truth or the crimes of 'inaction, indifference, and insensitivity' that are the hallmarks of the role of such beneficiaries?[15] Like victims and oppressors, there are also varieties of beneficiaries and bystanders. For example, some who benefited from apartheid were engaged in the struggle to overthrow it, and some victims of apartheid who were co-opted into the system became its beneficiaries. These distinctions and qualifications are important, yet they do not alter the broad picture. The truth is that if the majority of whites were not perpetrators in any direct sense, we were all beneficiaries. And many who knew better survived through maintaining silence against apartheid's injustices, just as many today cope with the guilt of the past through denying any complicity in apartheid. To get at such truth so deeply suppressed in the white consciousness would have required that the TRC probe the collective psyche like some Jungian analyst writ large.

Another difficulty in getting at the truth had to do with the male-dominated structure of the Commission and the fact that the majority of those who did appear before the TRC were black women. The tendency to narrow the focus of investigation to experiences of sexual violence sometimes reduced women to passivity and detracted significantly from their participation in political action and the liberation struggle. 'Woman' became a category determined by conventions and assumptions about women victims so that the truth of their real experiences was not fully told either at the hearings or through the media.[16] Many of them 'were neither broken victims nor detached witnesses'.[17] Even the attempts to gather the truth in this way were, it has been argued, 'intrinsically violent or violating' or at least misleading in what they purport to represent (human experience of violence and pain) and in their intention in so doing (to prevent future lapses into comparable violence).[18]

The TRC clearly had difficulty in getting at the whole truth for other reasons as well, reasons relating to the capacity of those engaged in telling the truth. One was the problem of memory and recall, another was the inevitability of not being able to tell everything whether for lack of time or for other, perhaps emotional reasons. Telling the truth about human rights violations, or listening to the other's account, is often a traumatic experience. Hence the TRC saw the vital need of providing emotional support and counselling for those involved in the

process. Of course, the TRC could not provide long-term therapy, a subject that is of considerable concern given the trauma
that was often associated with testifying,[19] and the possibility of
re-traumatization.[20] That is the pastoral role of other agencies,
especially Churches and other faith communities.

A further reason why the TRC was hindered in its task of
getting at the truth was that while victims tended to give detailed
accounts of their experience, perpetrators were often unwilling
to acknowledge the complete range of their activities even when
applying for amnesty. The TRC was not a court of law and therefore it had to depend on moral persuasion and the threat of not
granting amnesty. Amnesty was, in fact, a truth-seeking tool.[21]
This sometimes resulted in the truth being told to the advantage
of the perpetrator and the embitterment of the victim. 'The only
exceptions' as Frederick van Zyl Slabbert noted, were 'those
individuals who were almost forced to make a confession because
they were revealed through normal legal process as people with
an obvious burden of guilt'.[22] In other words, it is not only how
we perceive the truth that matters, but how the truth is told. The
perfunctory telling of the truth may be reasonably accurate yet
fail to touch the wellsprings of conscience or bring about any
change.

This problem was dramatically demonstrated by one of the
most sickening of all the applications for amnesty at the TRC,
that of the former security policeman Gideon Nieuwoudt for the
murder of activist Siphiwe Mtimkulu in the mid 1980s.

The story has been graphically recaptured in a documentary
film for South African television with the apposite title, *Where
Truth Lies*.[23] Prior to the amnesty hearing, the police, including
Nieuwoudt, had done everything possible to cover themselves,
including lying under oath in court. It was only as a result of
Mtimkulu's mother's persistence in trying to uncover the truth of
what had happened to her son that the culprits finally acknowledged their guilt and sought for amnesty. But even then, as the
documentary so dramatically shows, the telling of the truth was
still obfuscated by lies. It was not only a case of discovering where the truth lies, but also discovering that under such

circumstances even in telling the truth, there are lies that keep the truth hidden. In the documentary shot over two days we are shown the visit of Nieuwoudt to the Mtimkulu family to ask the family for forgiveness. There was a reluctant willingness on the part of Siphiwe's mother to grant forgiveness to her son's murderer on the basis of her faith in God. But there was considerable hesitation and opposition from other members of the family who persisted in asking Nieuwoudt whether or not he was responsible for poisoning and finally shooting Siphiwe.

Eventually, totally unscripted and unanticipated, Siphiwe's son, now a teenager, whose presence till then was in the shadows of the room, suddenly grabbed a heavy object (it happened to be a large ceramic dog) and hurled it at Nieuwoudt, cracking his head. There was pandemonium in the room as family, friends and the camera crew were thrown into confusion. Eventually the situation was brought under control and Nieuwoudt was rushed to hospital. Siphiwe's orphaned son had the last word. 'I could not listen to him continuing to tell lies'. Nieuwoudt was later granted amnesty, but we are left still wondering whether the truth was really uncovered, a feeling that even there in the amnesty proceedings, truth can still lie.

In retrospect, no one could seriously have expected the TRC to uncover the 'whole truth and nothing but the truth' and, perhaps even less so, the telling of the truth in ways that immediately fostered a spirit of reconciliation. The task of reconstructing the truth on the basis of evidence which was contradictory or sanitized, or based on the testimony of previous informers, inevitably made the process complex and contested.[24] Getting at the truth is, after all, a dialogical process, always multifaceted, always incomplete and, as in the case of the TRC, ironically built 'on the back of lies, of untruth and deceit'.[25] Truth-tellers never have the benefit of total vision, they always see the truth from a particular perspective, and there are many mechanisms that distort and obfuscate reality and memory. So we dare not give equal weight to all versions of what happened, and we need to recognize and acknowledge that much still remains hidden and in need of uncovering if dealing with the past is to be more complete.

What is remarkable, however, is not that much remains hidden and inaccessible, or that some of that retrieved was partial and diminished, but that so much was uncovered. As a result of the TRC we now have the vivid images of TV coverage and the TRC Report of five volumes of raw data etched into our common consciousness and conscience. No court of law could have provided us with such vivid images and painful stories, such agonizing debates and torturous confessions that became the stock-in-trade of the TRC. As Janet Cherry puts it: 'many of the mysteries of the apartheid era were revealed in this way'.[26] So even if some of the material contained in the TRC Report is false, and some only partly true, the vast amount of documentation, and especially the narratives of the victims, must surely significantly approximate the truth of what happened. To suggest otherwise is to fly in the face of overwhelming testimony, much of it corroborated by independent research and investigation. But it is also mischievous to suggest otherwise because it lends credence to those who, like Holocaust deniers, deny that apartheid was as bad as claimed. Even though some of what the TRC unearthed was previously known or suspected, we now have an overwhelming collection of evidence that leaves no one in doubt about a great deal of what happened during the apartheid era. What the TRC did in this regard, then, was to help reclaim a history that had been denied and shredded. After the TRC no one can honestly deny that apartheid was a monstrous crime. If nothing else was achieved by the TRC, this was a giant step forward.

But, to turn to a further issue we have identified, even if it is possible, is it necessary and always helpful to uncover and know all the truth for the sake of reconciliation? Critics of the TRC who declared that uncovering the truth does not always lead to reconciliation, and can just as easily lead away from it, are undoubtedly correct to a certain degree. There is nothing inevitable about truth being the road to reconciliation. Those familiar with Susan Howatch's novel, *Sins of the Fathers*, may recall Alicia's remark to her husband Cornelius on acknowledging her affair with his friend and business partner, Jake:

'People talk a lot of trash about how awful hypocrisy is, but they just don't know a damn thing. Hypocrisy saves one's sanity. It's the shield you hide behind when the truth is too terrible to face. How many people really have the courage to live wholly in the truth?'[27]

Pastoral counsellors know that telling the truth does not always bring about healing. We may also know this more directly from our own experience. So there are grounds for arguing that if the aim in telling the truth is reconciliation, only telling some of the truth may be appropriate, especially at the outset. In so far as it is possible, the whole truth might need to come out at some stage, but only when the healing process is mature enough to handle it, and even then it may never fully be confessed.

Christianity, it should be noted, does not proclaim that 'truth-telling' automatically brings about reconciliation between people. Writes Rowan Williams:

Since the Fall concealment is necessary and good in the sense that there is plenty in human thought, feeling, and experience that *should not* be part of shared discourse. We are alienated, divided, and corrupted; but to bring this into speech (and to assume we thereby tell a better or fuller truth) is to collude with sin.[28]

Telling the truth, as Bonhoeffer noted, 'means something different according to the particular situation in which one stands'.[29] Truth-telling can and has been cynically used as a destructive weapon or tool. Truth then becomes a lie. That is why hiding the truth, or even telling a lie for the sake of preserving life, can sometimes be of greater moral value than telling the truth.

Bonhoeffer's understanding of truth as 'living truth' obviously can be abused as when we adapt the truth to suit our circumstances, but so can the principle that the truth must be told no matter the circumstances, the position adopted by Immanuel Kant. The fact is, Bonhoeffer argued, 'the ethical cannot be detached from reality, and consequently continual progress in learning to appreciate reality is a necessary ingredient in ethical action',[30] including telling the truth. Hence it is not a question as to *whether* the truth should be told, but *how* and *when* and to *whom* it should be told, and therefore, for what purpose. This is certainly not to be understood as an excuse for not seeking the truth or struggling to restore justice. That suggests a lack of moral and political will to pursue the path of reconciliation rather than a strategy for doing so. As Miroslav Volf says, 'within social contexts . . . *the embrace itself* – full reconciliation – cannot take place until the truth has been said and justice done'.[31] But he adds the salutary comment that 'there is far too much dishonesty in the single-minded search for truth, too much injustice in the uncompromising struggle for justice'.[32]

The TRC, we must recall, was not seeking to establish the truth purely for its own sake, nor simply for the forensic purposes of legal prosecution, nor for the sake of revenge, but for the sake of reconciliation, whether at a personal or national level. And while we must acknowledge that there is nothing inevitable about truth being the road to reconciliation, we also need to recognize that this does not gainsay the necessity of telling the truth in pursuing reconciliation. It is the inevitability of the connection and the nature of the truth told that is contentious and the extent to which the truth that is uncovered impacts upon and changes our lives. The critical issue facing us in seeking reconciliation is not whether we now know all truth about the past, or even whether we know sufficient of it. The critical issue is what we *do* with the truth that has been uncovered.

The TRC may not have uncovered the whole truth, but it has provided the raw data for the inevitably long and painful bodily encounter with the truth that is part of the on-going process of reconciliation. A process that extends far beyond truth commissions and involves not just the victims and perpetrators of past crimes, but all of us. In this process the creative skill of dramatists, writers, poets, investigative reporters, film and documentary makers make a decisive contribution.[33]

Truth only becomes the truth *for us* when we interact with it, that is, when it begins to impact on our lives, changing not only our perspective but also changing us and our relationship to the 'other'. There is, I submit, something obscene about watching the horrors of crimes against humanity at a safe, remote distance, without recognizing that we, too, are participants and that those events challenge us to the core. It is precisely in this regard that the artist fulfils an intensely personal and yet critical public role. As in Sue Williamson's 'Truth Games' or the film *Secrets and Lies* or Krog's searing *Country of My Skull*, we are drawn into the process of truth-telling and discover that the truth is not something 'out there', something that can be clinically told and accurately captured in news report and journal article. Truth happens, it encounters us, and forces us to decide what we should do about it. Truth emerges in the process of interaction in which we too are participants, in which we too are called to engage bodily. As one of the speakers at the opening of Williamson's 'Truth Games' in Grahamstown said:

> Part of the power of the visual arts, is that they can remind us of our own physicality: we too have bodies. In this strange late-twentieth century, so marked by a sense of relativism, and the decline of absolutes, there is, we become increasingly aware, one absolute that holds fast: that is that we all, as human subjects, live within the body, and that while it is a site of pleasure, is can also become a place of terror. From Bosnia to Kosovo to Sierra Leone, to the Eastern Cape, the final battleground is the human body.[34]

If the truth we now know is shelved in the multi-volume TRC Report and becomes a matter of interest only to archivists and researchers, it may serve some historical purpose but not that of national reconciliation. If it becomes a political tool, selectively misread in the interests of party and group, then it will serve the purpose of further division, taking us away from rather than towards national reconciliation. If the truth as we know it is not further explored, if our knowledge is not deepened through on-going dialogue, and if it is not embodied in the educational formation of post-apartheid generations, we will have missed a

wonderful opportunity to further the case of national reconciliation. If the truth that has been uncovered does not serve to
prevent us from repeating the past in whatever guise, we will not
have advanced in our journey towards national reconciliation. If
the truth does not call forth remorse and humility on the part of
beneficiaries and bystanders, together with a willingness to work
for the common good, it will not achieve its goal.

The truth liberates and sets free, the truth heals and restores,
but only when the truth is lived and done. Truth serves the cause
of reconciliation and justice only when it leads to a genuine
metanoia, that is, a turning around, a breaking with an unjust
past, and a moving towards a new future. From a biblical perspective, the failure to listen to the truth and become transformed
by it has dire consequences. Truth that might have led to
forgiveness and healing becomes truth that judges and condemns
in deeds of righteous anger. This is one reason why we need to
listen to the sounds of vengeance and fury in order to appreciate
the words of grace and forgiveness.

Listen to the sound of fury

The message of the great eighth-century Hebrew prophets of
social righteousness is that Yahweh alone is the redeemer of
Israel and the world, but Yahweh's work of salvation can be
hindered as well as hastened by the response of peoples and
nations. When stubbornly hindered, when oppression and injustice is allowed to flourish, when truth is subverted, and when
there is no sign of repentance, Yahweh loses patience and
executes vengeance. A classic text is Isaiah 59:

> Justice is turned back,
>   and righteousness stands at a distance;
> for truth stumbles in the public square,
>   and uprightness cannot enter.
> Truth is lacking,
>   and whoever turns from evil is despoiled.

The Lord saw it, and it displeased him
    that there was no justice.
He saw that there was no one,
    and was appalled that there was no one to intervene;
so his own arm brought him victory,
    and his righteousness upheld him.
He put on righteousness like a breastplate,
    and a helmet of salvation on his head;
he put on garments of vengeance for clothing,
and wrapped himself in fury as in a mantle.
    (Isa. 59.14–17 NRSV)

But how, we may well ask, does God execute vengeance against oppression and injustice? What are the instruments Yahweh chooses for this purpose? If there are agents of reconciliation, are there not also agents of wrath and vengeance?

We tread here on difficult and dangerous terrain. We are aware of the argument that the destruction of the World Trade Center Towers in New York on 11 September 2001 was such an act, committed in the name of God or Allah to express anger at the wanton immorality and unrighteousness of American society and its global 'state terror'. How would the Hebrew prophets have interpreted such an event, keeping in mind that this is not unlike the destruction of Jerusalem at the hands of the Babylonians, about which they warned? To say the least, the question of vengeance is full of ambiguity. On the one hand, oppression cries out for redress, for the restoration of moral order. On the other hand, wanton destruction, even in the name of liberation and justice, fills us with moral revulsion.

Allow me to tell the story of what happened during a doctoral seminar at the time when the TRC was in session. Having heard about the research of a student at another university whose dissertation was on the TRC, I invited her to give an account of her work in progress. A middle-aged woman, Ginn Fourie, working in sociology, was engaged in research around the so-called 'Heidelberg Tavern Massacre' that occurred on 31 December 1993, six months before the first democratic elections. The

Heidelberg Tavern is located not far from the University of Cape Town and at the time attracted a fair number of students and other young people. That Friday evening four masked men burst into the tavern and fired several rounds of AK47 bullets into the crowd. Many people were injured and a number killed. Later the men, young black men, were arrested and sentenced to life imprisonment. During the TRC they applied for amnesty on the grounds that they were members of APLA (the armed wing of the Pan Africanist Congress) and that the shootings had been politically motivated. They did not believe that reconciliation was possible because liberation had not yet been achieved. Ginn Fourie's research centred on these four men, and her presentation to this point was academic though lively. But we had no idea what had led her to undertake her study until very quietly, almost as an afterthought, she said: 'My daughter Lyndi was killed in the massacre, and I want to find out whether or not we can become reconciled to each other!'

There was a deathly silence in the seminar room by the time Ginn Fourie had completed her story, a silence that lasted for what seemed a long time. When at last the silence was broken a conversation began that took our hitherto academic enquiry to a deeper level than we had ever previously been. Our discussion about reconciliation was no longer theoretical, but neither was it purely emotional or 'romantic theologizing'. What we had heard and experienced forced us to think even more critically about the reality of reconciliation as a costly process and a painful journey. What was it, after all, that led to the Heidelberg Massacre but the bitter experience of oppression and injustice on the part of those who finally, in an outburst of rage, pulled the triggers and unleashed a frenzy of death? For them the negotiated settlement was a sell-out of all their hopes for a truly transformed nation in which justice was finally achieved. Their outrage was a rage for justice, though the path chosen in its pursuit was violent vengeance.

During their trial Ginn Fourie asked permission to speak to the four accused. Thus began a relationship with the young men, which included visiting them in prison. This created the space within which they could meet 'face-to-face' without which any chance of embarking on the path of healing and reconciliation would have been stillborn. At the request of one of them, Humphrey Gqomfa, the suggestion was also made that they embark on a programme of counselling together.[35] At the time of writing this had not happened. But in her research paper published later, in which she appealed for a process of counselling and debriefing for all those who had received amnesty from the TRC, Fourie wrote these words:

> Once the debriefing groundwork has been done, perhaps our dream – Humphrey Gqomfa's and my own, of having counselling together at nation-wide conferences for survivors and perpetrators – can come about. We cannot afford to wait for second, third and fourth generation descendants of this traumatic and ongoing violence. We must take the initiative in attempting to understand the 'other' and so start the process of reconciliation and healing in our broken land.[36]

The demand for vengeance or retribution is a very natural inclination for those who have been grievously hurt and, indeed, for of all of us who, in the face of gross violations of human rights, have any sense of morality. One of the most remarkable aspects of the TRC is that, as far as can be ascertained, there have been no acts of vengeance perpetrated by victims against those who caused their suffering and told their side of the story to the TRC. But the demand for vengeance is not something to be dismissed as primitive or without warrant, for it arises out of the abhorrence of that which is patently evil and a desire to see justice done. As such it is also something widely acknowledged, legitimated and even required in certain religious and cultural social codes. 'Christians', Gregory Jones reminds us, 'have too often supported forgiveness, love, and forbearance, while failing to acknowledge the moral force of anger, hatred, and vengeance'.[37]

Vengeance is a constant theme in both the Old and New Testaments. In the former, it refers, somewhat ambiguously, both to just punishment for crime and vindictive revenge. Vengeance is only appropriate when the innocent become victims of crime and oppression, but even then this is not a licence to engage in malicious retaliation. Punishment, as mandated by the *lex talionis* (Exod. 21.23–25), should fit the crime and not be unrestrained and excessive. God's law does not sanction revenge and expressly rules out excessive reprisal.[38] Also rejected is the 'wrath of Jonah', that narrow self-righteous nationalist anger directed at other peoples and groups.[39] God's vengeance is always positive, restoring the balance in society caused by human wickedness and bringing encouragement to those who are oppressed by punishing their oppressors (Isaiah 61.1–4; Ps.58).

In his discussion of the Sermon on the Mount, Bonhoeffer affirms the injunction 'an eye for an eye, and a tooth for a tooth' (Lev. 24.20) as part of the Old Testament law on a par with the Ten Commandments, and therefore as right, just and valid.[40] Jesus himself 'affirms the power of retribution to convict and overcome evil, and to ensure the community of disciples as the true Israel'.[41] But the dominant emphasis in the New Testament, especially in the teaching of both Jesus and Paul, is the discouragement of human vengeance and instead reliance on God's action (Rom. 12.17–21).[42] The underlying theology here is yet again shaped by the vicarious suffering of Christ, the one who takes the place of the 'other' and transforms the wrath of vengeance into the mercy of forgiveness. What is so tragic is that for much of Christian history the real meaning of the cross has been abused by blaming the Jews for the death of Jesus and taking vengeance against them. Equally diabolical is the way in which the cross has been used as the symbol of crusades and of war fought to defend 'Christian civilization'.

The question of vengeance has been hotly debated in South Africa. Willa Boesak explored the subject systematically as a legitimate Christian response to oppression in his book *God's Wrathful Children*.[43] Drawing on the history of the black struggle against oppression from its earliest times, historical trajectories (the Zealots, Thomas Müntzer and Malcolm X) and on biblical sources, Boesak affirmed the validity of vengeance as an act of justice, recompense, retribution and reward, but rejected vengeance as blind destructive fury. The aim of his study was to discern the difference between the two and the correlation between human and divine vengeance. His conclusion was that 'poverty, oppression, and human brokenness elicit the wrath of God and the rage of the oppressed' and demand a 'redress of those conditions'.[44]

Acts of vengeance and retribution are the sounds of fury, an expression of righteous anger against those who undermine or destroy human life and social well-being. They reflect a legitimate concern for justice, and thus affirm the biblical understanding of God as the one to whom vengeance ultimately belongs (Deut. 32.35; Rom. 12.19 *et al.*). If we are truly going to understand the relationship between justice and forgiveness in the process of reconciliation from a biblical perspective, we must keep in mind that 'God's wrath' against evil is presupposed.[45] Only those who are truly angered by injustice can really begin to practise forgiveness or know what it means. Miroslav Volf rightly reminds us that

> God's wrath is an indispensable presupposition of reconciliation and justification. For at the heart of reconciliation lies the twin belief that evil must be named as evil and that the restoration of communion with the evildoer is not based (indeed, *cannot* be based!) simply on justice done.[46]

The paradox is that the single-minded pursuit of justice can lead to destructive vengeance, just as the pursuit of reconciliation without justice perpetuates evil.

We will not be able to resolve the problem of vengeance, determining whether or when it may be regarded as a genuine act of God, irrespective of its agents. We have to live with the ambiguity. But it would be folly not to recognize that the rage for justice is a wake up call for us to pursue justice. It is nothing new to recognize that oppression and poverty amidst wealth and plenty is a sure recipe for revolt and acts of vengeance. Perhaps we are more acutely aware of this today given the excessive wealth of a privileged minority in the world, and the massive poverty of millions across the globe. Liberation from poverty is as great a challenge as liberation from apartheid, perhaps greater, and as long as we are unable to overcome it, poverty will be the major stumbling-block on the road to national reconciliation. So there is a sense in which the desire for vengeance must be seen as a blessed rage for justice, blessed because it is a divine call to repentance and reparation before it is too late.

Listening to the rage of the victims of oppression is not only a necessary step in the process of preventing further outbreaks of violent fury, it is also a step in the process of recognizing that victims are not simply passive objects of oppression. Fourie refused to be classified as a victim to be treated with pity, and she refused to treat those who killed her daughter as victims. In a sense, of course, they were all victims. Fourie had lost a daughter, but she recognized that as a white person she was also a beneficiary. The young men were victims of apartheid, and yet they were also activists who made certain choices that led them to acts of terror. But all of them had the choice of working towards the restoration of humanity and relationships, of rising above their anger and hatred and becoming joint victors rather than victims. So the rage for justice may be seen also as a protest against victimhood, an affirmation of power amidst powerlessness, albeit the power of blind fury.

What is truly remarkable in the struggle for justice, however, is not the sound of fury, but the word of forgiveness, a key moment in the process of reconciliation. Yet it is only when we listen to the outrage of victims that we can begin to appreciate their offer of forgiveness. What led Ginn Fourie to forgive those who had murdered her daughter and to support the granting of amnesty to them was an understanding of the experience that had nurtured such outrage and a growing awareness that forgiveness was essential for her own healing and that of her daughter's murderers.

Forgiveness as wisdom and power

Writing at the time of the institution of the TRC, Kadar Asmal, a leader within the ANC and currently Minister of Education, expressed the hope that it would provide the possibility for the victims 'to fulfil a civic sacrament of forgiving'.[47] Asmal's evocative suggestion brings us to the heart of the TRC process. Yet the question of forgiveness was one of the most hotly contested issues during the course of the TRC. Part of the confusion derived from the translation of terms into the African vernacular.[48] What was often communicated was that if perpetrators told the truth they should automatically be forgiven. But truth-telling alone, as we have noted, could not bring about reconciliation. Indeed, once the truth-telling was over it was still very difficult for victims to understand why perpetrators had done what they did to inflict pain, suffering and death on them and their loved ones. If reconciliation was dependent on that understanding it was a forlorn hope. Under what circumstances, then, can forgiveness be expected, and what exactly does it mean to forgive whether in personal or political relations?

'Forgiveness' is a word that easily trips off our tongues, especially if we are not the victims of oppression and injustice. It is easy for us who are not victims to tell them to forgive their enemies; it is also relatively easy for oppressors to ask for forgiveness. The problem is that forgiveness can be manipulated by the dominant in such a way that it strengthens their position and weakens that of the victim. Forgiveness thus becomes a tool in the manipulation of power relations, making the oppressed even more a victim of injustice. Thus the TRC Commissioners were increasingly aware of the danger of enforcing victims to forgive, recognizing that for some it was important to hold back forgiveness and even express feelings of vengeance. However we approach the subject, genuine forgiveness, like true repentance, is a painful process and not something that can be turned on like a tap.

Forgiveness from the perspective of the gospel only makes sense against the background of God's demand that we change, and begin to seek God's justice in society. The forgiveness of God proclaimed in the gospel makes no sense at all unless understood in the light of God's judgement on sin and oppression, and God's costly gift of reconciliation. Forgiveness as such does not rule out anger or just punishment, and certainly does not excuse those who oppress and victimize. Hence Donald Shriver's observation that 'forgiveness thrives in the tension between justice-as-punishment and justice-as-restoration'.[49] If the perpetrators of crimes get away with what they did, then the rule of law is undermined; but if their punishment has no redemptive possibility it deepens the divisions in society, increases enmity and resentment, prevents reconciliation and encourages vengeance. What forgiveness rules out is that malicious and vindictive vengeance that perpetuates the cycle of violence. The victims of apartheid, Willa Boesak argues, have to find a way between 'indifferent cheap grace and the tempting laws of the jungle' in carving 'out an option that will enkindle the depth and seriousness of political forgiving'.[50]

Jesus called his disciples to forgive those who wronged them seventy times seven; he also counselled them to love their enemies, and neither take vengeance nor harbour resentment. (Matt. 5.39; Lk. 6.35; cf. Rom. 12.14–21) This unconditional forgiveness is at the heart of the Christian gospel. In keeping with Jesus' teaching, Desmond Tutu insisted that 'the victims of injustice and oppression must ever be ready to forgive. That is a gospel imperative'.[51] But what do these counsels of perfection mean in practice, especially within the political arena?

While it is true that a great many of the victims of apartheid were Christian, most of us find it very difficult to practice Jesus' teaching on unconditional forgiveness even when wronged only slightly by others. Even the Christian Church is, as Rowan Williams reminds us, 'unsure of how to handle forgiveness, reducing it to the possibility of reparation or drowning it in a rhetoric of a forgiving and forgetting God'. In doing so, 'the notion of offence itself evaporates, and there is no real injury to be healed by mercy'.[52] But if the crucifixion of Jesus means anything, it means that God had to descend into hell in order to redeem the world. Redemption could not come through a polite word of cheap grace, otherwise the words of Jesus from the cross – 'Father, forgive them for they know not what they do' – would have been adequate on their own. Jesus would not have had to experience being forsaken by God, or endure death itself. This is why the ethics of forgiveness must be rooted in the message of divine forgiveness, for otherwise it oscillates, as Paul Tillich observed, 'between legalism and sentimentality'.[53]

Shriver has cogently argued the case that forgiveness must not be kept in religious captivity but be allowed to enter the ranks of ordinary political virtues. It is therefore essential that it 'acquire more precise, dynamic, and politically contexted definition than it has usually enjoyed'.[54] Given the nature of power and the realities of politics, the mere suggestion that forgiveness be seen as a political virtue seems wishful thinking. But, for Shriver, forgiveness displays moral courage:

> the facing of still-rankling past evils with first regard for the truth of what actually happened; with resistance to the lures of revenge; with empathy – and no excusing – for all the agents and sufferers of the evil; and with real intent on the part of the sufferers to resume life alongside the evildoers or their political successors. That is the moral courage of forgiveness.[55]

Warring parties usually regard forgiveness in the political realm as a sign of weakness rather than strength, and likewise deem the restoring of justice for the enemy as undermining control rather than the only way to achieve the common good. However, forgiveness does not mean political naiveté, though it might appear childlike, and even foolish. Political forgiveness is a risk taken on the basis of mature insight and political acumen, and one that displays moral courage. Addressing a youth conference in Czechoslovakia in 1932, Bonhoeffer, aware of the imminent danger in the rearmament of Europe, spoke of the urgent need to work for international peace on the basis of the forgiveness of sins. 'The forgiveness of sins', he declared, 'still remains the sole ground of peace, even where the order of external peace remains preserved in truth and justice.'[56]

Of course, there is a distinction between personal and political forgiveness, as Bonhoeffer elsewhere reminds us. 'For the Church and the individual believer there can only be a complete breach with guilt and a new beginning which is granted through the forgiveness of sin, but in the historical life of nations there can always be only the gradual process of healing'.[57] Nonetheless, what is important in both instances is that wounds are healed in a process of which forgiveness is a key element, and that no further wounds are inflicted. There are signs that there is today a growing international awareness of such an approach, even if couched in secular terms.[58] There are alternative ways of pursuing politics than those that spawn the spiral of violence and escalate into war, ways that build on a commitment to moral accountability, pardon and reparation. And, in a paradoxical way, these ways serve the long-term self-interests of people and nations precisely because they serve the interests of the common good. As Tutu so clearly recognized, it 'is ultimately in our own best interest to become forgiving, repentant, reconciling and reconciled people, because without forgiveness, without reconciliation we have no future'.[59]

Reflecting on this in the light of his own experience of German history from the Third Reich to the Reunification of East and West, Jürgen Moltmann writes:

> The open acknowledgement of guilt and an inward turning away from the ideologies of violence, the forgiveness of guilt, and the beginning of a new shared and just life: all this becomes the sign of the hew humane politics.[60]

Moltmann goes on to say that he believes the 'basic elements of the church's practice of repentance and forgiveness' can be transferred 'into the policies whereby democracies come to terms with the crimes committed under dictatorships, with the violations of human rights and their consequences'.[61] He further suggests that the TRC in South Africa might provide the world with a model for doing this.

Let us now turn to consider forgiveness in terms of interpersonal relations, but with the intention of showing how this connects with forgiveness in the political realm, by reflecting again on Ginn Fourie's experience following the shooting of her daughter in the Heidelberg Tavern Massacre. Fourie noted several stages on her journey 'from tragedy to healing':

- Owning the feelings of excruciating pain, grief and loss of Lyndi.
- Accepting the graciousness of God's forgiveness and love in my own life.
- Somehow absorbing the violence of Lyndi's death, which I sense as a miracle.
- Feeling empathy for the prisoners in their fear and confusion at the criminal trial.
- Offering forgiveness to Lyndi's killers, who I regarded as evil men.
- Episodes of direct communication with the perpetrators, where I tried to be honest about my pain and fears and listened to reasons for their hurt and hate.
- The perpetrators' acceptance of responsibility for the hideous crimes which they had committed and their apologies.
- The perpetrators' gracious act of accepting my forgiveness and the healing for us all, symbolized by embracing.
- Lastly a vision for reconciliation on a larger national scale.[62]

What we see in these comments on her journey to forgive is Fourie's empathy for the humanity of her daughter's killers despite what they had done. She endeavoured to stand where they stood, to truly meet them in the space between, and to see things from their point of view without surrendering her own self-respect or deep hurt. This enabled her to build a relationship that not only had personal significance but also potential political consequences.[63] In recognizing the mutuality of guilt, forgiveness thus became a creative act, restoring humanity and making the restoration of community possible. What becomes apparent in this process is that through forgiveness the status of both victim and perpetrator change, and as their relationship is renegotiated they become different people at peace both with themselves and with each other. This is corroborated by other research done on the TRC process.

In her study of two of the most notorious of all the TRC cases of gross human rights violations, Pumla Gobodo-Madikizela cogently argues that 'the encounters that led to forgiveness between first generation perpetrators and family members of their victims' through the TRC 'are unprecedented in the history of atrocities in the 20th century'.[64] She further asserts that the

> TRC was a unique process in that while exposing the deeds of many perpetrators, it empowered victims in a way that no court could have done and elevated their status by making them the centre of its proceedings, honouring them while shaming the perpetrators in public... In the eyes of many victims who took the stand and spoke in public about their suffering justice was restored.[65]

Forgiveness thus became a 'two way process' in which both victim and perpetrator were 'able to share a common idiom of humanity, a sense of *human* relationship between them'.[66] There was a shared emotional experience, the perpetrator showing empathy with the victim's suffering, and the victim recognizing the pain of the perpetrator. Through remorse, the perpetrator identified with the victim, enabling the latter to forgive and become part of the rehumanizing process. Both were bound together. Just as the violence perpetrated by the likes of Eugene de Kock dehumanized both him and his victims, so, in the words of Goboda-Madikizela, 'through the forgiving embrace of the women widowed as a result of his actions, de Kock was welcomed into the world of moral humanity'.[67] In the process, victims themselves were 'relieved of the burden of anger, hatred and uncertainty evoked by the memory of their trauma',[68] and symbolically 'brought back to life'.[69]

In all this, there is a sense in which there is a 'turning of the tables' so that the power that once resided in the hands of the perpetrator is now in the hands of the victim. Forgiveness demonstrates that victims are no longer trapped in their 'victim-hood', but have overcome the evil that sought to destroy their humanity and make them victims. It turns victims into survivors, and enemies into friends; but even more, forgiveness enables those who forgive to overcome their bitterness and redeem their future, and those who sinned against them to recover their own humanity. But what if the perpetrators of crimes do not show any remorse? Indeed, many of the perpetrators of apartheid crimes showed little sign of remorse or repentance, and some-times used the occasion as a means to justify their deeds. Does this affect the efficacy of forgiveness as a means to healing and reconciliation?

The TRC amnesty process did not require perpetrators to express regret, remorse, or make apology, and very few of them made any attempt to do so.[70] The amnesty provisions were, in fact, part of the political compromise agreed to during the very last stage of the negotiations and only later was this linked to the task of the TRC.[71] These provisions excluded 'crimes committed for personal gain, or out of personal malice, ill will, or spite', but 'neither an apology not any sign of remorse was necessary to be granted amnesty'.[72] This political compromise was a weakness in the TRC process because from a moral point of view it is highly problematic to pardon those who show no regret. Yet it must be acknowledged that it is very difficult to evaluate remorse, for how do we actually 'see into the heart' of the 'other' and deter-mine whether or not expressions of remorse are genuine? This is difficult enough to ascertain in the confessional, let alone the amnesty court hearings. When perpetrators did show remorse it was often convincing for those best positioned to judge, namely the victims themselves, but they were not those responsible for administering the amnesty protocols.

The lack of remorse shown by many perpetrators who appeared before the TRC was a corollary of the plea by the former agents and advocates of apartheid to 'let bygones be bygones' in the interests of national reconciliation. This was what they believed reconciliation was about. But in fact it betrayed an attitude far removed from a genuine desire for reconciliation. In doing so, it cheapened the suffering of victims, disregarding the sacrifice of those who struggled against apartheid, and dishonouring the memory of those who suffered and died. This last observation raises a further issue for victims, for it is not only the lack of remorse that is problematic, but the question whether the living can really forgive people on behalf of others who died? No wonder some victims were reluctant to forgive, not out of a desire for revenge but out of respect for the dead. If they were willing to forgive, it is no wonder they refused to forget.

Amnesty, as many have said, does not mean amnesia. So, too, forgiveness requires remembering, not forgetting, what happened to loved ones, comrades and oneself. But forgiveness also implies remembering the past in ways that heal relationships, build community and thus anticipate a new future. Paradoxically, such remembrance is also a way of forgetting without denying the past. Thus, with his native Croatia in mind, Miroslav Volf writes of the need to put the past behind us.

> if we must remember wrongdoings in order to be safe in an unsafe world, we must let go of their memory in order to be fully redeemed . . . only those who are willing ultimately to forget will be able to remember rightly.[73]

Telling the truth about the past alone does not heal; it might lead, in fact, to acts of violent vengeance. Remembering then becomes a fanning the embers of a dying fire so that it bursts into flame again and devours us. The only way to redeem the past is through the healing of memories, thereby putting to rest that which can only foster bitterness and revenge. Genuine forgiveness, then, does not mean brushing the past aside and regarding injustice lightly, but on knowing how to remember rightly. Forgiveness arises out of a deep awareness of the evil that has been perpetrated, but knows how to deal with that evil in a way that leads to healing. Nelson Mandela expressed this well when he wrote: 'In prison my anger towards whites decreased, but my hatred for the system grew. I wanted South Africa to see that I loved even my enemies while I hated the system that turned us against one another'.[74] What is so remarkable about the example of Mandela is that he not only recognized this connection between justice and reconciliation, but he also saw the need to take the first step towards reconciliation, the step of forgiveness, as a means to restoring justice. Understood in this way, forgiveness becomes a creative act and its agents true artists.

From this perspective, forgiveness is always the prerogative of victims. The appropriate time for forgiving will be chosen by them; the place of forgiveness will be their place; the words of forgiveness, their words. Forgiveness, like vengeance, is a protest against being reduced to victims. It is another way of expressing power amidst powerlessness, but only now it is not an expression of destruction but of healing. From the perspective of the cross, forgiveness transforms the victim into the victor who embraces the 'other' in love rather that the victor who triumphs over the 'other' in judgement. Given all this, we must take special note of the testimony of victims who have learned to forgive, and of the fact that many of the victims who appeared before the TRC did not express any desire for vengeance. They wanted the truth to come out so that they could meaningfully forgive, and where possible receive what was their rightful due.

During a visit to South Africa in 1992, Emilio Castro, a former General Secretary of the World Council of Churches, reminded us that the victim is 'the one who has the key to a real and fundamental reconciliation, because it is in the victim that Jesus Christ is present'.[75] Just as we cannot force victims to forgive, so forgiveness when it occurs does so because victims, mirroring God's own forgiveness, take the initiative:

Forgiveness does not require . . . acts of reparation which *prove* that I am in earnest. On the contrary, forgiveness is prevenient – it *enables* reparation, expiation, atonement. To attach conditions to forgiveness is to attach conditions to love – but there are no such conditions, for love is free, for nothing.[76]

This points to the Christian conviction that those whom we forgive 'need not be perceived as innocent in order to be loved, but ought to be embraced *even when they are perceived as wrong-doers*'.[77] Forgiveness is therefore something gratuitous, not something earned by perpetrators, even though its effectiveness is dependent on the extent of their remorse, repentance and acknowledgement of accountability.

The ability and willingness to forgive is a sign of moral courage and strength, and as such it is also a sign of wisdom. Forgiveness is the exercising of power in weakness and wisdom in apparent foolishness. As the poet and songwriter Vusi Mahlasela reminds us:

> Here lies the wisdom
> The wisdom of forgiveness
> With bright colours of life
> A gift to all humanity
>
> Here lies the power
> The power of love
> With the soulful understanding
> of necessity for a change
>
> Why all these compromises
> When we know what to do
> Lets take the spear
> And put it right inside this evil monster
> Learn to be free
> And learn to be in harmony
> With the rest of the world
> Learn to be free
>
> So we can learn to forgive
> Because an eye for an eye
> Will only lead our world to blindness.[78]

6

Covenanting together to Restore Justice

Those of us who gathered in the large, modern and dignified Senate hall of the University of South Africa on the evening of 28 March 1979, at the start of an international conference on the interpretation of history, did not anticipate that we would witness an event of primitive violence. The hall was full of academics drawn from around southern Africa, and included dignitaries from the city. Professor F. A. van Jaarsveld, the much respected Afrikaner historian, in full academic dress, had just begun his keynote address[1] when the main doors of the Senate hall burst open. A dozen or so khaki-clad men marched into the hall and down the stairs to the podium. Grabbing hold of the speaker, they proceeded to pour hot tar and feathers over him. Pandemonium broke loose on the platform as scuffles broke out amidst attempts to rescue Professor van Jaarsveld. The rest of us in the vast auditorium were mesmerized by what was happening before our eyes, as though watching a cobra preparing to strike. Then, cracking a long whip, the leader of the group snatched the microphone and, in a stentorian voice filled with anger, declared that this action was necessary to protect the honour of the Afrikaner volk. Almost as suddenly as the group had entered the hall, they marched out leaving us shocked and dazed, to ponder what we had seen and heard.

Little did we know at the time that we had been witnesses of the public birth of a new right-wing paramilitary movement, the Afrikaner Weerstandsbeweging (Afrikaner Resistance Movement) or AWB, an organization that was to become notorious during the final years of the struggle against apartheid. Under its leader, Eugene Terre'Blanche, the very same person who cracked the whip in the UNISA Senate hall, the AWB engaged in acts of violent terror that threatened to destabilize South Africa during the critical years of transition to democracy. But what was it that led them that evening in 1979 to 'tar and feather' the doyen of Afrikaner historians, an academic devoted to Afrikaner identity and supportive of its cause? Van Jaarsveld had indicated to the press before the event that he was going to provide an alternative reading to the traditional Afrikaner story of the vow (*Gelofte*, translated 'covenant' in English) made between the Voortrekkers and God on the eve of the Battle of Blood River, 16 December 1838.

This vow was written down by Sarel Cilliers, a Boer leader, some 25 years later. According to Cilliers' account, the Voortrekkers pledged to God that they would remember the day as a holy Sabbath in perpetuity if God granted them victory over the Zulu army. This event became the key to the interpretation of Afrikaner history during the early decades of the twentieth century, celebrated every year on *Geloftedag*, the Day of the Covenant. As a people divinely saved from the might of the Zulu army, with considerable help we may add from the power of the gun, they had been divinely elected to become the rulers of South Africa. Professor van Jaarsveld's sin in the eyes of the AWB was not that he questioned the Afrikaner sense of divine calling, but that he questioned the accuracy of some of the claims made in the twentieth-century account of the narrative. It had become embellished by Afrikaner mythmakers in order to create a united Afrikaner nation over against both British imperial hegemony and the threat posed by a black African majority. The vow or covenant thus became a cornerstone of the ideology of apartheid, the heartbeat of Afrikaner civil religion as celebrated in the Voortrekker monument in Pretoria.[2] It provided divine justification for maintaining a separate Afrikaner nation, for the policy of apartheid and the entrenchment of white power.

Given this background, it may be regarded as audacious to attempt to revive the notion of covenant in the interests of national reconciliation in South Africa. The same might also be argued in countries such as Northern Ireland, where Protestants have been nurtured on a similar interpretation of history. Certainly the notion of covenant can be used for nationalistic ends, and often has been. But the concept of national reconciliation can also be used to foster a perverted patriotism at the expense of other nations. So what is of paramount importance is not the notion of covenant, or national reconciliation for that matter, but the values, ethical concerns, and theological and anthropological insights that give it form and structure.[3] If we can retrieve the notion of covenant from the narrow and exclusive way in which it has been used, and restore its inclusive meaning and the moral commitments that it demands, then it has considerable potency for the reconstruction of South Africa. For the idea of covenant, truly understood both theologically and politically, can provide the framework within which we can think and act together to overcome and heal the past, restructure power relations, restore justice and develop a common vision for the future. Nelson Mandela recognized this when, in his inaugural address as President of South Africa on 10 May 1994, he declared:

> We enter into a covenant that we shall build a society in which all South Africans, both black and white, will be able to walk, without any fear in their hearts, assured of their inalienable right to human dignity – a rainbow nation at peace with itself and the world.

There are, today, two memorials at the scene of the Battle of Blood River. The long-standing Voortrekker memorial celebrating the Vow and, across the river, the Zulu Museum opened in 1998. The latter was built to keep alive the heroic memory of the Zulu warriors and to tell their side of the story. But it was also intended to be a sign of reconciliation, inaugurated as it was with a Covenant of National Reconciliation. Unfortunately the two memorials do not reflect this intention. On the contrary, they symbolize division: the one designed as a Voortrekker laager, the other representing the horns of advancing Zulu impies. Built and maintained separate from each other, with no convenient bridge across the river to make them easily accessible to those who wish to hold both sides of the story together, their location, memorabilia and celebrations, especially at the Voortrekker site, nurture sectarian interpretations and keep past enmities alive.[4] They reflect opposing powers and civilizations confronting one another across an unbridgeable chasm. In so many respects South Africa remains as divided as ever, giving substance to President Mbeki's notion of 'two nations'.[5]

There are many other places today, such as the Voortrekker Museum in Pietermaritzburg and Robben Island Museum in Cape Town, where reconciliation is far more evident, and where effort is being made to remember the past in ways that heal. Indeed, there are many such developments that engender hope. These symbols and signs of reconciliation need highlighting. But the challenge of bridging Blood River, symbolic of other contested spaces and arenas in which division is so evident, remains the ultimate test, for it reflects the fundamental conflict of group interests and power that has dogged South Africa's history for so long.

Reconciliation is about building bridges, about allowing conflicting stories to interact in ways that evoke respect, build relationships and help restructure power relations. This means that we have to go beyond an agreement to co-exist across those rivers that divide and find ways to engender common endeavour. That is the only way to make the covenant of national reconciliation a reality. Building bridges requires effort on both sides of the river. If victims are called upon to forgive as we discussed in the previous chapter, what is the response of oppressors and beneficiaries? That is the agenda for this final chapter. But first some further thoughts on the covenant as the framework within which we can best understand the process of reconciliation.

Beyond the social contract

Theologically speaking, the doctrine of reconciliation is located within the framework of God's covenant with creation, a covenant made new in Jesus Christ. God's covenant means a gracious commitment on the part of God to heal and restore God's relationship with the world so that it might be brought to perfection. Creation is an ongoing task requiring divine intervention in acts of recreation and renewal. This covenantal understanding of reconciliation cannot be directly applied in the political arena because those involved are not God and humanity, but human parties seeking to live together in the same time and space. Moreover, they are by no means parties that share a common world-view. Yet there is an analogous relationship, for covenant implies a new commitment to one another that transcends simply agreeing to co-exist, with hostility continuing to simmer beneath the surface and periodically breaking out in another round of violence. In William J. Everett's words:

> the idea of covenant points to the way in which new relationships, not rooted in the inevitability of repeating communally inherited habits of hatred and cycles of revenge, are forged through intentional acts of entrustment.[6]

Forging such relations means respecting difference without allowing difference to foster sectarianism and division. It means recognizing the way in which power has been abused in serving self-interest and developing structures of inequality and injustice, and seeking ways to achieve equity rather than the protection of vested interests. A covenantal relationship, in other words, goes further than a social contract because it is concerned about reconciliation rather than mere co-existence.

This notion of covenant has informed some Christian traditions in their understanding of the Church and the way in which they have conceived of the nature of the state.[7] The history of this development, particularly in France, Scotland and New England need not detain us, but it has 'awesome political potency'[8] as a means to limit the power of sovereigns and activate the respon-

sible exercise of power by the people. Whatever its drawbacks, a
covenant relationship is qualitatively different from that of a
social contract. Whereas in social contract theory everyone in
society is equal by virtue of nature, in covenant theory everyone
is equal by virtue of both being in the image of God and being
sinful. Hence ancient distinctions of rank and privilege are
theoretically undermined. A covenant relationship thus goes
beyond the individualism of liberal democracy to affirm human
solidarity and sociality, and therefore a commitment that transcends self-interest and serves the common good.

One major reason why those in power at the time of the
transition from apartheid to democracy agreed to engage in the
process was that self-interest would be best served by doing so.
The decision was essentially a practical, utilitarian, rather than
a moral one. The politics of transition were indicative of this
approach, for the apartheid government through its state
security apparatus did much to compromise and even thwart the
process of transition in order to gain additional self-interested
advantages. There was very little mutual trust. Indeed, the period
between 1990, when Mandela was released from prison, and
1994 when he was inaugurated as President, was one of the most
bloody and violent periods in South African history. One that
threatened to disrupt the process and plunge the country into
chaos. Much of this was revealed during the TRC. Clearly what
was happening was an attempt to control the process in such a
way that the power and self-interests of the dominant group
would be served. Hence the introduction of the amnesty clause
late in the Kempton Park negotiations, a move on the part of the
National Party government that both saved the process from
collapsing and ensured that those responsible for apartheid's
crimes would not easily be brought to book. This was the context
in which it was agreed at the last moment by both sides to establish the TRC so that amnesty could be dealt with on a proper
basis and within the broader context of seeking national reconciliation. The TRC was, in fact, part of the compromise that
made the transition to democracy possible. Such compromises
might seem a betrayal of principle, however within the context of

negotiating an end to violent conflict they are morally necessary and defensible if mechanisms are put in place to renegotiate power relations and restore justice.

In the course of events, however, the TRC took the process beyond what some had expected in the direction of establishing a more covenantal basis on which the new South Africa could be established. But the ambiguities implicit in the process, confusing 'Holy Grail' and secular contract, demonstrated that it was difficult to proceed in this way on the basis of the normal game of playing power-politics. Hence the tensions that emerged between the TRC and both the former regime and the new government. Nonetheless, the shift from a social contract based on compromise to a more covenantal form of democracy was cemented by the introduction of institutional structures that would provide ways and means for embodying national reconciliation and ensuring that the process was not undermined. Hence the adoption of what is one of the most significant democratic constitutions in the world, and the establishment of the Constitutional Court to protect it. Other structures were also put in place, such as the Human Rights Commission and the Gender Commission. In other words, for the sake of the common good, the state promoted and adopted mechanisms to ensure that individual or group self-interest was kept in check.

Covenant is, as we have noted before, theologically speaking the framework within which reconciliation is to be understood and within which it becomes a reality. It is God's gracious covenant with Abraham that sets in motion the 'grand narrative' of redemption, and for Christians it is the new covenant in Christ that makes it possible for Gentiles to participate in God's saving purpose. In other words, God's reconciliation is contingent on the covenant. The covenant makes reconciliation possible; reconciliation makes the promise of the covenant a reality. Recognition of this dialectic is important, for it is not only necessary that the covenant be negotiated on a truly moral and inclusive basis, but that we recognize the extent to which human beings break faith in keeping their covenant obligations. The covenant is not a static relationship but one that requires constant renewal and affirmation. Volf speaks to this issue when he relates the message of the cross to the covenant.[9] A covenantal relationship requires a willingness to see things from the perspective of the 'other', a willingness for *self*-sacrifice in keeping the covenant, and an unconditional commitment to the relationship so that any breakdowns occur within rather than outside the relationship.

Just as there were demands made upon ancient Israel by the covenant, above all the demand to pursue social justice, so the renewal of the covenant carries with it the demand to do justice and seek peace. Thus the covenant is not only one of God relating to humanity, but of God drawing humanity into the task of caring for and transforming the social order and the environment as a whole. God's covenant therefore has direct social, political and ecological consequences. At the same time, we cannot apply the classic substance of the theology of the covenant directly to the political realm. This would lead inevitably to the utopian and theocratic fallacy of trying to create the kingdom of God on earth. That is where many committed to a covenantal approach in the past went wrong, and some continue to make the same mistake. Today's utopia becomes tomorrow's dystopia, where power that once served a noble goal is abused in serving a new ignoble end. What we must rather do is to think analogically about the covenant in order to discern its potency for justice within the political arena, recognizing that there can be no symmetry between God's covenant with humanity, and our covenant with each other. Yet there are significant points of reference even in this regard. While there is no symmetry in terms of power relations or responsibility for the past, it is usually the case that one side must initiate the process and make it possible for the 'other' to respond. But the process obviously requires commitment and participation from both sides, and the sooner the better.

In the last chapter we considered the relationship between truth-telling and forgiveness, the first being the necessary task of perpetrators, the second being the gratuitous offer extended to them by their victims. Such forgiveness becomes, in turn, a generous invitation to the perpetrators and benefactors to accept the forgiveness offered and to respond in ways that are appropriate. Forgiveness is gratuitous and therefore does not demand penitence, remorse, lament or reparation. However, if the latter are not part of the response, those pardoned have not really appropriated the gift and entered the covenant relationship. They inevitably end up trying to justify themselves rather than becoming participants in the creation of a restored humanity.

If forgiveness is the prerogative of the victim, accepting responsibility for and being liberated from past wrongs is the corollary for perpetrators and beneficiaries. If 'white South Africa' is to be in covenant with the rest of South Africa in its transformation we have to take responsibility for what we have done to our fellows in the name of God. Stated in another way, we have to come to terms with the truth that has been uncovered through the TRC, acknowledge our guilt in ways that heal and renew, and find ways to move beyond the past in covenant with the rest of South Africa. This is a basic first step in responding to the initiative of an offered forgiveness and thus crossing those rivers that still divide. Without this step national reconciliation remains beyond realization.

Acknowledging guilt

South Africa's past history is too complex to reduce to a simplistic scheme. Yet there is no way in which we can overcome the alienation resulting from our past unless we do recognize the broad sweep of its character as a struggle between settlers for control and dominance, and of indigenous people for liberation and justice. Whatever the nuances required to tell this story in its varied details, the bare bones are beyond doubt. This means that there are two dominant pasts that need to be overcome and brought together in a way that makes healing and reconciliation possible. Those who have been the instruments and benefactors of oppression have to deal with their past in a way that sets them free from shame and guilt whether acknowledged or repressed, as well as from the attempt to cling to unjust privilege to the disadvantage of others. And those who have been their victims have to remember the past rightly, so that they are set free from a soul-destroying bitterness and uncontrollable desires for vengeance. In the process of reconciliation both of these need to happen in ways that interact with and mutually support each other.

One of the most serious lacunae in the TRC process, one beyond the control of the Commission itself, was the failure of the majority of white South Africans to become involved or even approve of its work.[10] Of course, many perpetrators gave testimony in order to obtain amnesty, but the vast majority of beneficiaries of apartheid were notable for their absence and silence.[11] There are several possible reasons for this lack of participation. Many whites undoubtedly did not feel personally responsible for apartheid, despite the fact that all benefited from it and at least the majority voted to keep the National Party government in power. There was also a spirit of defiance, a sense of regarding the TRC as something of a charade, designed to make whites feel guilty. But there was also a deeper issue involved, at least amongst some, namely a sense of shame. This was not only the public shaming of those who had committed the crimes, but the more general sense of shame that these crimes had been perpetrated in the name and for the sake of all whites.

Shame can be the first step on the way to repentance and change. But too often it is what James Fowler in his discussion of North American culture labels 'toxic shame',[12] shame that leads to a denial of truth and reality and therefore shame that is potentially destructive. This parallels a widespread phenomenon in many African societies. One of my students once told me that his mother always insisted that he should never admit blame for some wrong that he committed. The reason was that to 'lose face' was to surrender one's dignity. But to 'lose face' is, I would argue, not being willing or able to face the 'other' and therefore to enter into a proper relationship with another who has been hurt by my action. Inevitably this leads to blaming the 'other', even to the extent of finding scapegoats for one's own failure. As those engaged in trying to bring an end to violence and division in Northern Ireland know so well, the sectarianism on which this breeds 'builds and relies on a culture of blame'.[13] Blaming others and seeking ways to escape the pain and shame of acknowledging guilt often leads to self-destructive behaviour, whereas recognizing and accepting responsibility for guilt, helps rehumanize both the perpetrator *and* the victim.

Whatever the reasons, the failure of many whites in particular to enter meaningfully into the TRC process signalled an inability and an unwillingness to deal with the past in a way that acknowledged shame and guilt and opened up the possibility of healing and reconciliation. Almost 30 years ago, the psychiatrist Karl Menninger raised the pertinent question, embodied in the title of his book, *Whatever Became of Sin?* 'Is no one any longer guilty of anything?' he asked:

> Guilty perhaps of a sin that could be repented and repaired or atoned for? Is it only that someone may be stupid, or sick or criminal – or asleep? Wrong things are being done, we know; tares are being sown in the wheat field at night. But is no one responsible, no one answerable for these acts? Anxiety and depression we all acknowledge, and even vague guilt feelings; but has no one committed any sins?[14]

Menninger's analysis of the plight of contemporary society, marked by injustice, oppression, violence, corporate greed and environmental blight, to mention but a few examples of estrangement, led him to recover the concept of sin in order to do justice to reality.

Despite the limitations of language or historical misconceptions, the doctrine of sin is an attempt to help us understand better ourselves as well as our social relations. It is not motivated by any 'doom and gloom' desire to make us all feel bad or more depressed about the state of the world or our own condition. On the contrary, an understanding of our solidarity in sin (the proper meaning of 'original sin') is a necessary step along the road to reconciliation. This is so if for no other reason than that it reminds us that none of us is faultless. All of us, whether oppressors, benefactors or victims, are caught up together in a web of human fallenness and fallibility. This means that the doctrine of original sin is essentially anti-moralistic.[15] An important implication is that the process of reconciliation cannot take place if we approach it from a position of moral righteousness, apportioning blame and claiming innocence. The doctrine of sin means that we are all in this mess together, none is innocent even though not all are equally guilty except, as we shall suggest, in a metaphysical or ontological sense. We may be uneasy about 'denying innocence to victims' and wary of adding the burden of guilt to their already 'heavy load of suffering'.[16] But the fact that all have sinned does not mean that all sins are equal, only that none is entirely faultless. 'The aggressor's destruction of a village and the refugees' looting of a truck and thereby hurting their fellow refugees are equally sin, but', Volf rightly insists, 'they are *not* equal sins; the rapists' violation and the women's hatred are equally sin, but they are manifestly *not* equal sins.'[17]

Just as there are distorted understandings of sin, so there is an unhealthy neurotic or masochistic sense of guilt that binds us to the past and prevents us from changing.[18] *Feeling* guilty for something that is clearly not real (as distinct from *being* guilty) may be the result of a superego shaped by repressive parents, bad religious experience, and so forth. That is what Freudian psychoanalysis seeks to overcome. There was good reason for that critique, but we must avoid the opposite danger of denying guilt when it needs to be faced and dealt with. Guilt is not an anachronistic idea derived from the Dark Ages that has been explained away by psychoanalytic or evolutionary theory.[19] We need to recognize that the pendulum has swung, and that what we now need is to recover a healthy sense of shame and guilt in order to regain a sense of moral responsibility and accountability. If sin means that we have done wrong; guilt means that we recognize that we are responsible for having done so, and deserve to be punished. This is why the recovery of genuine forgiveness is also so necessary, for it is not the threat of punishment that awakens genuine shame and guilt, but the generous offer and gift of forgiveness. A proper sense of guilt is, in the words of David E. Roberts, a pioneer in relating psychotherapy and Christian faith, 'a sign that we have not become totally insensitive, hard-ened and irrecoverable'.[20]

In his study of the Nuremberg Trials[21] the German philoso-pher Karl Jaspers[22] speaks of guilt as an original, inevitable aspect of our humanity.[23] Such ontological or metaphysical guilt, struggle, death and suffering, is an 'ultimate situation' that presents all of us as human beings with insoluble problems from which we can never finally escape. Even if the 'momentary aspect' of such situations may change, or their 'shattering force' is obscured, they remain essentially the same. 'I must die, I must suffer, I must struggle, I am subject to chance, I involve myself inexorably in guilt.'[24] Such 'metaphysical' guilt is part of being human.[25] Tillich referred to this as 'tragic guilt' or the 'universal destiny of estrangement'.[26] There is, as a result, a solidarity between people making each of us co-responsible for everything unjust. Accepting our shared responsibility for this has the capacity to bring about 'a transformation of human self-consciousness before God' that 'may lead to a new source of active life . . . where arrogance becomes impossible'.[27] As none of us is guiltless in this sense, none of us but only God can judge others.

Alongside such metaphysical guilt, Jaspers refers to three other different yet interconnected and often overlapping types of guilt: criminal, political and moral.[28] Such distinctions are useful in helping us recognize the complexity of the issues, even though we should not draw rigid boundaries between them. Criminal guilt is the result of breaking the law, being found guilty and punished by an appropriate court of law. Political guilt, especially in a democratic society, derives from the fact that citizens are respon-sible for the way in which they are governed. It is also possible to be guilty of political crimes, but not morally guilty, as in break-ing an unjust law or in seeking to overthrow a tyrannical regime. Moral guilt means that I am responsible for all my deeds and therefore every deed is subject to moral judgement. In this instance the only possible judge can be conscience, and penance and reparation the only appropriate response.

So far so good, but what about the notion of 'collective guilt' not just in the metaphysical sense but in the sense of being jointly responsible for crimes against humanity? Tillich rejected the idea on the grounds that a social group 'has no natural, deciding centre' as is the case with an individual person; it is a 'power structure, and in every power structure certain individuals determine the actions of all individuals who are parts of the group'.[29] Others rightly argue that the notion of 'collective guilt' can lead to unjust condemnation and acts of vengeance. But it is difficult to get away from the notion of collective guilt. 'What else can one feel or should one feel', asks David Roberts, 'as he thinks of the collective crimes of war and injustice in which he is directly or indirectly implicated?'[30] Collective guilt, whether it is the collectivity of a colonial power, Nazi leadership, the apartheid government cabinet or the wider collectivity of those who kept them in power is, it seems to me, an undeniable reality. While certain individuals may lead the rest of us along the path of criminality, we usually have the freedom to go along with – or stand against – the stream. Here we are at the heart of what is meant by being a 'bystander' to and a 'beneficiary' of apartheid. There is abundant evidence to support Menninger's description of sin as 'collective irresponsibility'.[31] No matter how true it may be that only an individual, never a group, can be judged guilty,[32] there is, Jaspers wrote, 'a sort of collective moral guilt in a people's way of life which I share as an individual, and from which grow political realities'.[33] By the same token, it is this feeling of collective guilt which leads the individual to the 'task of renewing human existence from its origin'.[34]

Yet, even within this collectivity there are various gradations of guilt and appropriate forms of punishment. After all, who really was responsible for the crimes of apartheid, and in which sense are they guilty? The architects of apartheid, the National Party leaders, the security forces and foot soldiers, the local or international bankers who financed the regime, those Churches who gave apartheid legitimation, the foreign governments who gave their tacit support, black homeland leaders, the many benefactors from the system? The list could be extended much further to include all those who benefited from the oppression of others.

The reluctance of many whites in South Africa to acknowledge some guilt for apartheid, or even to accept the fact that we are beneficiaries of what was an unjust system, is still something that has to be dealt with if national reconciliation is to become a reality.[35] But even confessing guilt for certain crimes may become a technique whereby the guilty even gain an advantage over their victims without undergoing any change or making any restitution. Just as 'people turned from Nazis into democrats in five minutes after 1945',[36] so few white South Africans publicly acknowledge that they previously supported apartheid. There is good reason, then, why a confession of guilt should be delayed until the enormity of the crime has been exposed. Otherwise the confession may be reduced to vague generalities and become a way of escape from accepting full responsibility.[37] The very act of confessing guilt, like its opposite, defiant self-isolating pride, can be used as a means to avoid dealing with the problem.[38] A general amnesty that prevents any public exposure of the truth is a more blatant way of achieving the same end.

There are dangers in widening the scope of guilt, especially if we fail to recognize types and grades of guilt. Nazi propaganda was particularly successful in blurring the distinction between themselves and other Germans. This tactic succeeded to the extent that the Allies themselves abandoned any distinction between Germans.[39] But a clear distinction could be drawn, for instance, between the Nazi leaders and their willing henchmen and women within the Gestapo, and the average German citizen swept along by the euphoric tide of patriotism. And, indeed, between such leaders and followers, and those who were engaged in acts of resistance, and those Germans who were communists or gay or Jewish, and who thereby became Nazism's victims. Even amongst resisters meaningful distinctions could be made. After all, some opposed National Socialism from the beginning, while others only did so when it directly affected them. And what about the guilt of those who emigrated and from a safe distance expressed self-righteous criticism of those who remained behind and eventually succumbed to Nazi dictates and propaganda? We could push this line of argument further, because there is a sense in which the average German who was seduced by Nazi propaganda also became a victim. Consider those who were drafted into the army and suffered bitterly on the eastern front, those who lost sons in the process, and those whose homes if not lives were destroyed by the bombing of Dresden. In assessing guilt fairly we have to take into account the extent to which people were really free to dissent, the extent to which they actually knew what was happening around them, and their motivation for doing what they did.

Jasper's typology of guilt enables us to recognize the criminality of some actions, and the rights of the victims for just recompense. It enables those who honestly and rightly do not see themselves as criminally guilty, to acknowledge, nonetheless, political complicity and moral failure. It helps others, who were faithful in their resistance to Nazism and apartheid, to discern possible moral guilt. And it enables us all to discern our common humanity before God, and therefore our shared need for transformation. Whether or not that transformation of soul, so necessary for the rebirth and reconstruction of society, takes place, depends on whether or not we are willing to acknowledge whatever our own guilt and choose the path of renewal. Only in this way could the Nuremberg Trials be prevented from becoming 'a factor of doom' rather than providing 'a basis for hope for the future world order'.[40] After all, was it only Germans who created the Nazi monster? Was it not the demand of impossible reparations made at Versailles in 1919 that prepared the ground? Was it only Germans who allowed Hitler to achieve power and extend his totalitarian reign of terror over Europe?[41] Was it not also, amongst other players, the Vatican that, through its concordat with Hitler provided 'the first great endorsement of the Nazi regime?'[42] Were the racist ideologies of National Socialism confined to Germany? The German situation simply could not be separated from the world situation.[43] To discuss the German-guilt problem, or apartheid crimes, or Serbian ethnic cleansing, or Rwandan genocide, is to reflect on the frailty and failures of our own humanity. In Jaspers' words:

Everywhere people have similar qualities. Everywhere there are violent, criminal, vitally capable minorities apt to seize the reins if occasion offers, and to proceed with brutality.[44]

What happened in Germany, and what has happened in South Africa, has occurred and can do so elsewhere. After all, did not British colonial policy help create apartheid? Did not Westminster refuse to listen to the pleas of black South African leaders for basic human rights and, instead, approve the Union Constitution of 1910 that excluded all but a few blacks from the franchise? Is racism confined to white South Africans, or is it something that has become endemic to European, indeed, global culture?

We do not grasp the significance of guilt by simply regarding it in forensic terms any more than the doctrine of the atonement can be properly understood in juridical terms. Søren Kierkegaard's comment is apposite: he 'who only learns to recognise his guilt by analogy with the decisions of police justice or the supreme court never really comprehends that he is guilty'. In the same way, if God is understood as a judge in the Roman sense writ large rather than the God of prophetic justice, then the 'fear of God' does not evoke penitence, gratitude and moral responsibility, but a distorted sense of guilt with all its negative consequences. Kierkegaard's further comment is equally apposite. If the courts or public opinion declare someone not guilty, 'he becomes about the most ludicrous and pitiable of all men, a paragon of virtue who is a little better than people generally are, but not quite so good as the parson'.[45] This is one reason why the TRC and similar truth commissions can serve the task of reconciliation better than any court of law or the equivalent of a Nuremberg Trial. A genuine sense of guilt is something far more profound than any judicial declaration of guilt.

Whether necessary for amnesty or not, an honest recognition of guilt and genuine remorse is necessary for the healing of perpetrators and makes forgiveness, and therefore the healing of victims, more probable. One reason is that remorse, understood as a 'painful awakening to a reality that has been denied',[46] or 'the backbite of conscience'[47] is an important, albeit traumatic, step on the road to recovering one's identity and self-respect. We need to recognize ourselves in our guilt, and therefore come to appreciate that accepting responsibility for the past will in fact set us free from its destructive potential. Acknowledging guilt is thus not an end in itself, it is a step towards what the New Testament calls *metanoia* or repentance, that is, a willingness to acknowledge fault, turn around, and begin to live life on a new basis both personally and socially.[48]

Corporately, such remorse found expression in the Old Testament practice of lamentation connected with the destruction of Jerusalem and exile in Babylon. This profound outburst of corporate grief is parallel to the grieving process so necessary at the time of a loved one's death, and without which it is difficult to come to terms with the new situation and start life afresh. To 'mourn now', as Jesus taught in the Beatitudes, is precisely what lament means. It is an attitude of sorrow and remorse for what has happened, and therefore of humility both before God and others without which reconciliation is not possible. With this in mind Denise Ackermann, a South African feminist theologian, has spoken of our 'need to *lament* the injustice and the pain of the past before we can hope for meaningful reconciliation'.[49] 'The call to lament', she writes, 'is an appeal to all, both to the victims and to the repentant perpetrators of suffering, to engage in public acts of mourning which will enable true reconciliation and healing to take place.'[50] She continues:

> To lament psychologically, culturally, socially and as people of faith because of shame, guilt, disillusionment and disenchantment, is at the core of the contemporary struggle to find meaning and identity as whites in contemporary South Africa.[51]

Repentance, remorse, lamentation, all lead to a new commitment to restore, as the prophet Joel described, 'the years that the locusts have eaten'. That is, to restore justice. But what precisely is justice, and how does it relate to the exercise of love on the one hand, and to the exercise of power on the other?

Reconnecting love, power and justice

Following on from his fine study of reconciliation in *Exclusion and Embrace*, Miroslav Volf developed some of his ideas in a later article in which he criticized the *Kairos Document*, as well as myself by name, for giving primacy to justice rather than reconciliation.[52] Volf acknowledges that for Paul reconciliation with God always implies reconciliation with the 'other', and therefore it demands justice.[53] However, he insists that the struggle for justice must not be regarded as an end in itself, but rather as a means to achieving reconciliation 'whose ultimate goal is a community of love.'[54] Justice, in other words, is subordinate to reconciliation.[55] Using his metaphor of embrace, Volf makes four interrelated claims. First, 'the will to embrace is unconditional and indiscriminate'; second, 'truth and justice are preconditions of actual embrace'; third, 'the will to embrace is the framework for the search for justice'; and fourth, 'embrace is the goal of the struggle for justice'.[56]

Many who supported the intention of the *Kairos Document* had difficulty with the way in which it dealt with the relationship between justice and reconciliation. Within that historical context, the *kairos* of South Africa in the mid 1980s, we believed that what was confessed in the *Kairos Document* was necessary and right. But that does not mean that we would say exactly the same today. There is always a danger of treating justice and reconciliation as ahistorical ideals, or regarding them as invariably following a sequential pattern, the one leading to the other. Volf's nuanced discussion does not exclude the inseparable relationship between justice and reconciliation especially if, as he says, 'we reshape the concept of justice'. This, as he argues, 'is precisely what we find in the biblical traditions: the grace of embrace has become part and parcel of the idea of justice'.[57] But even so, he still insists that 'true justice will always be on the way to embrace'.[58] Whereas I would argue that reconciliation and justice are both part of the process and the goal, both means and ends. The problem with the *Kairos Document* was that while it distinguished between cheap and costly reconciliation, it did not distinguish between various forms of justice even though it spoke clearly enough about justice in terms of God's reign.

There is, unfortunately, no coherent understanding of justice in the modern world. Many people think they know what justice means but, as Duncan Forrester points out, they usually 'understand justice in a way that suits their individual and collective interests'.[59] This has serious negative ramifications for any society, but especially for those that are multicultural, making it difficult to establish criteria that have broad acceptance. What justice might mean to different sectors of South African society varies from restoring 'law and order', the restoring of 'the rule of law', to the restoring of the land and its resources. The first concerns the dealing with rampant crime; the second has to do with ensuring that due process is followed; and the third is about social and economic justice. The more culturally pluralistic and economically divided a society, the more disparate the concepts of justice and the greater the contest around its achievement. After all, whose justice are we talking about?[60] The justice that requires due process in order that perpetrators of crimes are not unfairly punished, or the redressing of the injustices that have come about as a result of colonialism and apartheid? It can be argued that the punishment meted out by a 'necklacing' or lynching mob is a form of rough justice, but it is clearly not the kind of justice that re-establishes moral order or heals society.

Willa Boesak had such questions in mind when he compared the ways in which different understandings of justice have been expressed in more militant forms of Islam, Judaism, African resistance and Christianity around the question of vengeance.[61] In doing so he distinguished between punitive, corrective, compensatory, redemptive justice and the vindication of God's name and honour. Each of these embodies what might be regarded as a necessary element in the pursuit of justice as a whole. Punishment for crimes is legitimate and necessary for social order. Repentance for misusing God's name in oppressing others is necessary so that God's concern for justice is upheld. Correcting centuries of unjust social and political practices, as through the redistribution of land and resources, is essential. Compensation or reparation for loss of livelihood, education, health and the death of loved ones – however inadequate this must be – is a demand of justice. But, Boesak concluded, each of these has to be considered within the broader framework of the aim of restoring justice. That is, justice understood as redemptive and reconciling, justice as the exercise of love and power in a way that heals relationships and builds community.

In a more recent discussion of these issues, Christopher Marshall provides a similar yet different kind of list to that of Boesak. He speaks of natural and rough justice, distributive and retributive justice, commutative and remedial justice, poetic and practical justice, each of which is inevitably partial and fallible.[62] Marshall's impressive discussion of the issues based on a careful exegesis of the New Testament leads him to a conclusion that takes the case for restorative justice further. He insists that whatever truth there may be in other forms of justice, the Christian tradition is about 'restorative' or what he calls 'covenant justice'. That is, the justice that rebuilds God's intended network of relationships. This is not something in addition to the gospel of God's saving grace or doctrine of atonement; restorative justice is precisely what Paul's interpretation of the gospel is about.[63] 'Justification by faith', writes Marshall, 'is a manifestation of restorative justice.'[64] From a Pauline perspective, then, it is the restoring of justice that is the whole point of reconciliation.[65] Likewise, the Gospel writers, Marshall maintains, 'consider Jesus' entire life and ministry (also) to be a demonstration of divine justice'.[66] Jesus' declaration that he had not come to destroy but fulfil the Torah implies a deep respect for the demands of God's justice in personal and social relations. But the way in which Jesus understood God's justice and the manner in which he set about fulfilling its aims differed radically from both pharisaic legalism and Roman jurisprudence.

Covenantal justice is quite distinct from Roman and Greek law,[67] for while it may involve punishment, it never rests there, for the goal of God's justice is healing and reconciliation. The biblical notion of justice, like reconciliation, is about relationships, and especially about the quality of relationship, whether understood in terms of interpersonal or group relations, or our relationship with God and creation as a whole. Kathryn Tanner rightly perceives that this redefinition of justice requires that 'Christians work for a just society that corresponds to a covenant of grace'.[68] Such a view of justice is not hard-hearted, especially towards those who are poor, disreputable or unable to plead their own cause, but merciful. God's justice is the justice of restored relations, an understanding of justice inseparable even if distinguishable from love, and one which finds expression in liberation from oppression and reconciliation within both personal and social relations. We recall the medieval vision, represented so well by Dante in his *Paradiso*, that the establishment 'of universal love is a necessary condition of the reign of justice'.[69] Of course, there can be no perfect justice unless we think in eschatological terms about the ultimate reign of God's righteousness. But for Dante, the approximation of such justice was possible on earth if only greed and covetousness could be overcome by charity.

Restorative justice is not, however, a weak form of justice, a dilution of the normal legal process. Nor does it necessarily exclude other forms of justice, even retribution or the use of punishment as a deterrent. Restorative justice is rather the attempt to 'to recover certain neglected dimensions that make for a more complete understanding of justice'.[70] Its emphasis is on rehabilitation, on compensation, on the recovery of dignity and the healing of social wounds.[71] This is precisely what is at the heart of justice in the biblical tradition; it is relational and social, it requires both embrace and the overcoming of oppression in all its forms. That is why, from a Christian perspective love and justice belong together, for love, in Forrester's words, 'gives the clue to the inner nature of justice; and justice without love becomes distorted into something diabolic and tyrannical'.[72] Yet how do love and justice relate to power? For power too has to do with relationships whether we speak interpersonally or politically. The will-to-power is the source of human alienation and estrangement; yet without the proper exercise of power, justice is not possible.

In his classic study of love, power and justice, Paul Tillich showed the intrinsic connection between them even though recognizing that the connection is continually broken apart by sin. Writing of personal relations, he spoke of a 'creative justice' in which love and justice are maintained through listening, giving and forgiving.[73] Creative justice seeks ways to overcome hostility that are not immediately apparent, but which become so through listening to the 'other', through conversation, and through 'speaking the truth in love'. In other words, creative justice is part and parcel of the process of reconciliation. On the broader social stage, Tillich argued that centres of power evolve which bring people together rather than divide them, and in doing so they exercise the power of love and justice, even though they may yet again fall apart in the course of events.[74] The Church, for example, is called to be such a centre of power, just as the TRC functioned in this way as an instrument of the state in forging a relationship between forgiveness and justice.

Underlying all of this is the Christian conviction that ultimately love, power and justice together define the nature of God as evident in God's creative and redemptive work. Of course, this raises the spectre of the problem of theodicy that cannot be dealt with here except to say that from the Christian perspective God does not exercise power in a way that contradicts justice or love. In Tillich's words:

> Love destroys, as its strange work, what is against love. It does so according to justice, without which it would be chaotic surrender of the power of being. Love, at the same time, as its own work, saves through forgiveness of that which is against love. It does so according to the justifying paradox without which it would be a legal mechanism.[75]

If you speak of God as loving, gracious and merciful, you cannot logically end up with a concept of divine justice that contradicts those attributes.[76] Divine power is revealed in the suffering and vicarious love of the cross that forgives perpetrators yet condemns injustice in exercising the creative and redemptive justice of God. God's justice, power and love are revealed in the fact that the just dies for the unjust, thereby justifying and embracing the ungodly in a new covenantal relationship. Thus restorative justice has to do with renewing God's covenant and therefore the establishing of just power relations without which reconciliation remains elusive. It is not a justice that separates people into the good and the bad, the ritually clean or the ethnically acceptable, but one that seeks to bind them together in mutual care and responsibility for each other and for the larger society.

Restorative or covenantal justice is by no means the only or even dominant understanding of what justice means. But it is only as we seek to restore the power relationships that have been broken by human rights abuses that we really lay the necessary foundations for preventing further abuses and enabling healing. This obviously implies a system of justice based on human rights, the administration of which benefits all sectors of society and inculcates respect for the rule of law, not least by holding accountable those who violate human rights. Whether or not it achieves these goals is, of course, the acid test for its validity as an alternative to justice as punishment alone.[77] This is why the granting of amnesty by the TRC was such a contentious issue. As the South African artist William Kentridge put it: 'As people give more and more evidence of the things they have done, they get closer and closer to amnesty, and it gets more and more intolerable that these people should be given amnesty.'[78]

But whatever the limitations of the TRC, precisely because its focus was on restorative justice it was able to provide possibilities for future prosecutions of significant numbers of perpetrators in a way that would not have been possible through the courts. Moreover, it brought judgement to bear on the structures of oppression and injustice in a way that went beyond the limitations of a court of law. After all, legal trials are about individual culpability, not the iniquities of a social system and its transformation. This has been true of many other truth commissions, as Hayner indicates, 'partly due to the limited reach of the courts, and partly out of recognition that even successful prosecutions do not resolve the conflict and pain associated with past abuses'.[79] So while the TRC could not bring about justice in the way and in the sense that courts might do so, it did break open possibilities for restoring justice.

In this regard it should be noted that the Amnesty Committee of the TRC functioned far more as a legal court than was true of the TRC as a whole. This indicates perhaps more than anything else the ambiguous role of the TRC as a cross between confessional and court. But despite the problems that resulted, the fact that forgiveness and justice were connected, even if not fully realized within the total work of the TRC, contributed to its role in facilitating the process of reconciliation and restoring justice. By way of contrast, perhaps it was because the Nuremberg Trials were only a court of law and not a national confessional, that Jaspers expressed his disappointment 20 years after that it had not led to the healing of Germany but only exacerbated the hurt.[80]

The restoration of justice requires a great deal more than could be achieved through the TRC, even though justice was restored for some victims to a meaningful extent. When we talk about restoring justice in the context of reconciliation in South Africa, and most other places as well, the focus must be on social and economic justice. If this is not the case, then maintaining 'law and order' and pursuing 'due process' can be abused in ways that perpetuate injustice as was often the case during apartheid. This raises the important question of reparation, the collective form of doing penance, and in many ways the key to restoring justice. Reparation means more than simply helping all those who have suffered and are in need. Reparation is not simply being kind or going the extra mile; reparation is not engaging in welfare – reparation is seeking to undo what should never have been done in the first place. Reparation is restorative justice in action. For Jaspers it required affirmative action on behalf of 'those deported, robbed, pillaged, tortured and exiled by the Hitler regime'.[81] In the South African context such reparation requires redistribution of land and wealth, as well as affirmative action with regard to access to resources, education, employment, housing and health care.

The record of governments worldwide in implementing the recommendations of truth commissions, not least the TRC, has not been good.[82] There are several reasons for this. One is a lack of political will and commitment. Related to this is the fact that present governments have to pay for the sins and faults of previous regimes. But usually the main reason is the lack of resources and, even where this is not an insurmountable problem, new governments often lack capacity to implement the recommendations. So yet again, victims of past oppression can become victims of good intentions but no delivery on promises. It is too easy to pay lip-service to the rights and moral claims of the victims of a society without honouring that claim. This has always been a ploy on the part of those seeking to give their cause moral justification. The American Civil War and the South African War (1899–1902) were morally justified on the basis of liberating slaves or defending the rights of blacks. But this rationalization does not bear much scrutiny, indeed, such hypocrisy abuses moral claims and undermines moral values. If the TRC's recommendations regarding reparation are not taken seriously we will be guilty of something similar. The victims will remain victims. This will also and inevitably undermine the building of a moral culture. But any society that is serious about justice, and especially the restoration of justice within the context of national reconciliation, has to take the voice of the victims of injustice as primary and refuse to allow that voice to be silenced.

In many places, most notoriously in Zimbabwe today, but not only there, the restoring of justice and therefore reconciliation is above all inseparable from the question of land distribution and property rights. Negative reactions to what is happening in Zimbabwe, especially with regard to its presidential election, should not obfuscate the issue that lies behind the social upheaval in that country. Itumuleng Mosala rightly perceived that black alienation in southern Africa was, in the first instance, not from white people, but alienation 'from our land, our cattle, our labour'.[83] And, therefore, reconciliation with white people is bound up with the restoration of that which restores livelihood, human dignity and connections with the land. Noteworthy in this regard is that the Greek word for 'law', namely *nomos*, derives from the word *nemo*, 'to distribute' or 'deal out', in the sense of assigning land or pasture.[84] But it is far more a biblical rather than a Graeco-Roman perspective on the meaning of justice, as is evident in the sabbatical and jubilee year teaching in the Torah. Everett makes the point well in terms of the covenant:

> covenant making, in its biblical origins, was a way to begin a new life together with the land. Without this new possibility, there is no reason to come together in an intentional, constructive way to secure that new future. Without this possibility of a shared future on the basis of a new covenant, reconciliation is impossible.[85]

The redistribution of land is not easy to achieve after so long a period of colonialism and apartheid, but far-reaching steps must be taken. The redistribution of wealth is never easy or without pain but it is vital, and those who were privileged in the past need to accept this responsibility as a liberating and healing opportunity. It is not simply a matter of government trying to make reparation; it is also the responsibility of those who are privileged. Covenanting for the restoration of justice is a commitment to share and therefore a way of building a moral community. Without the development of a sense of co-responsibility for the human situation, political liberty and democratic freedom are impossible. While it is impossible to redress all the wrongs that have been perpetrated against the victims of colonial injustice and apartheid, reparation means that concrete steps have to be taken which will lead to a more equitable and just society. The transformation of education, health services and every other aspect of public life in such a way that justice and equity are achieved, is essential if justice is to be a reality. This is why the objectives of the worldwide Jubilee movement, or the South African campaign 'Homes for All', and many other similar programmes are so important. But all of this obviously requires a fundamental transformation of the individual, even though the path of transformation will be different for every person.

The liberation of the privileged is essential for the liberation of the oppressed, a dictum that applies globally as well as locally and regionally. This is not a stratagem of privatized piety, but an act of far-reaching political consequence. But the liberation of the privileged cannot happen without the aid of those who were victims, their willingness also to accept the 'other', in this case those who were on the other side of the apartheid divide. There is a profound sense in which restoring justice and achieving reconciliation is only possible through what Duncan Forrester calls the 'generosity of the victim'.[86] The reason is simply the harsh fact that it is impossible to really restore everything that has been lost by the victim. How does one restore the life of a loved one who has been murdered by security forces? How does one restore the land in full to Native Americans, to Australian Aborigines, to the Khoi and San in South Africa? Generosity, writes Forrester, 'is a way of broadening and deepening the understanding of justice'.[87] He continues: 'If the oppressors are willing to say, "I am sorry", and to make what restitution is possible, even if it is largely token and symbolic, then creative justice becomes possible through the generosity of the victim.'[88]

The recognition that there can never be perfect justice in this world no matter how much we seek to redress past injustices, explains in part the biblical expectation of a 'last judgement'. What is at stake is the conviction that ultimately the universe is moral, that injustice and oppression will not go unpunished, and that the suffering of victims is not for naught. This belief in divine retribution has, as Marshall so aptly describes it, led to 'a hell of a problem'. But his careful survey of the New Testament evidence leads him to conclude that even though 'punishment has a significant place in the presentation of divine justice . . . the purpose of this punishment is ultimately reparative or redemptive in design'.[89] Divine punishment is ultimately reserved for the principalities and powers of evil. That it why God's judgement holds out the promise of hope for the cosmic restoration of 'all things', as Paul taught. Thus closely linked to this sense of judgement is, however, the greater sense of hope that permeates the Christian tradition. Hence the prophetic vision of a 'new covenant', of the coming to birth of a 'new heaven and a new earth', of God's will being done on earth 'as it is in heaven'. This hope reaches beyond death, but like God's justice, it is a hope that anticipates God's future gift of a 'new earth', of cosmic reconciliation, in the present.

A new covenant forged in hope

A few weeks before the first democratic election in South Africa in 1994 I participated in an academic symposium that focused on the question as to whether or not the elections could be 'free and fair'. Virtually all of the participants present were social and political scientists; I was the only theologian. Hard-nosed statistics and political realism drove the discussion throughout the day, and as the day progressed the mood became more sombre and pessimistic. There was so much intimidation and violence in certain parts of the country that everything pointed away from the elections fulfilling the necessary criteria. Having agreed with a great deal of what was said, I began to share the mood, yet there was always something nagging in my consciousness that prevented me from succumbing to the prevailing pessimism. Finally, in an act of exasperation, I blurted out that no matter what the statistics and the wisdom of political science might tell us, they could never have the last word. From a faith perspective, I added, nothing could happen to bring about change in South Africa unless people lived and acted in hope. Politics might be the art of the possible but, to indulge in a cliché, theology is about the art of the impossible and unexpected.

There is, as we saw earlier in Chapter 2, an intrinsic connection between ultimate hopes and penultimate indicators and signs of that hope. Within that 'space between the times', reconciliation can take on a new dynamic as people together participate in developing a common vision for the future and in seeking to make that vision a reality. This shared vocation, as Everett calls it, helps overcome 'a fixation on the past, with its infinite complexity of sin and victimage, each act crying out for publicity and reparation'. These acts, 'of an often incomprehensible brutality', Everett continues, 'must be approached from the standpoint of the miraculous opening up of a possible new order founded not on the consequences of the past and its compensations but on the new covenant forged in the midst of new hopes'.[90]

Christian eschatology, the doctrine of the 'last things', is not simply about hope for justice in the future but about the impact which God's future has on our present experience. The Marxist critique was quite right in calling the bluff on the way in which eschatology was used to keep the poor in their place with promises of eternal reward. Though, paradoxically, in the history of the struggles of the poor and oppressed it has often been the case that the 'more other-worldly the focus . . . the more this-worldly its relevance. The more we are able to trust God finally to transform the situation, the more we are lifted out of the mire of despair and set free to launch small-scale initiatives of resistance.'[91] Jesus' proclamation of the 'reign of God', that is, God's justice, always pointed beyond the present, but in a way that brought hope to those who suffered now and demanded repentance and obedience from those who were responsible for their condition and plight. This much is obvious from Jesus' parables of judgement in the Synoptic Gospels. In John's Gospel neither God's judgement nor salvation awaits us only in the future, they are present realities revealed in the death of Christ and related to the way in which we respond to God's merciful justice. Judgement day is every day, just as today is the day of salvation. How we respond to this possibility and offer determines whether the future opens up in a way that restores justice or not.

How to relate eschatological hope and contemporary political realities has been a dominant theme in Christian theology for much of the twentieth century, finding classic expression in Jürgen Moltmann's *Theology of Hope*.[92] For Moltmann the 'sin of despair' is the sin of not taking seriously the covenant promise of God and therefore not doing justice but wallowing in resignation, inertia and melancholy.[93] Hope, on the other hand, is the only realistic way to live because it takes seriously 'the possibilities with which all reality is fraught'.[94] Those who trust in God's covenant promise, that is, those who live in hope, will never be prepared to accept given evils as the last word. They 'can no longer put up with reality as it is, but begin to suffer under it, to contradict it'.[95] At least two consequences flow from this. The first is that the Church, when true to its covenant relation to God, is 'a constant disturbance in human society' because it refuses to allow things as they are to remain set in concrete.[96] The second and related consequence is that such hope leads to creative action, for new thinking and planning spring from hope.[97] Hope, as distinct from wishful thinking or utopian longing, is precisely that which makes us creatively alive to possibilities in history.

Part of the problem with the widespread secular world-view is the inability to imagine alternatives other than those permitted by scientific rationality in the unfolding of history. Modernity leaves little room for the element of surprise, for the humanly unpredictable. But history is full of surprises, however we may account for them. If we are serious about reconciliation and restoring justice in the world, then Hannah Arendt's insight on the matter is surely one that we need to heed. 'The miracle that saves the world', she writes, is 'natality', that is, the birth of new people with the capacity of participating in new beginnings. She continues:

> Only the full experience of this capacity can bestow upon human affairs faith and hope, those two essential characteristics of human existence which Greek antiquity ignored altogether, discounting the keeping of faith as a very uncommon and not too important virtue and counting hope among the evils of illusion in Pandora's box. It is this faith and hope for the world that found perhaps its most glorious and most succinct expression in the few words with which the Gospels announced their 'glad tidings': 'A child has been born to us.'[98]

From the cradle to the cross, Jesus' life and ministry highlighted this surprising, unexpected element in the way in which God acts, and the fact that it is only the childlike who really have the eyes to see and the ears to hear what is truly happening. And, more especially, to discern what can happen and to risk participating in new beginnings.

Many of those who were engaged in the struggle against apartheid will testify that it was the hope of an end to oppression and the hope of the birth of a new nation which sustained them through the years of suffering, struggle, prison and exile. Often hope was disappointed and on the verge of despair and defeat. Like many who have cried out to God throughout history, 'How long, O Lord?' But hope for the future of South Africa became a source of creative power and vision that eventually led to fundamental change. Shortly after he was arrested and imprisoned in 1943, Bonhoeffer wrote words from prison that were a great encouragement to some of us during that time:

> It may be that the day of judgement will dawn tomorrow; in that case, we will gladly stop working for a better future. But not before.[99]

These words express what it means to live in hope. It is often wiser to be pessimistic, at least in the sense of there being less chance of being proven wrong, avoiding disappointment and ridicule. But, as Bonhoeffer commented, 'optimism that is will for the future should never be despised, even if it is proved wrong a hundred times; it is health and vitality . . . '.[100] Such hope is not based on illusion or wishful thinking, and we must be careful that we do not create false hopes of utopia which lose touch with concrete reality and actually prevent us from achieving the necessary goals. We know only too well that utopia is beyond our grasp. But hope remains a powerful and necessary antidote to despair – despair about crime, about violence, about abuse and ongoing violations of human rights. Hope is all about the vision of what we believe our world can and should be. Hope is a vision of what we believe our country can and should be. Hope enables us to believe that we can achieve some meaningful expression of justice, reconciliation and healing here and now even though the ultimate goal must always remain beyond our grasp.

Covenanting to restore justice, covenanting together as a people reconciled to God and one another, covenanting to restore relations with the 'other', requires then a commitment to live and work in anticipation of what God promises. Such hope, as Vusi Mahlasela reminds us, has to become the obsession of our lives.

In the beginning it was said 'Let there be light'
In these times I say Let there be Hope
'Cause so many flickering in the state of uncertainty and
    suspense
Though atrocities, suffering and decay may prevail
When we start to hope change takes form
Through our born trust we leave sad memories behind us
'Cause this is the time for hope

I don't know much, but I do know
That out of fear there is hope
I wish I could find better words to say
To bring it into the open.

This hope is the obsession of life
But I do know that I can sing
In clouds of words to you
Perhaps you may still feel nothing
Out of your weakness
But one thing I have always hoped
Is for you to be with hope.[101]

Hope as the obsession of life! What else is the Christian gospel of reconciliation about than life lived within the covenant of God's promise of new life, new worlds, new possibilities breaking into the old?

Notes

Chapter 1

1 The programme is run by the International Center for Transitional Justice based in New York. Its president is Dr Alex Boraine former deputy chair of the Truth and Reconciliation Commission in South Africa. The co-sponsor of the programme is the Institute for Justice and Reconciliation in Cape Town. Funding is provided by the Open Society Foundation. On the work of the Institute for Justice and Reconciliation see www.ijr.org.za

2 Priscilla B. Hayner, *Unspeakable Truths: Confronting State Terror and Atrocity*, New York: Routledge, 2001.

3 Alex Boraine, Levy Janet and Ronel Scheffer, (eds.), *Dealing with the Past: Truth and Reconciliation in South Africa*, Cape Town: Idasa, 1994; Alex Boraine and Janet Levy, (eds.), *The Healing of a Nation?* Cape Town: Justice in Transition, 1995.

4 www.forgiving.org The Campaign is funded by the Templeton Foundation under the patronage of Archbishop Desmond Tutu, former US President Jimmy Carter, and eminent psychologist Professor Robert Coles of Harvard. There is also an International Forgiveness Institute at the University of Wisconsin.

5 One comprehensive study of the issues that I received too late for any thorough consideration, though I have briefly noted its contents in a few places, is Raymond G. Helmick SJ and Rodney L. Petersen, (eds.), *Forgiveness and Reconciliation: Religion, Public Policy, and Conflict Transformation*, Philadelphia: Templeton Foundation Press, 2001.

6 Antjie Krog, *Country of My Skull*, Johannesburg: Random House, 1998, p. 109.

7 Jakes Gerwel, 'National Reconciliation: Holy Grail or Secular Pact?' in Charles Villa-Vicencio and Wilhelm Verwoerd, (eds.), *Looking Back Reaching Forward*, Cape Town: University of Cape Town Press, 2000, p. 280.

8 Gerwel, 'National Reconciliation: Holy Grail or Secular Pact?', p. 284.

9 Gerwel, 'National Reconciliation: Holy Grail or Secular Pact?', p. 286.

10 Bhiku Parekh, 'The Voice of Religion in Political Discourse', in Leroy S. Rouner, (ed.), *Religion, Politics, and Peace*, Notre Dame: University of Notre Dame Press, 1999, p. 74.

11 Horacio Verbisky, quoted in Hayner, *Unspeakable Truths*, p. 160.

12 Wolfhart Pannenberg, *Systematic Theology*, vol. 2, Grand Rapids: Eerdmans, 1994, p. 443.

13 Dietrich Ritschl, *The Logic of Theology*, Philadelphia: Fortress Press, 1986, p. 181.

14 Ritschl, *The Logic of Theology*, p. 181.

15 Ritschl, *The Logic of Theology*, pp. 181–2.

16 Parekh, 'The Voice of Religion in Political Discourse', p. 73.

17 Joseph Liechty and Cecelia Clegg, *Moving Beyond Sectarianism: Religion, Conflict and Reconciliation in Northern Ireland*, Dublin: Columba Press, 2001, p. 44.

18 Erik Doxtader, 'Reconciliation in a State of Emergency: The Middle Voice of 2 Corinthians', *Journal for the Study of Religion* 14 no. 1 (2001), pp. 48–9.

19 Dietrich Bonhoeffer, *Letters and Papers from Prison*, London: SCM Press, 1971, p. 300.

20 Desmond Tutu, *No Future Without Forgiveness*, London: Rider, 1999.

21 For an introduction to the debate about narrative theology, see Stanley Hauerwas and L. Gregory Jones, (eds.), *Why Narrative? Readings in Narrative Theology*, Grand Rapids: Eerdmans, 1989.

22 Gerwel, 'National Reconciliation: Holy Grail or Secular Pact?', p. 279.

23 Rowan Williams, *On Christian Theology*, Oxford: Blackwell, 2000, p. 266.

24 Quoted in Mxolisi Mgxashe, 'Reconciliation: A Call to Action', in Villa-Vincencio and Verwoerd, *Looking Back Reaching Forward*, p. 218.

25 Rowan Williams, *The Wound of Knowledge*, London: Darton, Longman & Todd, 1990, p. 2.

26 Hayner, *Unspeakable Truths*, p. 155.

27 The Zulu word *ukubuyisana* which is often used to translate reconciliation literally means 'to return to each other' in the sense of mutual forgiveness. See Mark Hay, *Ukubuyisana: Reconciliation in South Africa*, Pietermaritzburg: Cluster Publications, 1998, p. 1.

28 Basil John Hendricks, 'The Notion of Reconciliation as Part of the Emerging Coloured Identity', MA diss., University of Cape Town, 1996.

29 See Kadar Asmal, Louise Asmal and Ronald Suresh Roberts, *Reconciliation Through Truth*, Cape Town: David Philip, 1996, pp. 51–2.

30 Albert Luthuli, *Let My People Go!*, London: Collins, 1962, p. 231.

31 The Mayibuye Centre at the University of the Western Cape is the main

archive of the liberation movement in South Africa and has extensive documentation on the subject in all its dimensions.

32 *Cottesloe Consultation*, Consultation of the South African Member Churches of the World Council of Churches, ed. Leslie A. Hewson (1961).

33 John W. de Gruchy, *The Church Struggle in South Africa*, Grand Rapids: Eerdmans, 1979, pp. 115–20.

34 See the essays in Klaus Nürnberger and John Tooke, (eds.), *The Cost of Reconciliation in South Africa*, Cape Town: Methodist Publishing House, 1988.

35 Tony Balcomb, *Third Way Theology*, Pietermaritzburg: Cluster Publications, 1993.

36 *The Kairos Document*, Johannesburg: Institute for Contextual Theology, 1986, p. 9, art. 3.1.

37 *Journal of Theology for Southern Africa* 58 (March 1987); John W. de Gruchy, 'The Struggle for Justice and the Ministry of Reconciliation', in Nürnberger and Tooke *The Cost of Reconciliation in South Africa*, pp. 166–80.

38 Itumeleng Mosala, *Biblical Hermeneutics and Black Theology in South Africa*, Grand Rapids: Eerdmans, 1989.

39 The remarkable story of these talks is told in Nelson Mandela, *Long Walk to Freedom: The Autobiography of Nelson Mandela*, Johannesburg: Macdonald Purnell, 1994.

40 Louw Alberts and Frank Chikane, (eds.), *The Road to Rustenburg*, Cape Town: Struik, 1991.

41 See the Rustenberg Declaration in Alberts and Chikane, *The Road to Rustenburg*, pp. 275–86.

42 See the discussion of the issues in Asmal et al., *Reconciliation Through Truth*, pp. 18–19.

43 See the discussion of the issues in Alex Boraine, *A Country Unmasked: Inside South Africa's Truth and Reconciliation Commission*, New York: Oxford University Press, 2000, pp. 117–18, 269–70, 275–6.

44 A Xhosa word which means human solidarity.

45 *The Truth will set you Free*, SACC Brochure, 1995, p. 24.

46 Quoted in Mgxashe, 'Reconciliation: A Call to Action', p. 218. For a brief summary of the Recommendations in the TRC Report see the brochure *Time to Act: The Recommendations of the Truth and Reconciliation Commission*, published by the Institute for Justice and Reconciliation in Cape Town. See also the TRC webpage: www.truth.org.za

47 Priscilla Hayner, 'Same Species, Different Animal: How South Africa Compares to Truth Commissions Worldwide', in Villa-Vicencio and Verwoerd, (eds.), *Looking Back Reaching Forward*, p. 41.

48 For Archbishop Tutu's own comments on his appointment and its implication, see Tutu, *No Future Without Forgiveness*, p. 71.

49 See James C. Cochrane, John W. de Gruchy and Steve Martin, (eds.), *Facing the Truth: South African Faith Communities and the Truth and Reconciliation Commission*, Cape Town: David Philip, 1999, pp. 67–8; Boraine, *A Country Unmasked*, pp. 267–8.

50 See Kadar Asmal's critical comments on the TRC's granting amnesty without requiring contrition, and on the danger of morally equating the crimes of apartheid with those of the liberation movements in Asmal et al., *Reconciliation Through Truth*, pp. 23–6. These issues are dealt with from the perspective of the TRC in Boraine, *A Country Unmasked*, pp. 269–86, 300–14.

51 See, for example, Tinyiko Maluleke, 'The Truth and Reconciliation Discourse: A Black Theological Evaluation', in James C. Cochrane et al., (eds.), *Facing the Truth*, pp. 101–13; Mahmood Mamdani, 'A Diminished Truth', in Wilmot James and Linda van de Vijver, (eds.), *After the TRC: Reflections on Truth and Reconciliation in South Africa*, Cape Town: David Philip, 2000, pp. 58–61; Frederick van Zyl Slabbert, 'Truth Without Reconciliation, Reconciliation Without Truth', in James and van de Vijver, *After the TRC*, pp. 62–72.

52 This description made by President Thabo Mbeki in his opening address to the conference on 'National Reconciliation' in 1998, in the National Assembly, Cape Town.

53 Gerwel, 'National Reconciliation: Holy Grail or Secular Pact?', p. 281.

Chapter 2

1 James Denney, *The Christian Doctrine of Reconciliation*, London: James Clarke, 1959, p. 6.

2 Karl Barth, *Church Dogmatics: The Doctrine of Reconciliation*, Church Dogmatics, vol. IV/1, Edinburgh: T&T Clark, 1961, p. 3.

3 P. T. Forsyth, *The Work of Christ*, London: Independent Press, 1952, pp. 56, 81.

4 Wolfhart Pannenberg, *Systematic Theology*, vol. 2, Grand Rapids: Eerdmans, 1994, p. 400.

5 Mark C. Taylor, *Altarity*, Chicago: University of Chicago Press, 1987, p. xxix.

6 See Cilliers Breytenbach, *Versöhnung. Eine Studie Zur Paulinschen Soteriologie*, Neukirchen: Neukirchen Verlag, 1989.

7 I owe this suggestion to Dr Ralf K. Wüstenberg. See Wüstenberg's dissertation (Habilitation) on reconciliation in which he also uses the TRC as a case study. Ralf Wüstenberg, 'Die Politische Dimension der Versöhnung: Eine Systematisch-Theologische Studies Zum Umgang mit Schuld Nach Den Systemumbrüchen in Südafrika und Deutschland', Habilitationsschrift, Heidelberg, 2002.

8 Rowan Williams, *On Christian Theology*, Oxford: Blackwell, 2000, p. 6.

9 See J. N. D. Kelly, *Early Christian Doctrines*, London: A&C Black, 1968, pp.163–4, 375; Otto Weber, *Foundations of Dogmatics*, vol. 2, Grand Rapids: Eerdmans, 1983, pp. 177–91.

10 See Dietrich Bonhoeffer, *Creation and Fall: A Theological Exposition of Genesis 1–3*, Dietrich Bonhoeffer Works, vol. 3, Minneapolis: Fortress Press, 1997.

11 See, for example, the critique of the Christian grand narrative in Michael Goldberg, 'God, Action, and Narrative: Which Narrative? Which Action? Which God?', in Stanley Hauerwas and L. Gregory Jones, (eds.), *Why Narrative? Readings in Narrative Theology*, Grand Rapids: Eerdmans, 1989, p. 348.

12 Rowan Williams, *The Wound of Knowledge*, London: Darton, Longman & Todd, 1990, p. 2.

13 Ralph Martin, *Reconciliation: A Study of Paul's Theology*, Atlanta: John Knox Press, 1981, p. 81.

14 Martin, *Reconciliation*, p. 5.

15 The noun (reconciliation) καταλλαγη four times (Rom. 5.11, 11.15; 2 Cor. 5.18, 19), and the verb (to reconcile) eleven times ἀποκαταλασσω (Eph. 2.16; Col. 1.20, 22), διαλλασσομαι (Matt. 5.24), καταλασσω (Rom. 5.10 twice; 1 Cor. 7.11; 2 Cor. 5.18, 19, 20), συναλασσω (Acts 7.26). On one occasion the English translators have used reconciliation to translate the Greek word for peace εἰρηνη (Acts 12.20).

16 Gerhard Kittel, (ed.), *Theological Dictionary of the New Testament*, vol. 1, trans. Geoffrey Bromiley, Grand Rapids: Eerdmans, 1977, pp. 255–9; Colin Brown, (ed.), *New International Dictionary of New Testament Theology*, Exeter: Paternoster Press, 1978, pp. 145–74.

17 See the discussion of the words in 'Reconciliation, Forgiveness', in Johannes P. Louw and Eugene A. Nida, (eds.), *Greek–English Lexicon of the New Testament Based on Semantic Domains*, vol. 1, New York: United Bible Societies, 1988, pp. 502–3.

18 J. Christiaan Beker, *Paul the Apostle: The Triumph of God in Life and Thought*, Philadelphia: Fortress Press, 1980, pp. 257–8.

19 Ralph P. Martin, 'Center of Paul's Theology', in Gerald F. Hawthorne and Ralph P. Martin, (eds.), *Dictionary of Paul and His Letters*, Downers Grove, IL: InterVarsity Press, 1993, p. 94.

20 Leonnard Goppelt, *Theology of the New Testament: The Variety and Unity of the Apostolic Witness to Christ*, Grand Rapids: Eerdmans, 1982, p. 139.

21 S. E. Porter, 'Peace, Reconciliation', in Hawthorne and Martin, *Dictionary of Paul and His Letters*, p. 695.

22 See 'Reconciliation, Forgiveness', Louw and Nida, *Greek–English Lexicon*, p. 502.

23 Martin, *Reconciliation*, pp. 109–10.

24 Erik Doxtader, 'Reconciliation in a State of Emergency: The Middle

Voice of 2 Corinthians', *Journal for the Study of Religion* 14 no. 1 (2001), p. 57.

25 Martin, *Reconciliation*, pp. 113–14, 119, 121–2.
26 See Martin, *Reconciliation*, pp. 71–89; Beker, *Paul the Apostle*, pp. 257–8.
27 Goppelt, *Theology of the New Testament*, p. 137.
28 Goppelt, *Theology of the New Testament*, p. 138.
29 Martin, *Reconciliation*, p. 154.
30 For a detailed exposition of Paul's theology of justification and justice along these lines, see Christopher D. Marshall, *Beyond Retribution: A New Testament Vision for Justice, Crime, and Punishment*, Grand Rapids: Eerdmans, 2001, pp. 35–69.
31 Marshall, *Beyond Retribution*, p. 59.
32 Martin, *Reconciliation*, p. 232.
33 Timothy Gorringe, *God's Just Vengeance*, Cambridge: Cambridge University Press, 1996, p. 77.
34 Jan Milic Lochman, *Reconciliation and Liberation: Changing a One-Dimensional View of Salvation*, London: Christian Journals, 1980, p. 102.
35 Martin, *Reconciliation: A Study of Paul's Theology*, p. 225.
36 H. A. Hodges, *The Pattern of the Atonement*, London: SCM Press, 1955, p. 11.
37 Lynette Jean Holness, 'Christology from Within: A Critical Retrieval of the Humanity of Christ, with Particular Reference to the Role of Mary', PhD diss., University of Cape Town, 2001.
38 Gustavo Gutiérrez, *A Theology of Liberation*, trans. Matthew J. O'Connell, revised edn, Maryknoll, NY: Orbis, 1988, p. 97.
39 For a comprehensive discussion of the centrality of sacrifice in Christian theology and practice, see F. C. N. Hicks, *The Fullness of Sacrifice: An Essay in Reconciliation*, London: SPCK, 1953.
40 See especially Gustav Aulén, *Christus Victor: An Historical Study of the Three Main Types of the Idea of Atonement*, London: SPCK, 1953, pp. 20–3.
41 Lochman, *Reconciliation and Liberation*, p. 103.
42 St Anselm, *Basic Writings: Proslogium, Monologium, Cur Deus Hom & The Fool by Gaunilon*, trans. S. N. Deane, La Salle, IL: Open Court, 1968.
43 Anselm, *Basic Writings*, pp. 279–80. See also Pannenberg, *Systematic Theology*, vol. 2, p. 404.
44 On this development, see Pannenberg, *Systematic Theology*, vol. 2, pp. 405–16.
45 Marshall, *Beyond Retribution*, pp. 60–9.
46 Gorringe, *God's Just Vengeance*, pp. 7–12.
47 Gorringe, *God's Just Vengeance*, p. 11.

48 Gorringe, *God's Just Vengeance*, p. 81.

49 Quoted in Nathaniel Micklem, *The Doctrine of Our Redemption*, London: Eyre & Spottiswoode, 1948, p. 101.

50 Hans Küng, *On Being a Christian*, London: Collins, 1977, p. 424.

51 Shailer Mathews, *The Atonement and the Social Process*, New York: Macmillan, 1930, p. 174.

52 Holness, 'Christology from Within'.

53 John W. de Gruchy, 'From Political to Public Theologies: The Role of Theology in Public Life in South Africa', Opening Address at Colloquium in Honour of Duncan Forrester, Edinburgh, October 2001.

54 Albrecht Ritschl, *The Christian Doctrine of Justification and Reconciliation*, trans. H. R. Mackintosh and A. B. Macaulay, second edn, Edinburgh: T&T Clark, 1902. This is the only volume translated into English.

55 Ritschl, *The Christian Doctrine of Justification and Reconciliation*, p. 319.

56 Ritschl, *The Christian Doctrine of Justification and Reconciliation*, p. 357.

57 Walter Rauschenbusch, *A Theology for the Social Gospel*, Nashville: Abingdon Press, 1917.

58 See James Richmond, *Ritschl: A Reappraisal*, London: Collins, 1978, pp. 131–2. On the relationship between Barth and Ritschl, and especially on the continuities between them, see Richmond, *Ritschl*, pp. 278–80. See Barth's criticism of Ritschl's understanding of sin, and his failure to appreciate fully the significance of God's holiness Barth, *Church Dogmatics*, IV/1, pp. 381–2, 490. Albrecht Ritschl was one of the mentors of Reinhold Seeberg, Bonhoeffer's *Doktorvater*, and his influence can been seen in Bonhoeffer's theology as well. See Eberhard Bethge, *Dietrich Bonhoeffer: A Biography*, Minneapolis: Fortress Press, 2000, pp. 70, 86, 88, 910.

59 Forsyth, *The Work of Christ*, p. 66.

60 Forsyth, *The Work of Christ*, p. 54.

61 Forsyth, *The Work of Christ*, pp. 56–7.

62 Forsyth, *The Work of Christ*, pp. 82, 87–90.

63 Forsyth, *The Work of Christ*, pp. 76–7.

64 Barth, *Church Dogmatics*, IV/1, p. 317.

65 See John Webster, *Karl Barth*, London: Continuum, 2000, pp. 147–60.

66 Karl Barth, *Ethics*, Edinburgh: T&T Clark, 1981, p. 445.

67 See Barth's article on 'Church and State' (also referred to as 'Justification and Justice') in Karl Barth, *Community, State, and Church: Three Essays*, trans. Will Herberg, Garden City, NY: Doubleday Anchor, 1960.

68 See particularly Barth's exposition in *Church Dogmatics*, IV/1, pp. 157–210.

69 Timothy Gorringe, *Karl Barth: Against Hegemony*, Oxford: Oxford University Press, 1999.

70 Hendrikus Berkhof, *Christian Faith: An Introduction to the Study of Faith*, Grand Rapids: Eerdmans, 1979, p. 302.

71 On the significance of the work of René Girard for theology in this regard, see Pannenberg, *Systematic Theology*, vol. 2, p. 422.

72 Dietrich Bonhoeffer, *Sanctorum Communio: A Theological Study of the Sociology of the Church*, Dietrich Bonhoeffer Works, vol. 1, Minneapolis: Fortress Press, 1998, p. 147.

73 Bonhoeffer, *Sanctorum Communio*, p. 155.

74 Dietrich Bonhoeffer, *Ethics*, New York: Macmillan, 1965, p. 297.

75 Bonhoeffer, *Ethics*, p. 197.

76 Bonhoeffer, *Ethics*, p. 206.

77 Bonhoeffer, *Ethics*, p. 232.

78 Bonhoeffer, *Ethics*, p. 195.

79 Bonhoeffer, *Ethics*, p. 204.

80 Bonhoeffer, *Ethics*, p.70.

81 Bonhoeffer, *Ethics*, pp. 212–13.

82 Bonhoeffer, *Ethics*, p. 26.

83 Bonhoeffer, *Ethics*, p. 86.

84 Bonhoeffer, *Ethics*, p. 220.

85 Lochman, *Reconciliation and Liberation*.

86 Lochman, *Reconciliation and Liberation*, pp. 106–7.

87 On the difference between 'concrete' and 'abstract utopia', see Karl Mannheim, *Ideology and Utopia: An Introduction to the Sociology of Knowledge*, New York: Harcourt, Brace & World, 1936, pp. 192–9.

88 Lochman, *Reconciliation and Liberation*, p. 111.

89 Emilio Castro, 'Reconciliation', in Michael Kinnamon and Brian E. Cope, (eds.), *The Ecumenical Movement: An Anthology of Key Texts and Voices*, Geneva: World Council of Churches, 1997, p. 65.

90 Castro, 'Reconciliation', p. 66.

91 Anne Carr, *Transforming Grace: Christian Tradition and Women's Experience*, San Francisco: Harper & Row, 1988, p. 187.

92 Joseph Liechty and Cecelia Clegg, *Moving Beyond Sectarianism: Religion, Conflict and Reconciliation in Northern Ireland*, Dublin: Columba Press, 2001, p. 292.

Chapter 3

1 For an account of this achievement, see Roberto Morozzo della Rocca, *Vom Krieg Zum Frieden. Mosambik: Geschichte einer Ungewöhnlichen Vermittlung*, Hamburg: Verlag Dienste in Übersee, 1997; Andrea Bartoli, 'Forgiveness and Reconciliation in the Mozambique Peace Process', in Raymond G. Helmick SJ and Rodney L. Petersen, (eds.),

Forgiveness and Reconciliation: Religion, Public Policy, and Conflict Transformation, Philadelphia: Templeton Foundation Press, 2001, pp. 351–84.

2 The Community has also played an important role in many other conflict situations (Albania, Burundi, Kosovo, Guatemala, Algeria and the Democratic Republic of the Congo) and is presently involved in Christian–Muslim relations following a Consultation held by the Community at which both Christian and Muslim representatives from South Africa were present.

3 See the Corrymeela webpage: www.corrymeela.org

4 See the journal *Reconcile: Peace and Reconciliation in Practice* for details of the work of the International Centre for Reconciliation and the Community of the Cross of Nails at Coventry Cathedral.

5 See J. L. Gonzalez Balado, *The Story of Taizé*, London: Mowbray, 1980; and Kathryn Spink, *The Life and Vision of Brother Roger of Taizé*, London: SPCK, 1986.

6 *The Rule of Taizé*, Taizé: Les Presses de Taizé, 1961.

7 Spink, *Brother Roger*, p. 134.

8 Balado, *The Story of Taizé*, p. 28.

9 In comparison with the total number of parishes and congregations in South Africa, to use my own country as an example, those that provide evidence for such a claim are certainly not in the majority and there are some appalling examples to the contrary. But from my own experience they are by no means few and some of them have been quite remarkable in what they have achieved against enormous odds. See, for example, Rob Robertson, *St Antony's Activists: Turning Dreams into Deeds*, Cape Town: R. J. D. Robertson, 1999. Examples of what the Churches are now doing about reconciliation can also be gleaned, inter alia, from the ecumenical newspaper *Inselelo* published by the Diakonia Council of Churches in Durban, and the ecumenical magazine *Challenge* (www.challengemag.co.za). On the role of the Churches in the transition to democracy see John W. de Gruchy, *Christianity and Democracy: A Theology for a Just World Order*, Cambridge: Cambridge University Press, 1996, pp. 205–24.

10 Roger Schutz, *This Day Belongs to God*, London: Faith Press, 1960, p. 15.

11 Joseph Liechty and Cecelia Clegg, *Moving Beyond Sectarianism: Religion, Conflict and Reconciliation in Northern Ireland*, Dublin: Columba Press, 2001, pp. 197–204

12 Dietrich Bonhoeffer, *Sanctorum Communio: A Theological Study of the Sociology of the Church*, Dietrich Bonhoeffer Works, vol. 1, Minneapolis: Fortress Press, 1998, p. 127.

13 Chris Loff, 'The History of a Heresy', in John W. de Gruchy and Charles Villa-Vicencio, (eds.), *Apartheid Is a Heresy*, Grand Rapids: Eerdmans, 1983, pp. 10–23.

14 C. F. Beyers Naudé, *My Decision*, Farewell Sermon, 3 November, Johannesburg: Christian Institute, 1963.

15 James Gustafson, *Treasure in Earthen Vessels: The Church as Human Community*, Chicago: University of Chicago Press, 1976, p. 13.

16 Gustafson, *Treasure in Earthen Vessels*, p. 13.

17 Desmond Tutu, *No Future Without Forgiveness*, London: Rider, 1999, p. 213.

18 See especially Clifford Green, *Bonhoeffer: Theology of Sociality*, Grand Rapids: Eerdmans, 1999.

19 Bonhoeffer, *Sanctorum Communio*, pp. 189–91.

20 See Bonhoeffer, *Sanctorum Communio*, p. 86.

21 Bonhoeffer, *Sanctorum Communio*, p. 80.

22 Bonhoeffer, *Sanctorum Communio*, p. 80.

23 Bonhoeffer, *Sanctorum Communio*, p. 117.

24 Bonhoeffer, *Sanctorum Communio*, p. 121.

25 Bonhoeffer, *Sanctorum Communio*, p. 153.

26 Bonhoeffer, *Sanctorum Communio*, pp. 146–8.

27 Bonhoeffer, *Sanctorum Communio*, p. 155 n. 88.

28 Bonhoeffer, *Sanctorum Communio*, p. 157.

29 Bonhoeffer, *Sanctorum Communio*, p. 178.

30 Bonhoeffer, *Sanctorum Communio*, p. 184.

31 Bonhoeffer, *Sanctorum Communio*, p. 191.

32 See Bonhoeffer, *Sanctorum Communio*, p. 198.

33 cf. Von Soosten, Editor's Afterword to the German edition, published in the ET, Bonhoeffer, *Sanctorum Communio*, p. 303.

34 Dietrich Bonhoeffer, *Letters 1933–1935*, Dietrich Bonhoeffer Werke, vol. 13, München: Chr. Kaiser Verlag, 1994, p. 399.

35 Bonhoeffer, *Sanctorum Communio*, p. 173.

36 Kadar Asmal, Louise Asmal and Ronald Suresh Roberts, *Reconciliation Through Truth*, Cape Town: David Philip, 1996, p. 49.

37 See, for example, Mark Hay, *Ukubuyisana: Reconciliation in South Africa*, Pietermaritzburg: Cluster Publications, 1998.

38 John Howard Yoder, 'Sacrament as Social Process: Christ the Transformer of Culture', *Theology Today* 48 no. 1 (April 1991), pp. 33, 41.

39 Dietrich Bonhoeffer, *Discipleship*, Dietrich Bonhoeffer Works, vol. 4, Minneapolis: Fortress Press, p. 233.

40 Loff, 'The History of a Heresy'.

41 Dietrich Bonhoeffer, *Life Together; Prayerbook of the Bible*, Dietrich Bonhoeffer Works, vol. 5, Minneapolis: Fortress Press, 1996, p. 110.

42 See the critique in Wolfhart Pannenberg, *Christian Spirituality*, Philadelphia: Westminster Press, 1983, pp. 16–20.

43 Psalms 6, 32, 38, 51, 102, 130, 143.

44 John T. McNeill, *A History of the Cure of Souls*, New York: Harper, 1951, pp. 98–99.

45 'Reconciliation', in Mary Collins, Joseph A. Komonchak and Dermot A. Lane, (eds.), *The New Dictionary of Theology*, Dublin: Gill & Macmillan, 1987, p. 830.

46 See, for example, the prohibitions and purification rules in the book of Leviticus. There is a useful summary of some of the issues dealt with here in Harmon L. Smith, *Where Two or Three Are Gathered: Liturgy and the Moral Life*, Cleveland, OH: Pilgrim Press, 1995, pp. 81–89.

47 Richard Kieckhefer, 'Major Currents in Late Medieval Devotion, in Jill Raitt, (ed.), *Christian Spirituality*, vol. 2, *High Middle Ages and Reformation*, New York: Crossroad, 1989, pp. 102–5.

48 See Karl Rahner, 'Forgotten Truths Concerning Penance', in *Theological Investigations Volume II*, London: Darton, Longman & Todd, 1963, pp. 153–62.

49 Max Thurian, *Confession*, London: SCM Press, 1958, pp. 26–29.

50 Thurian, *Confession*, p. 27.

51 On the importance of mutual confession of sins within the life of the church community, see Bonhoeffer, *Life Together*, pp. 108–18.

52 See Thurian, *Confession*. The United Church of Christ in the USA has included in its Book of Worship both an Order for Reconciliation of a Penitent Person, and an Order for Corporate Reconciliation. See *Book of Worship*, New York: United Church of Christ, 1986.

53 C. G. Jung, *Modern Man in Search of a Soul*, New York: Harcourt, Brace, 1933, p. 227.

54 Victor White, *God and the Unconscious: An Encounter between Psychology and Religion*, London: Collins Fontana, 1967, p. 188.

55 White, *God and the Unconscious*, pp. 181–2.

56 O. Hobart Mowrer, *The Crisis in Psychiatry and Religion*, Princeton, NJ: Van Nostrand, 1961.

57 Mowrer, *The Crisis in Psychiatry and Religion*, p. 190.

58 Rahner, 'Forgotten Truths Concerning Penance', p. 160.

59 Antjie Krog, *Country of My Skull*, Johannesburg: Random House, 1998.

60 Antonio Moreno, *Jung, Gods and Modern Man*, London: Sheldon Press, 1974, p. 44.

61 See Smith, *Where Two or Three Are Gathered*, pp. 90–1.

62 Dietrich Bonhoeffer, *Ethics*, New York: Macmillan, 1965, p. 292.

63 'Reconciliation', in Collins et al., *The New Dictionary of Theology*, pp. 830–6.

64 Michael Sievernich, 'Social Sin and Its Acknowledgment', in Mary Collins and David Power, (eds.), *The Fate of Confession, Concilium* 190, Edinburgh: T&T Clark, 1987, pp. 52–63.

65 'Reconciliation', *The New Dictionary of Theology*, p. 836.
66 See the *Rite of Reconciliation* published by the South African Council of Churches in 1996 to be used in relation to the work of the Truth and Reconciliation Commission.
67 Bonhoeffer, *Sanctorum Communio*, p. 119.
68 J. Beckmann, (ed.), 'Stuttgart Confession', Guttersloh: C. Bertelsmann Verlag, 1950, pp. 26–7.
69 Franklin Littell, 'From Barmen (1934) to Stuttgart (1945): The Path of the Confessing Church in Germany', *Journal of Church and State* 3 (May 1961), p. 49.
70 Willem Adolf Visser 't Hooft, *Memoirs*, London: SCM Press, 1973, p. 193.
71 Visser 't Hooft, *Memoirs*, p. 193.
72 See the discussion in Bonhoeffer, *Sanctorum Communio*, pp. 120–1.
73 Bonhoeffer, *Ethics*, p. 111.
74 Bonhoeffer, *Ethics*, p. 113.
75 See James C. Cochrane, John W. de Gruchy and Steve Martin, (eds.), *Facing the Truth: South African Faith Communities and the Truth and Reconciliation Commission*, Cape Town: David Philip, 1999; for a personal account by one of the TRC Commissioners and a NGK theologian, see Piet Meiring, *Chronicle of the Truth Commission*, Vanderbijpark, RSA: Carpe Diem, 1999, pp. 265–85.

Chapter 4

1 On 11 September 2001 two American airliners were hijacked and flown into the twin towers of the World Trade Center in New York. This resulted in the destruction of the skyscrapers and the death of over 3,000 people. A further airliner was likewise hijacked and flown into the Pentagon in Washington DC, with the further loss of several hundred lives. These terrorist attacks on the symbols of economic and military power in the United States were undertaken by Al Qaeda, a militant Islamic organization. There has been widespread comment and debate on these events, and the 'War on Terrorism' subsequently initiated by President George W. Bush of the United States. Amongst the more perceptive theological commentaries is Rowan Williams, *Writing in the Dust: After September 11th*, Grand Rapids: Eerdmans, 2002.
2 For a brief statement on resurgent Islam, see J. Paul Rajashekar, '"Islamic Fundamentalism": Reviewing a Stereotype', *The Ecumenical Review* 41 no. 1 (January 1989), pp. 64–72. Abdulkadar Tayob usefully distinguishes between revivalism, reformism and Islamism within the contemporary Islamic resurgence. Abdulkadar Tayob, *Islamic Resurgence in South Africa: The Muslim Youth Movement*, Cape Town: University of Cape Town Press, 1995, pp. 16–37.

3 David Westerlund and Ingvar Svanberg, (eds.), *Islam Outside the Arab World*, Richmond, Surrey: Curzon Press, 1999.

4 Faried Esack, *Qur'an, Liberation and Pluralism: Towards an Islamic Perspective of Inter-Religious Solidarity against Oppression*, Oxford: Oneworld Publications, 1997, pp. 224–8.

5 For comment on PAGAD (People against gangsterism and drugs) in relation to the Muslim community in South Africa, see Abdulkadar Tayob, 'Southern Africa', in *Islam Outside the Arab World*, pp. 118–19.

6 Hans Küng and Jürgen Moltmann, (eds.), *Islam: A Challenge for Christianity, Concilium* 1994/3, London: SCM Press, 1994, pp. vii–viii.

7 Karl-Josef Kuschel, *Abraham: Sign of Hope for Jews, Christians, and Muslims*, New York: Continuum, 1995, p. 253.

8 Charlotte Klein, *Anti-Judaism in Christian Theology*, London: SPCK, 1978; James H. Charlesworth, (ed.), *Jews and Christians: Exploring the Past, Present, and Future*, New York: Crossroad.

9 Following the seventh-century theologian, John of Damascus.

10 Hans Küng, *Christianity and the World Religions*, London: Collins, 1987, pp. 123–6.

11 Eqbal Ahmad, 'Islam and Politics', in Byron Haines, Yvonne Yazbeck Haddad and Ellison Findlay, (eds.), *The Islamic Impact*, Syracuse, NY: Syracuse University Press, 1984, p. 14. For discussion of what is often regarded as the high point of the relationship between the three faiths, see Mark R. Cohen, *Under Crescent and Cross: The Jews in the Middle Ages*, Princeton: Princeton University Press, 1994.

12 Bernard Lewis, *The Jews of Islam*, Princeton: Princeton University Press, 1984, p. 191.

13 Ataullah Siddiqui, *Christian–Muslim Dialogue in the Twentieth Century*, London: Macmillan, 1997, p. 199.

14 Ahmad, 'Islam and Politics', pp. 8–9.

15 Quoted in David A. Kerr, 'Islamic Da 'Wa and Christian Mission: Towards a Comparative Analysis', *International Review of Mission* 89 no. 353 (April 2000), p. 168.

16 See the report on Christian–Muslim dialogue sponsored by the World Council of Churches in *Issues in Christian–Muslim Relations: Ecumenical Considerations*, Geneva: World Council of Churches, nd, p. 3.

17 See Gilles Kepel, *The Revenge of God: The Resurgence of Islam, Christianity and Judaism in the Modern World*, Cambridge: Polity Press, 1994, p. 13.

18 Ahmad, 'Islam and Politics', p. 24.

19 See Kuschel, *Abraham*, p. 177.

20 Ahmad, 'Islam and Politics', p. 14.

21 Akbar S. Ahmed, *Postmodernism and Islam: Predicament and Promise*, London: Routledge, 1992.

22 Ahmed, *Postmodernism and Islam*, p. 48.

23 Ahmed, *Postmodernism and Islam*, p. 36.

24 Ahmad, 'Islam and Politics', p. 18.

25 See Esack, *Qur'an, Liberation and Pluralism*, pp. 106–7.

26 Abdulaziz Sachedina, 'Islamic Theology of Christian–Muslim Relations', *Journal for Islamic Studies* 18 (1998), pp. 21–2.

27 Ahmed, *Postmodernism and Islam*, p. 48.

28 Ahmed, *Postmodernism and Islam*, p. 48.

29 Kuschel, *Abraham*, p. 228.

30 Siddiqui, *Christian–Muslim Dialogue in the Twentieth Century*, p. 198.

31 Kerr, 'Islamic Da 'Wa and Christian Mission', p.168.

32 Kuschel, *Abraham*, p. 213.

33 For brief introductions to Christianity in South Africa, see John W. de Gruchy, 'Settler Christianity', in Martin Prozesky and John W. de Gruchy, (eds.), *Living Faiths in South Africa* Cape Town: David Philip, 1995, pp. 28–44; Charles Villa-Vicencio, 'Mission Christianity', in *Living Faiths in South Africa*, pp. 45–71; and John W. de Gruchy, 'Christianity in Twentieth Century South Africa', in *Living Faiths in South Africa*, pp. 83–115.

34 For a brief history of Judaism in South Africa, see Jocelyn Hellig, 'The Jewish Community in South Africa', in Prozesky and de Gruchy, *Living Faiths in South Africa*, pp. 155–76.

35 Milton Shain, *The Roots of Antisemitism in South Africa*, Johannesburg: Witwatersrand University Press, 1994; Patrick Furlong, *Between Crown and Swastika: The Impact of the Radical Right on the Afrikaner Nationalist Movement in the Fascist Era*, Johannesburg: Witwatersrand University Press, 1991, pp. 46–69.

36 Claudia Braude in the discussion that followed the symposium on The Truth Commission, *Jewish Affairs* (Spring 1996), p. 36.

37 Under the auspices of Gesher, an organization formed to promote reconciliation in post-apartheid South Africa.

38 Geoff Sifrin, 'The Truth Commission: Jewish Perspectives on Justice and Forgiveness in South Africa: Introducing the Issues', *Jewish Affairs* (Spring 1996), p. 30.

39 Franz Auerbach, 'The Truth Commission: Jewish Perspectives on Justice and Forgiveness in South Africa: In Support of the Truth Commission', *Jewish Affairs* (Spring 1996), p. 32.

40 Auerbach, 'The Truth Commission: In Support of the Truth Commission', p. 32.

41 See Samuel Schimmel, 'Joseph and his brothers: A Paradigm for Repentance', *Judaism: Quarterly Journal of Jewish Life and Thought* 37 no. 1 (Winter 1998), pp. 60–5.

42 Steven Friedman, 'The Truth Commission: Jewish Perspectives on Justice and Forgiveness in South Africa: Some Questions', *Jewish Affairs* (Spring 1996), p. 33.

43 Friedman, 'The Truth Commission: Some Questions', p. 34.

44 Esack, *Qur'an, Liberation and Pluralism*, p. 112.

45 For a brief history of Islam in South Africa, see Ebrahim Moosa, 'Islam in South Africa', in *Living Faiths in South Africa*, ed. Martin Prozesky and John W. de Gruchy, Cape Town: David Philip, 1995.

46 Moosa, 'Islam in South Africa', p. 130.

47 Jamiatul Ulama Transvaal, 'Submission to the TRC', *Journal for Islamic Studies* 17 (1997), p. 95.

48 Those in Natal and Transvaal were influenced by Sufism and by jurist-theologians, the *'ulama*. See Moosa, 'Islam in South Africa', p. 139.

49 See Tayob, *Islamic Resurgence in South Africa*, pp. 161–83.

50 Jamiatul Ulama Transvaal, 'Submission to the TRC', p. 95; Muslim Judicial Council, 'Submission to the TRC', *Journal for Islamic Studies* 17 (1997), pp. 101–2.

51 Muslim Youth Movement, 'Submission to the TRC', *Journal for Islamic Studies* 17 (1997), p. 106.

52 Esack, *Qur'an, Liberation and Pluralism*, pp. 109–10.

53 Muslim Judicial Council, 'Submission to the TRC', pp. 101–2.

54 Muslim Judicial Council, 'Submission to the TRC', pp. 103–4.

55 Muslim Youth Movement, 'Submission to the TRC', p. 108.

56 Muslim Youth Movement, 'Submission to the TRC', p. 108.

57 See Tayob, *Islamic Resurgence in South Africa*.

58 Tayob, *Islamic Resurgence in South Africa*, pp. 152–3; Esack, *Qur'an, Liberation and Pluralism*, pp. 32–4.

59 Esack, *Qur'an, Liberation and Pluralism*, pp. 109–10.

60 For an overview, see Muhammed Haron, 'The Truth and Reconciliation Commission and the Muslim Community in South Africa', *Journal for Islamic Studies* 17 (1997), pp. 92–3.

61 Muslim Judicial Council, 'Submission to the TRC', p. 104.

62 Jamiatul Ulama Transvaal, 'Submission to the TRC', p. 99.

63 See the account in Esack, *Qur'an, Liberation and Pluralism*, pp. 238–9.

64 See Esack, *Qur'an, Liberation and Pluralism*, p. 252, n. 11.

65 See Peter Ochs in David F. Ford, (ed.), *The Modern Theologians: An Introduction to Christian Theology in the Twentieth Century*, Blackwell: Oxford, 1997, pp. 607–21.

66 W. H. T. Gairdner, *Edinburgh 1910: An Account and Interpretation of the World Missionary Conference*, Edinburgh: Oliphant, Anderson & Ferrier, 1910, pp. 71–2.

67 Gairdner, *Edinburgh 1910*, p. 75.

68 For an overview of the WCC initiatives, see 'Meeting in Faith', in *Meeting in Faith*, Twenty Years of Christian–Muslim Conversations Sponsored by the World Council of Churches, ed. Stuart Brown, Geneva: World Council of Churches, 1989; *Guidelines on Dialogue with People of Living Faiths and Ideologies*, Geneva: World Council of Churches, 1993.

69 Siddiqui, *Christian–Muslim Dialogue in the Twentieth Century*, pp. 163–9.

70 Siddiqui, *Christian–Muslim Dialogue in the Twentieth Century*, p. 194.

71 San Antonio Statement (1989), para. 28, quoted in *Issues in Christian–Muslim Relations*, World Conference on Mission and Evangelism, San Antonio, Geneva: World Council of Churches, 1989, p. 5.

72 Kuschel, *Abraham*, p. 225.

73 See, for example, the work of the Children of Abraham Institute at the University of Virginia, USA and, in particular, the work of Dr Peter Ochs.

74 Kuschel, *Abraham*, p. 203.

75 Kuschel, *Abraham*, pp. 204–24.

76 Kenneth Cragg, *Muhammed and the Christian*, London: Darton, Longman & Todd, 1984, p. 124.

77 Seyyed Hossein Nasr, *Ideals and Realities of Islam*, San Francisco: HarperCollins, 1986, p. 35.

78 Kuschel, *Abraham*, p. 197.

79 William Montgomery Watt, *Muslim–Christian Encounters: Perceptions and Misperceptions*, London: Routledge, 1991, p. 114.

80 Sachedina, 'Islamic Theology of Christian–Muslim Relations', p. 5.

81 Sachedina, 'Islamic Theology of Christian–Muslim Relations', p. 6.

82 Sachedina, 'Islamic Theology of Christian–Muslim Relations', p. 12.

83 There is a dearth of material that deals explicitly with reconciliation in Islam. For what follows I am indebted to lectures by Fr Chr. Troll who, when they were given in 1984, was Professor of Islamology at the Institute of Religious Studies in New Delhi, India. The lectures were published in Chr. Troll, *Encounter: Documents for Muslim–Christian Understanding, by the Pontifical Institute for the Study of Arabic and Islam, Rome* 103–104 (March 1984).

84 Samuel Schimmel, 'Judaism and Forgiveness', unpublished ms. p. 15.

85 Josef van Ess, in Küng, *Christianity and the World Religions*, p. 98.

86 Küng, *Christianity and the World Religions*, p. 111.

87 Quoted in Watt, *Muslim–Christian Encounters*, p. 127, from an article entitled 'Towards an Islamic Christology' published in *The Muslim World* 66 (1976), p. 187.

88 Karl Barth, *Church Dogmatics: The Doctrine of Reconciliation*, Church Dogmatics, vol. IV/1, Edinburgh: T&T Clark, 1961, pp.183–4.

89 See the discussion in Küng, *Christianity and the World Religions*, pp. 112–21.

90 van Ess, in Küng, *Christianity and the World Religions*, p. 107.

91 René Girard, *Things Hidden Since the Foundation of the World*, Stanford, CA: Stanford University Press, 1987, p. 429.

92 Nasr, *Ideals and Realities of Islam*, pp. 103–109.

93 Nasr, *Ideals and Realities of Islam*, p. 93.

94 Ahmad, 'Islam and Politics', p. 18.

95 Ahmad, 'Islam and Politics', p. 19.

96 For a discussion of the issues, see Khursid Ahmad, 'Islam and Democracy: Some Conceptual and Contemporary Dimensions', *Muslim World* 90 nos. 1–2 (Spring 2000), pp. 1–21.

97 Ahmad, 'Islam and Democracy', p. 17.

98 On the issues facing Muslims in countries where they are in a minority, see Westerlund et al., *Islam Outside the Arab World*.

99 For texts that express a liberal interpretation of Islam, see Charles Kurzman, (ed.), *Liberal Islam: A Sourcebook*, Oxford: Oxford University Press, 1998.

100 See the discussion in John W. de Gruchy, *Christianity and Democracy: A Theology for a Just World Order*, Cambridge: Cambridge University Press, 1995.

101 Kuschel, *Abraham*, p. 213.

102 Sachedina, 'Islamic Theology of Christian–Muslim Relations', p. 14.

103 Abdulaziz Sachedina, *The Islamic Roots of Democratic Pluralism*, New York: Oxford University Press, 2000.

104 Ahmad, 'Islam and Politics', p. 14.

105 Sachedina, 'Islamic Theology of Christian–Muslim Relations'.

106 Esack, *Qur'an, Liberation and Pluralism*, pp. 82–6.

107 Esack, *Qur'an, Liberation and Pluralism*, pp. 239–40.

108 Quote in Esack, *Qur'an, Liberation and Pluralism*, p. 240.

109 See Esack, *Qur'an, Liberation and Pluralism*, p. 241.

110 See Esack, *Qur'an, Liberation and Pluralism*, p. 246.

111 Dietrich Bonhoeffer, *Ethics*, New York: Macmillan, 1965, p. 99.

112 Lamin Sanneh, 'Faith and the Secular State', *New York Times*, 23 September 2001.

113 Kuschel, *Abraham*, p. 240.

114 Muslim scholars, such as the Indian Asghar Ali Engineer and the South African Faried Esack, would later produce accounts of Islam from a liberation perspective that paralleled Christian liberation theology. See Asghar Ali Engineer, *Islam and Liberation Theology*, New Delhi: Sterling Publishers, 1990.

115 Quoted in Diane D'Souza, 'Evangelism, Dialogue, Reconciliation: A Case Study of the Growth and Transformation of the Henry Martyn Institute', *Muslim World* 91 nos. 1–2 (Spring 2001), pp. 155–86. I am indebted to this article for my information on the Institute.

116 For a Muslim perspective, see Sachedina, 'Islamic Theology of Christian–Muslim Relations', p. 13.

117 Watt, *Muslim–Christian Encounters*, p. 151, quoting Mahmoud Ayoub, *Muslim World* 79 (1989) (Sura 21.105; Matt. 5.5).

Chapter 5

1 Priscilla B. Hayner, *Unspeakable Truths: Confronting State Terror and Atrocity*, New York: Routledge, 2001, p. 7.

2 A quotation from the *Truth and Reconciliation Commission of South Africa Report*, vol. 5, chap. 9, section 423, in Hayner, *Unspeakable Truths*, p. 157.

3 See Andries Odendaal, 'For All Its Flaws: The TRC as a Peacebuilding Tool', *Track Two: Constructive Approaches to Community and Political Conflict* 6 nos. 3 and 4 (December 1997), pp. 4–10.

4 See Sue Williamson, *Resistance Art in South Africa*, Cape Town: David Philip, 1989; Sue Williamson and Ashraf Jamal, *Art in South Africa: The Future Present*, Cape Town: David Philip, 1996. For a discussion of the role of art in public life with special reference to South Africa, see John W. de Gruchy, *Christianity, Art and Transformtion: Theological Aesthetics in the Struggle for Justice*, Cambridge: Cambridge University Press, 2001, pp. 191–202.

5 Sue Williamson, 'Artist's Statement' in the brochure for 'Truth Games': a series of interactive pieces around the hearings of the Truth and Reconciliation Commission of South Africa.

6 *Secrets and Lies* (1996). A review by Damian Cannon. Copyright © Movie Reviews UK 1997.

7 Martin Buber, *Between Man and Man*, London: Collins, 1961, p. 40.

8 See David Ford's exposition of Paul Ricoeur's insights on these issues, in David F. Ford, *Self and Salvation: Being Transformed*, Cambridge: Cambridge University Press, 1999, pp. 82–5.

9 Frederick van Zyl Slabbert, 'Truth Without Reconciliation, Reconciliation Without Truth', in Wilmot James and Linda van de Vijver, (eds.), *After the TRC: Reflections on Truth and Reconciliation in South Africa*, Cape Town: David Philip, 2000, p. 70.

10 See the discussion in Alex Boraine, *A Country Unmasked: Inside South Africa's Truth and Reconciliation Commission*, New York: Oxford University Press, 2000, pp. 288–92.

11 According to article 3 of its foundational Act.

12 Mahmood Mamdani, 'A Diminished Truth', in *After the TRC*, p. 59.

13 Mamdani, 'A Diminished Truth', p. 60.

14 For the use of this term see Victoria Barnett, *Bystanders: Conscience and Complicity During the Holocaust*, Westport, CN: Greenwood Press, 1999.

15 Barnett, *Bystanders*, p. 12, quoting Michael Marrus, *The Holocaust in History*, Hanover, NH: University Press of New England, 1987, 4p. 157.

16 Fiona C. Ross, 'Women and the Politics of Identity: Voices in the South African Truth and Reconciliation Commission', unpublished paper, ASA

Conference on 'Rights, Claims and Entitlements', University of Sussex, 2001.

17 Christina Stuckey quoted in Ross, 'Women and the Politics of Identity', p. 15.

18 Ross quoting Julie Taylor, 'Body Memories: Aide Memoires and Collective Amnesia in the Wake of the Argentine Terror', in Michael Ryan and Every Gordon, (eds.), *Body Politics: Disease, Desire and Family*, Boulder, CO: Westview Press, 1994, p. 201.

19 See Trudy de Ridder, 'The Trauma of Testifying', *Track Two* 6 nos. 3 and 4 (December 1997), pp. 30–3.

20 Hayner, *Unspeakable Truths*, pp. 141–2.

21 Hayner, *Unspeakable Truths*, p. 98.

22 Slabbert, 'Truth Without Reconciliation, Reconciliation Without Truth', p. 69.

23 Mark J. Kaplan, *Where Truth Lies*, African Renaissance, 1999. See also the account in Desmond Tutu, *No Future Without Forgiveness*, London: Rider, 1999, p. 188.

24 Janet Cherry, 'Historical Truth: Something to Fight for', in Charles Villa-Vicencio and Wilhelm Verwoerd, (eds.), *Looking Back Reaching Forward*, Cape Town: University of Cape Town Press, 2000, p. 137.

25 James C. Cochrane, John W. de Gruchy and Steve Martin, (eds.), *Facing the Truth: South African Faith Communities and the Truth and Reconciliation Commission* Cape Town: David Philip, 1999, p. 7.

26 Cherry, 'Historical Truth', p. 136.

27 Susan Howatch, *Sins of the Fathers*, London: Hamish Hamilton, 1980, p. 310.

28 Rowan Williams, 'The Suspicion of Suspicion: Wittgenstein and Bonhoeffer', in Richard H. Bell, (ed.), *The Grammar of the Heart*, San Francisco: Harper & Row, 1988, p. 44. See also the discussion in Gregory L. Jones, *Embodying Forgiveness: A Theological Analysis*, Grand Rapids: Eerdmans, 1995, p. 45.

29 Dietrich Bonhoeffer, *Ethics*, New York: Macmillan, 1965, pp. 363–72.

30 Bonhoeffer, *Ethics*, p. 367.

31 Miroslav Volf, *Exclusion and Embrace: A Theological Exploration of Identity, Otherness, and Reconciliation*, Nashville: Abingdon Press, 1996, p. 29.

32 Volf, *Exclusion and Embrace*, p. 29.

33 Slabbert, 'Truth Without Reconciliation, Reconciliation Without Truth', p. 71.

34 Jane Taylor, Dakawa Arts Centre, Grahamstown, July 1999.

35 Ginn Fourie briefly recounts her story in Ginn Fourie, 'The Psychology of Perpetrators of "Political" Violence in South Africa: A Personal Experience', *Ethnicity and Health* 5 no. 3/4 (2000), pp. 283–9.

36 Fourie, 'The Psychology of Perpetrators', p. 289.

37 Jones, *Embodying Forgiveness*, p. 244.

38 Christopher D. Marshall, *Beyond Retribution: A New Testament Vision for Justice, Crime, and Punishment*, Grand Rapids: Eerdmans, 2001, p. 80.

39 For use of this metaphor in relation to the Palestinian–Israeli problem, see Rosemary Radford Ruether and Herman J. Reuther, *The Wrath of Jonah: The Crisis of Religious Nationalism in the Israeli-Palestinian Conflict*, San Francisco: Harper & Row, 1989.

40 Dietrich Bonhoeffer, *Discipleship*, Dietrich Bonhoeffer Works, vol. 4, Minneapolis: Fortress Press, 2001, p. 132.

41 Bonhoeffer, *Discipleship*, p. 132.

42 Wayne T. Pitard, 'Vengeance', in *Anchor Bible Dictionary*, New York: Doubleday, 1997.

43 Willa Boesak, *God's Wrathful Children*, Grand Rapids: Eerdmans, 1995.

44 Boesak, *God's Wrathful Children*, p. 208.

45 Miroslav Volf, 'The Social Meaning of Reconciliation', *Interpretation* 54 no. 2 (April 2000), p. 167.

46 Volf, 'The Social Meaning of Reconciliation', p. 167.

47 Kadar Asmal, Louise Asmal and Ronald Suresh Roberts, *Reconciliation Through Truth*, Cape Town: David Philip, 1996, p. 49.

48 Ikomishoni Yenyaniso Noxolelwaniso: The Commission for Truth and Reconciliation.

49 Donald W. Shriver, *An Ethic for Enemies: Forgiveness in Politics*, New York: Oxford University Press, 1995, p. 32.

50 Boesak, *God's Wrathful Children*, p. 207.

51 Desmond Tutu, *The Rainbow People of God*, New York: Doubleday, 1994, p. 222.

52 Rowan Williams, *On Christian Theology*, Oxford: Blackwell, 2000, p. 272.

53 Paul Tillich, *Love, Power and Justice*, New York: Oxford University Press, 1960, p. 121.

54 Shriver, *Ethic for Enemies*, p. 7.

55 Shriver, *Ethic for Enemies*, p. 67.

56 Dietrich Bonhoeffer, *No Rusty Swords: Letters Lectures and Notes 1928–1936*, Collected Works of Dietrich Bonhoeffer, vol. 1, London: Collins, 1965, p. 165.

57 Bonhoeffer, *Ethics*, p. 118.

58 See the discussion in Brian Frost, *The Politics of Peace*, London: Darton, Longman & Todd, 1991.

59 Tutu, *No Future Without Forgiveness*, p. 127.

60 Jürgen Moltmann, 'Political Reconciliation', in Leroy S. Rouner, (ed.), *Religion, Politics, and Peace*, Notre Dame: University of Notre Dame Press, 1999, p. 28.

61 Moltmann, 'Political Reconciliation', p. 29.

62 Fourie, 'The Psychology of Perpetrators', p. 236.

63 See the discussion on this issue in Shriver, *Ethic for Enemies*, pp. 8–9.

64 Pumla Goboda-Madikizela, 'Legacies of Violence: An In-Depth Analysis of Two Case Studies Based on Interviews with Perpetrators of a "Necklace" Murder and with Eugene de Kock', PhD diss., University of Cape Town, 1999, p. 233. Pumla Goboda-Madikizela served on the Human Rights Violations Committee of the TRC. Her dissertation was based on research done on two case studies of gross violations of human rights. The first was the killing of Nosipho Zamela by young community marshals in Mlungisi township near Queenstown in the Eastern Cape in 1985 using the 'necklace' method. This was a gruesome form of murder, used by young 'comrades' in the black townships to punish informers and sell-outs, in which the victim was doused with petrol and then set on fire. The second was the atrocities perpetrated by Eugene de Kock, head of the notorious state security covert operations centre, Vlakplaas, for which he was sentenced in October 1996 to serve 212 years of life imprisonment.

65 Goboda-Madikizela, 'Legacies of Violence', p. 234.

66 Goboda-Madikizela, 'Legacies of Violence', p. 244.

67 Goboda-Madikizela, 'Legacies of Violence', p. 246.

68 Goboda-Madikizela, 'Legacies of Violence', p. 247.

69 Goboda-Madikizela, 'Legacies of Violence', p. 254.

70 For much of my discussion on the connection between forgiveness and remorse I am indebted to Goboda-Madikizela, 'Legacies of Violence', pp. 235–40.

71 Hayner, *Unspeakable Truths*, p. 41.

72 Hayner, *Unspeakable Truths*, p. 43.

73 Volf, *Exclusion and Embrace*, pp. 131–2.

74 Nelson Mandela, *Long Walk to Freedom: The Autobiography of Nelson Mandela*, Johannesburg: Macdonald Purnell, 1994, p. 559.

75 Emilio Castro, 'Reconciliation', in Michael Kinnamon and Brian E. Cope, (eds.), *The Ecumenical Movement: An Anthology of Key Texts and Voices*, Geneva: World Council of Churches, 1997, p. 67.

76 Timothy Gorringe, *God's Just Vengeance*, Cambridge: Cambridge University Press, 1996, p. 267.

77 Volf, *Exclusion and Embrace*, p. 85.

78 Vus: Mahlaselah 'Wisdom of Forgiveness', *Wisdom of Forgiveness* (BMG Africa CD). (Reproduced with permission).

Chapter 6

1 F. A. van Jaarsveld, 'A Historical Mirror of Blood River', in A. König and H. Keane, (eds.), *The Meaning of History*, Pretoria: University of South Africa, 1980, pp. 8–59.

2 F. A. van Jaarsveld, *The Afrikaner's Interpretation of South African History*, Cape Town: Simondium Publishers, 1964; T. Dunbar Moodie, *The Rise of Afrikanerdom: Power, Apartheid and the Afrikaner Civil Religion*, Berkeley: University of California Press, 1975.

3 See the discussion of this issue in Miroslav Volf, *Exclusion and Embrace: A Theological Exploration of Identity, Otherness, and Reconciliation*, Nashville: Abingdon Press, 1996, pp. 150–6.

4 I am indebted to Professor William Everett for his account of a visit to the sites in February 2002.

5 Duma Gqubule, 'What About the Black "Gatvol" Factor?' *Sunday Independent* (Johannesburg), 20 May 2001, p. 7.

6 William J. Everett, *Religion, Federalism and the Struggle for Public Life: Cases from Germany, India and America*, New York: Oxford University Press, 1997, p. 165.

7 For a discussion of the subject see John W. de Gruchy, *Christianity and Democracy: A Theology for a Just World Order*, Cambridge: Cambridge University Press, 1995, pp. 89–94.

8 Richard L. Greaves, *Theology and Revolution in the Scottish Reformation: Studies in the Thought of John Calvin*, Grand Rapids: Eerdmans, 1980, p. 124.

9 Volf, *Exclusion and Embrace*, pp. 154–5.

10 One research report states that only 37% of white South Africans approved of the TRC's work. James L. Gibson, and Helen Macdonald, *Truth –Yes, Reconciliation – Maybe: South Africans Judge the Truth and Reconciliation Process*, Research Report, Rondebosch, Cape Town: Institute for Justice and Reconciliation, 2001.

11 It is estimated that only about 40% of whites now acknowledge they were beneficiaries of apartheid's past. Gibson, *Truth – Yes, Reconciliation – Maybe*.

12 James Fowler, *Faithful Change: The Personal and Public Challenges of Postmodern Life*, Nashville: Abingdon Press, 1996.

13 Joseph Liechty and Cecelia Clegg, *Moving Beyond Sectarianism: Religion, Conflict and Reconciliation in Northern Ireland*, Dublin: Columba Press, 2001, p. 18.

14 Karl Menninger, *Whatever Became of Sin?*, New York: Hawthorne, 1973, p. 13.

15 Wolfhart Pannenberg, *Systematic Theology*, vol. 2, Grand Rapids: Eerdmans, 1994, p. 238.

16 Volf, *Exclusion and Embrace*, p. 81.

17 Volf, *Exclusion and Embrace*, p. 82.

18 LeRoy Aden, 'Distortions of a Sense of Guilt', *Pastoral Psychology* 15 no. 141 (February 1964). See also Dietrich Bonhoeffer, *Ethics*, New York: Macmillan, 1965, p. 113.

19 For a discussion on the compatibility of evolution and guilt from the

perspective of liberation theology, see Juan Luis Segundo, *Evolution and Guilt*, Dublin: Gill & Macmillan, 1980.

20 David E. Roberts, *Psychotherapy and a Christian View of Man*, New York: Charles Scribner's Sons, 1950, p. 108.

21 Karl Jaspers, *Die Schuldfrage: Zur Politischen Haftung Deutschland*, Heidelberg: Verlagen Lambert Schneider, 1946. ET Karl Jaspers, *The Question of German Guilt*, trans. E. B. Ashton, New York: Dial Press, 1947. For a detailed discussion of Jasper's book and its contemporary relevance see John W. de Gruchy, 'Guilt, Amnesty and National Reconstruction: Karl Jaspers' "Die Schuldfrage" and the South African Debate', *Journal of Theology for Southern Africa* 83 (June 1993), pp. 3–13.

22 Jaspers was an early victim of Nazi power. In 1933, at the age of fifty, he was prevented from exercising any of his administrative duties as a professor of philosophy at the University of Heidelberg. In 1937 he was denied the right to teach, and in April 1945, he and his Jewish wife Gertrud Mayer were scheduled for deportation to a concentration camp and extermination. Fortunately the Allied forces reached Heidelberg in time to prevent this tragedy. But its possibility demonstrates the extent to which Jaspers was at the receiving end of Nazi criminality; it also sets Jaspers apart from many other German philosophers and intellectuals of the time who were bewitched by National Socialism.

23 Charles Wallraff, *Karl Jaspers: An Introduction to His Philosophy*, Princeton: Princeton University Press, 1970, pp. 141–2.

24 Karl Jaspers, *The Way to Wisdom*, New Haven: Yale University Press, 1954, p. 20, quoted in Wallraff, *Karl Jaspers*, p. 142.

25 Jaspers, *The Question of German Guilt*, p. 100.

26 Paul Tillich, *Systematic Theology*, vol. 2, London: Nisbet, 1957, p. 53.

27 Jaspers, *The Question of German Guilt*, p. 36.

28 For another set of distinctions, namely responsibility for 'the sinful burden of history', accountability for wrong even if not evil action and 'effective participation by deed or omission', see Michael Sievernich, 'Social Sin and Its Acknowledgment', in Mary Collins and David Power, (eds.), *The Fate of Confession* , *Concilium* 190, Edinburgh: T&T Clark, 1987, pp. 58–63.

29 Tillich, *Systematic Theology*, vol. 2, p. 67. Gestrich follows Tillich on this issue, see Christoph Gestrich, *The Return of Splendor in the World*, Grand Rapids: Eerdmans, 1997, p. 252.

30 Roberts, *Psychotherapy and a Christian View of Man*, p. 108.

31 Menninger, *Whatever Became of Sin?* pp. 94–132.

32 Jaspers, *The Question of German Guilt*, pp. 41, 75–6.

33 Jaspers, *The Question of German Guilt*, p. 76.

34 Jaspers, *The Question of German Guilt*, p. 80.

35 See the discussion of denial in Melissa Steyn, *'Whiteness Just Isn't What*

It Used to Be': *White Identity in a Changing South Africa*, Albany, NY: State University of New York Press, 2001, pp. 104–7.

36 Victoria Barnett, *For the Soul of the People: Protestant Protest against Hitler*, New York: Oxford University Press, 1992, p. 223.

37 Jaspers, *The Question of German Guilt*, p. 115.

38 Jaspers, *The Question of German Guilt*, p. 108.

39 Hannah Arendt, 'Organized Guilt and Universal Responsibility', *Jewish Frontier* 12 no. 1 (January 1945), pp. 19–20.

40 Jaspers, *The Question of German Guilt*, p. 59.

41 Jaspers, *The Question of German Guilt*, pp. 90–1.

42 Jaspers, *The Question of German Guilt*, p. 93.

43 Jaspers, *The Question of German Guilt*, p. 24.

44 Jaspers, *The Question of German Guilt*, p. 99.

45 Søren Kierkegaard, *The Concept of Dread*, Princeton: Princeton University Press, 1957, p. 144.

46 Pumla Goboda-Madikizela, 'Legacies of Violence: An In-Depth Analysis of Two Case Studies Based on Interviews with Perpetrators of a "Necklace" Murder and with Eugene de Kock', PhD diss., University of Cape Town, 1999, p. 237.

47 P. Shabad, 'Remorse: The Echo of Inner Truth', *The Psychotherapy Patient* 5 (1988), p. 117, quoted in Goboda-Madikizela, 'Legacies of Violence', p. 238.

48 For a penetrating theological analysis of guilt, see Karl Rahner, 'Guilt and Its Remission: The Borderland between Theology and Psychotherapy', in *Theological Investigations Volume II*, London: Darton, Longman & Todd, 1963, pp. 265–81.

49 Denise Ackermann, 'On Hearing and Lamenting: Faith and Truth Telling', in H. Russel Botman and Robin M. Petersen, (eds.), *To Remember and to Heal*, Cape Town: Human & Rousseau, 1996, p. 52.

50 Ackermann, 'On Hearing and Lamenting', p. 55.

51 Ackermann, 'On Hearing and Lamenting', p. 55.

52 Miroslav Volf, 'The Social Meaning of Reconciliation', *Interpretation* 54 no. 2 (April 2000), pp. 168–70.

53 Volf, 'The Social Meaning of Reconciliation', p. 166.

54 Volf, 'The Social Meaning of Reconciliation', p. 163.

55 Volf, 'The Social Meaning of Reconciliation', p. 165.

56 Volf, 'The Social Meaning of Reconciliation', p. 171.

57 Volf, *Exclusion and Embrace*, p. 224.

58 Volf, *Exclusion and Embrace*, p. 225.

59 Duncan B. Forrester, *Christian Justice and Public Policy*, Cambridge: Cambridge University Press, 1997, p. 72.

60 Alasdair MacIntyre, *After Virtue*, Notre Dame: University of Notre Dame Press, 1981; Alasdair MacIntyre, *Whose Justice? Which Rationality?*, London: Duckworth, 1988.

61 Willa Boesak, *God's Wrathful Children*, Grand Rapids: Eerdmans, 1995, pp. 208–42.

62 Christopher D. Marshall, *Beyond Retribution: A New Testament Vision for Justice, Crime, and Punishment*, Grand Rapids: Eerdmans, 2001, p. 25.

63 Marshall, *Beyond Retribution*, pp. 35–95.

64 Marshall, *Beyond Retribution*, p. 59.

65 See also the critique of Volf in Marshall, *Beyond Retribution*, p. 26 n. 71.

66 Marshall, *Beyond Retribution*, p. 69.

67 Marshall, *Beyond Retribution*, p. 41.

68 Kathryn Tanner, 'Justification and Justice in a Theology of Grace', *Theology Today* 55 no. 4 (January 1999), p. 523.

69 See the introduction by Dorothy L. Sayers to Dante, *The Divine Comedy*, vol. 3, *Paradise*, Harmondsworth: Penguin, 1962, p. 51.

70 Charles Villa-Vicencio, 'Restorative Justice: Dealing with the past differently', in Charles Villa-Vicencio and Wilhelm Verwoerd, (eds.), *Looking Back Looking Forward*, p. 69.

71 Villa-Vicencio, 'Restorative Justice', *Looking Back Looking Forward*, p. 73.

72 Forrester, *Christian Justice and Public Policy*, p. 218.

73 Paul Tillich, *Love, Power and Justice*, New York: Oxford University Press, 1960, p. 84.

74 Tillich, *Love, Power and Justice*, p. 106.

75 Tillich, *Love, Power and Justice*, pp. 113–14.

76 See the discussion in Tanner, 'Justification and Justice in a Theology of Grace'.

77 Villa-Vicencio, 'Restorative Justice', *Looking Back Looking Forward*, p. 72.

78 William Kentridge commenting on his work at the New York Museum of Contemporary Art. Quoted in the *Cape Argus* (14 June 2001), p. 17.

79 Priscilla B. Hayner, *Unspeakable Truths: Confronting State Terror and Atrocity*, New York: Routledge, 2001, p. 14.

80 In a postscript to a new edition of *Die Schuldfrage*, published in Karl Jaspers, *Hoffnung und Sorge*, München: R. Piper, 1962, pp. 84–5; see also the perceptive insights in Donald W. Shriver, *An Ethic for Enemies: Forgiveness in Politics*, New York: Oxford University Press, 1995, pp. 80–8. It is noteworthy that the Nuremberg Trials were followed by the ambiguous but significant indictment of some 90,000 Nazis and the conviction of 7,000 by post-war German courts.

81 Jaspers, *The Question of German Guilt*, p. 118.

82 Hayner, *Unspeakable Truths*, p. 169.

83 Itumeleng J. Mosala, 'The Meaning of Reconciliation: A Black Perspective', *Journal of Theology for Southern Africa* 59 (June 1987), p. 22.

84 See Hans-Helmut Esser, 'Nomos', in Colin Brown, (ed.), *New International Dictionary of New Testament Theology*, vol. 2 (Exeter: Paternoster Press, 1976), p. 438.

85 Everett, *Religion, Federalism and the Struggle for Public Life*, p. 165.

86 Forrester, *Christian Justice and Public Policy*, pp. 231–4.

87 Forrester, *Christian Justice and Public Policy*, p. 232.

88 Forrester, *Christian Justice and Public Policy*, p. 232.

89 Marshall, *Beyond Retribution*, p. 198.

90 Everett, *Religion, Federalism and the Struggle for Public Life*, p. 165.

91 Richard Bauckham and Trevor Hart, *Hope Against Hope: Christian Eschatology at the Turn of the Millennium*, Grand Rapids: Eerdmans, 1999, p. 193.

92 Jürgen Moltmann, *Theology of Hope*, London: SCM Press, 1967. Even though Moltmann has developed and clarified his position since the publication of *Theology of Hope*, his basic thesis remains. See Jürgen Moltmann, *Experiences in Theology: Ways and Forms of Christian Theology*, London: SCM Press, 2000, pp. 87–93.

93 Moltmann, *Theology of Hope*, p. 22.

94 Moltmann, *Theology of Hope*, p. 25.

95 Moltmann, *Theology of Hope*, p. 21.

96 Moltmann, *Theology of Hope*, p. 22.

97 Moltmann, *Theology of Hope*, p. 35.

98 Hannah Arendt, *The Human Condition*, Chicago: University of Chicago Press, 1958, p. 247.

99 Dietrich Bonhoeffer, *Letters and Papers from Prison*, trans. Eberhard Bethge, SCM Press: London, 1971, pp. 15–16.

100 Bonhoeffer, *Letters and Papers from Prison*, p. 15.

101 Vus: Mahlaselah, 'Hope', *Wisdom of Forgiveness* (BMG Africa CD). (Reproduced with permission).

Select Bibliography

Asmal, Kadar, Louise Asmal, and Ronald Suresh Roberts, *Reconciliation Through Truth* (Cape Town: David Philip, 1996)

Barnett, Victoria, *Bystanders: Conscience and Complicity During the Holocaust* (Westport, CT: Greenwood Press, 1999)

Barth, Karl, *Church Dogmatics: The Doctrine of Reconciliation*, vol. IV/1 (Edinburgh: T. & T. Clark, 1961)

Bauckham, Richard and Trevor Hart, *Hope Against Hope: Christian Eschatology at the Turn of the Millennium* (Grand Rapids: Eerdmans, 1999)

Bonhoeffer, Dietrich, *Discipleship*, Dietrich Bonhoeffer Works, vol. 4 (Minneapolis: Fortress Press, 2001)

Bonhoeffer, Dietrich, *Ethics* (New York: Macmillan, 1965)

Bonhoeffer, Dietrich, *Sanctorum Communio: A Theological Study of the Sociology of the Church*, Dietrich Bonhoeffer Works, vol. 1 (Minneapolis: Fortress Press, 1998)

Boraine, Alex, *A Country Unmasked: Inside South Africa's Truth and Reconciliation Commission* (New York: Oxford University Press, 2000)

Boraine, Alex and Janet Levy (eds.), *The Healing of a Nation?* (Cape Town: Justice in Transition, 1995)

Boraine, Alex, Janet Levy and Ronel Scheffer (eds.) *Dealing with the Past: Truth and Reconciliation in South Africa* (Cape Town: Idasa, 1994)

Botman, H. Russel and Robin M. Petersen (eds.), *To Remember and to Heal* (Cape Town: Human & Rousseau, 1996)

Clegg, Joseph and Cecelia Liechty, *Moving Beyond Sectarianism: Religion, Conflict and Reconciliation in Northern Ireland* (Dublin: Columba Press, 2001)

Esack, Faried, *Qur'an, Liberation and Pluralism: Towards an Islamic Perspective on Inter-Religious Solidarity Against Oppression* (Oxford: Oneworld Publications, 1997)

Everett, William J., *Religion, Federalism and the Struggle for Public Life:*

Cases from Germany, India and America (New York: Oxford University Press, 1997)

Ford, David F., *Self and Salvation: Being Transformed* (Cambridge: Cambridge University Press, 1999)

Forrester, Duncan B., *Christian Justice and Public Policy* (Cambridge: Cambridge University Press, 1997)

Forsyth, P.T., *The Work of Christ* (London: Independent Press, 1952)

Fowler, James, *Faithful Change: The Personal and Public Challenges of Postmodern Life* (Nashville: Abingdon Press, 1996)

Frost, Brian, *The Politics of Peace* (London: Darton, Longman & Todd, 1991)

Frymer-Kensky, Tikva, David Novak, Peter Ochs, David Fox Samuel and Michael A. Signer (eds.), *Christianity in Jewish Terms* (Boulder, CO: Westview Press, 2000)

Goboda-Madikizela, Pumla, 'Legacies of Violence: An In-Depth Analysis of Two Case Studies Based on Interviews with Perpetrators of a "Necklace" Murder and with Eugene de Kock' (Ph.D. dissertation, University of Cape Town, 1999)

Gorringe, Timothy J., *God's Just Vengeance* (Cambridge: Cambridge University Press, 1996)

Gustafson, James, *Treasure in Earthen Vessels: The Church as Human Community* (Chicago: University of Chicago Press, 1976)

Hay, Mark, *Ukubuyisana: Reconciliation in South Africa* (Pietermaritzburg: Cluster Publications, 1998)

Hayner, Priscilla B., *Unspeakable Truths: Confronting State Terror and Atrocity* (New York: Routledge, 2001)

James, Wilmot and Linda van de Vijver (eds.), *After the TRC: Reflections on Truth and Reconciliation in South Africa* (Cape Town: David Philip, 2000)

Jones, Gregory L., *Embodying Forgiveness: A Theological Analysis* (Grand Rapids: Eerdmans, 1995)

Krog, Antjie, *Country of My Skull* (Johannesburg: Random House, 1998)

Kuschel, Karl-Josef, *Abraham: Sign of Hope for Jews, Christians, and Muslims* (New York: Continuum, 1995)

Mandela, Nelson, *Long Walk to Freedom: The Autobiography of Nelson Mandela* (Johannesburg: Macdonald Purnell, 1994)

Marshall, Christopher D., *Beyond Retribution: A New Testament Vision for Justice, Crime, and Punishment* (Grand Rapids: Eerdmans, 2001)

Martin, Ralph, *Reconciliation: A Study of Paul's Theology* (Atlanta: John Knox Press, 1981)

Meiring, Piet, *Chronicle of the Truth Commission* (Vanderbijpark, RSA: Carpe Diem, 1999)

Moltmann, Jürgen, *Theology of Hope* (London: SCM Press, 1967)

Nasr, Seyyed Hossein, *Ideals and Realities of Islam* (San Francisco: HarperCollins, 1986)

Nürnberger, Klaus and John Tooke (eds.), *The Cost of Reconciliation in South Africa* (Cape Town: Methodist Publishing House, 1988)

Prozesky, Martin and John W. de Gruchy (eds.), *Living Faiths in South Africa* (Cape Town: David Philip, 1995)

Raymond, S.J., G. Helmick and Rodney L. Petersen (eds.), *Forgiveness and Reconciliation: Religion, Public Policy, and Conflict Transformation* (Philadelphia: Templeton Foundation Press, 2001)

Rouner, Leroy S. (ed.), *Religion, Politics, and Peace* (Notre Dame: University of Notre Dame Press, 1999)

Shriver, Donald W., *An Ethic for Enemies: Forgiveness in Politics* (New York: Oxford University Press, 1995)

Siddiqui, Ataullah *Christian-Muslim Dialogue in the Twentieth Century* (London: Macmillan, 1997)

Tayob, Abdulkadar, *Islamic Resurgence in South Africa: The Muslim Youth Movement* (Cape Town: University of Cape Town Press, 1995)

Thurian, Max, *Confession* (London: SCM, 1958)

Tillich, Paul, *Love, Power and Justice* (New York: Oxford University Press, 1960)

Tutu, Desmond, *No Future Without Forgiveness* (London: Rider, 1999).

Villa-Vicencio, Charles and Wilhelm Verwoerd (eds.), *Looking Back Reaching Forward* (Cape Town: University of Cape Town Press, 2000)

Volf, Miroslav, *Exclusion & Embrace: A Theological Exploration of Identity, Otherness, and Reconciliation* (Nashville: Abingdon, 1996)

Williams, Rowan, *On Christian Theology* (Oxford: Blackwell, 2000)

Index

Printed in the United States
72588LV00005BA/1-33